THE AMERICAN WAY

A TRUE STORY OF NAZI ESCAPE, SUPERMAN, AND MARILYN MONROE

HELENE STAPINSKI AND BONNIE SIEGLER

Simon & Schuster

New York London Toronto Sydney New Delhi

Simon & Schuster
1230 Avenue of the Americas
New York, NY 10020

First Simon & Schuster hardcover edition February 2023

SIMON & SCHUSTER and colophon are registered
trademarks of Simon & Schuster, Inc.

For information about special discounts for bulk purchases,
please contact Simon & Schuster Special Sales at
1-866-506-1949 or business@simonandschuster.com.

The Simon & Schuster Speakers Bureau can bring authors
to your live event. For more information or to book
an event, contact the Simon & Schuster Speakers Bureau at
1-866-248-3049 or visit our website at www.simonspeakers.com.

Interior design by Bonnie Siegler

Manufactured in the United States of America

1 3 5 7 9 10 8 6 4 2

Library of Congress Cataloging-in-Publication Data
has been applied for.

ISBN 978-1-9821-7166-7
ISBN 978-1-9821-7168-1 (ebook)

For Omi and Opi

CAST OF CHARACTERS

JULES AND EDITH WITH HER MOTHER,
MARTHA FRIEDMANN (LEFT), AND SISTER, USHI (RIGHT)

THE SCHULBACKS, THEIR FAMILY, AND FRIENDS

JULES SCHULBACK . . . . *A young furrier from Berlin*

EDITH SCHULBACK (NÉE FRIEDMANN) . . . . *His wife*

HANNELORE (HELEN) SCHULBACK . . . . . . *Their oldest daughter*

EVY SCHULBACK . . . . *Their youngest daughter*

GOLDA . . . . *Jules's oldest sister*

SIMON . . . . *Golda's husband, a Berlin businessman*

PAUL AND DON . . . . *Golda's sons*

JEFFREY . . . . *Golda's grandson*

MOLLIE . . . . *Jules's second oldest sister*

DAVID SCHMERZ . . . . *Mollie's husband, a furrier*

SARA . . . . *Jules's third oldest sister*

CILLY . . . . *Jules's youngest sister*

MAX . . . . *Jules's brother*

ALBERT AND MARTHA FRIEDMANN . . . .
. . . . *Edith's parents, textile company owners in Berlin*

URSULA (USHI) FRIEDMANN . . . . *Edith's sister*

LEJA . . . . *Ushi's friend and coworker*

FAYE STERNBERG . . . . *Jules's cousin from the Bronx*

MURRAY STERNBERG . . . . *Faye's husband*

NEIL AND FRED STERNBERG . . . . *Faye's sons*

BONNIE . . . . *Jules's granddaughter*

JEFF . . . . *Bonnie's husband*

HARRY DONENFELD & CO.

HARRY DONENFELD...
...*A New York City printer, bootlegger, and publisher of Superman*

JACK LIEBOWITZ ....*Harry's business partner*

FRANK COSTELLO..............*A mobster and Harry's friend*

WALTER WINCHELL..
..............*Hearst newspaper columnist and radio broadcaster*

GUSSIE DONENFELD ....*Harry's wife*

IRWIN AND PEACHY DONENFELD ....*Harry's children*

SUNNY PALEY ....*Harry's mistress*

JERRY SIEGEL................*Writer and Superman's co-creator*

JOE SHUSTER.................*Artist and Superman's co-creator*

MAX GAINES.............................*Comic book publisher*

MAJOR MALCOLM WHEELER-NICHOLSON...................
....*Comic book publisher*

DR. FREDRIC WERTHAM ....*Psychiatrist and anti-comics crusader*

EUGENE MALETTA ....*A Queens publisher*

JACK KOSLOW...................................*A murderer*

SUPERMAN...........................*America's first superhero*

MARILYN AND HER SUPPORTING CAST

MARILYN MONROE . . . . *An actress*

JOE DiMAGGIO . . . . *A baseball player and Superman's biggest fan*

CLARK GABLE . . . .
. . . .*The King of Hollywood and the namesake for Clark Kent*

MILTON GREENE. . . .*Photographer and Marilyn's business partner*

AMY GREENE . . . . *A former model and Milton's wife*

ARTHUR MILLER . . . . . . *Playwright and Marilyn's third husband*

BILLY WILDER . . . . *A screenwriter and film director*

EUGENIA . . . . *Wilder's mother*

MAX . . . . *Wilder's father*

HOWARD HUGHES . . . . *Billionaire and RKO studio head*

HUGH HEFNER . . . . *Publisher of* Playboy

SAM SHAW . . . . *Photographer and Hollywood publicist*

JULES SCHULBACK

PROLOGUE

THE TEN-BLOCK WALK

NEW YORK CITY, 1954

JULES SCHULBACK LEFT HIS THIRD-FLOOR APARTMENT around midnight and stepped onto the sidewalk at Lexington and Sixty-First Street in Manhattan, carrying what looked like a black lunch box with chrome around the edges. He surveyed the familiar view, glancing at an upstairs window across the street that belonged, strangely, to a doll hospital. Its lights and red neon crosses had been turned off for the evening, hiding the buckets of miniature heads and arms and various doll parts that would spook visitors when they peeked from his apartment window in the daylight. But Jules found the doll hospital mildly amusing, as he did most things. He panned his gaze a few doors down and crossed the avenue to his fur shop.

Its treasures were locked up for the night. Jules inspected the darkened window, as he always did when passing by, partly to admire his display—frozen mannequins posed in the latest minks and fox stoles—but also to check that everything was all right in his absence. And it was.

Since it was a Tuesday night, the streets of Manhattan were mostly deserted, Jules's shadow one of the only ones cast by dim streetlamps and a moon that was just past full. The Chrysler Building loomed in the distance, only a few of its offices lit, the bright moon reflecting off the spiked metal helmet of its tower.

The temperature was in the fifties, chilly for early fall. In Jules's version of the story, a story he would retell again and again over the decades, a few Checker cabs flew by, a few crawled, looking for a fare, but Jules walked. Two blocks, then three, past shuttered drugstores and dry cleaners, past silent newsstands and grocery stores. Past a single bored cop on the beat, to whom he gave a respectful nod but didn't stop to chat up. Jules loved to chat and loved to spin a good story. But tonight he was a man with a mission, not just an insomniac out on a late-night stroll in the greatest city in the world. He did not have an American dream; he was already living it, right now, right here on these streets.

As he grew closer to his destination—East Fifty-First Street—Jules sensed a strange charge in the atmosphere, as if the molecules were being rearranged somehow, and a distant hum, even before he saw the crowd. He passed the all-night coffee shop with its pink neon and the onion-shaped green copper domes of the Central Synagogue on the corner of Fifty-Fifth Street—so much like the one he had left behind in Berlin. And sure enough, three blocks away he could see it: a bright glow up ahead.

As he drew nearer, the lights were brighter than daylight, the crowd deeper than those on the Forty-Second Street subway platform during the evening rush. His heart beating faster with each step, Jules realized there was something strange about this crowd. He couldn't identify it right away. It took a few beats. But then it hit him—there were only men here, their families and wives tucked safely into bed back in their apartments.

Like Yankee Stadium under the floodlights, men in hats and jackets and a smattering of ties stood around, excited for the game to begin. Some stood on fire escapes and the roofs of cars, perched on lampposts and atop traffic lights, all trying to find a good spot to glimpse the coming attraction—the American dream made flesh, with all its promises and curves. One of the Yankees was even here,

Joe DiMaggio, shaking hands and working the growing crowd of photographers and cops, loiterers and fans.

Jules dove straight in. He'd never been a timid man; if he had been, he wouldn't be here walking the Earth. Gently pushing his way through the crowd using his free hand and a few German-accented "Pardon mes" and "Excuse mes"—he was a gentleman after all—he got as close as he could to the commotion. There was the gaffer he had met yesterday, who tipped him off about tonight. They nodded in recognition.

Then the movie director flitted past in his fedora, nervously eyeing the growing throng. His name was Billy Wilder. They were both from Berlin, Jules knew, both escaped Jewish refugees. He caught Wilder's eye and held it for a moment, long enough to think that maybe Billy, too, knew what they had in common. As if Jules was marked somehow with invisible ink that only the fellow wounded could detect. Billy walked past, and Jules was suddenly reminded of his purpose here tonight. He squeezed his black box between his legs, screwed around with a few knobs, wound a small crank, knelt down into a narrow free space between bodies, and then placed the box up to his right eye. His Bolex 16 mm camera.

It was September 15, 1954, and it was no accident he was here. Jules was a thoughtful man who had always planned everything very carefully. Befriending that gaffer was just one of many steps that brought this furrier and amateur filmmaker to the front row of one of the most iconic moments in twentieth-century film history, one that he—and he alone—would save for posterity in living, moving color.

Jules looked around the artificially lit New York City street corner. Always so much life, so much to capture. He had tasted the bitterness of life, but this, this was the sweet part. He peeked through the lens of his Bolex, focused on Billy Wilder and the crew in front of him.

And suddenly, as if she knew he was coming, out stepped Marilyn Monroe. And . . . *Action.*

For Jules, staring the glamour of Hollywood in the face took more than a ten-block walk. His long, complicated journey to New York City, like those of most immigrant Jews during World War II, had taken bravery and cunning. But, against all logic, here he was, front and center, smack in the middle of the waking dream that was America.

Jules had almost not made it there that night. Had almost not made it to America. The odds had been against him, really. On dark nights when he couldn't keep the sorrow at bay, he would think of the family and friends he had left behind, many of them dead.

His story included not one but two escapes from Nazi Germany, of lies quickly imagined and creatively told, of ocean liners and fake identities and magic—the never-ending, never-tarnished magic of Hollywood. Some of those who came in and out of Jules's story—Clark Gable, Billy Wilder, Joe DiMaggio, and Marilyn Monroe—were real, of human flesh, with flaws and imperfections. Like Jules, each had escaped something, wearing a mask to survive, creating an alternate identity, using the powers that they, and only they, possessed. Dreaming and remaking themselves in a country that not only allowed reinvention but demanded it.

Others in his story were not real, like Superman, a fellow refugee—from another dying planet—whose incredible powers helped shine a light on the very horror that Jules had escaped, a horror so many had willfully ignored. Superman, too, needed an alternate self, a stuffed-shirt newspaper man—a regular guy. Those who created Superman had their own journey, too, sons of survivors, riding the first wave of an art form—the comics—that would one day crash into the Hollywood that Jules so loved.

And finally there was the man who Jules never really spoke to, the man who gave him life—and gave life to Marilyn and Superman as well.

Harry.

He was just a few blocks away from here, living his own American dream, with all the complications and grit that entailed. The early Mob connections, the bootlegging, and the girlie magazines had all given way to respectability, fortune, and fame. But on this night, this very same chilly autumn night when Marilyn stepped into the camera lights, Harry's life would start unraveling. A series of events was set in motion that would change Harry's life, leaving him—for the few years he had left on Earth—a mere observer of a world he'd created.

So many strands. So many stories. All crisscrossing and colliding into one another. The starlet. The king of Hollywood. The superhero. The publisher. The ballplayer. The filmmaker. And Jules. All traveling together through this extraordinary time. This night beneath the klieg lights was like the tip of the needle stitching those intricate threads together, but to truly see it, you have to go back in time.

Rewind the film, turn back the colorful page of panels, and start at the beginning.

ACT ONE

JULES AND EDITH ON A WEEKEND OUTING

CHAPTER 1

IN THE METROPOLIS

BERLIN, CIRCA 1929

WANNSEE LAKE WAS BIG AND BEAUTIFUL AND SURROUNDED by mansions and marinas, sailboats drifting by lazily in the distance. It was warm and sticky in crowded Berlin. But not here. Wannsee was breezy, the cool lake water a welcome reward for the long work-week. Being tan was suddenly chic, and sunbathing a new pastime, so young Germans traveled in droves on weekends to lie out and bake by the water. On summer Sundays, seventeen-year-old Jules Schulzbach would travel to Wannsee with his teenage girlfriend, Edith, who was two years younger. They'd rendezvous beneath the modern golden clock outside the Berlin Zoo train station, a popular meeting place, the smell of the elephants wafting out over the rattling train and traffic noise. It was a short train ride from the zoo station to Wannsee. Jules, fair skinned with light brown hair that turned even lighter in the sun, would rent a striped *Strandkorb*—a small portable roofed cabana—for himself and his love. They would spend the day swimming and then squeeze together, still damp, into their little cabana, watching the sunbathers bathe and the sailboats sail.

When the sun went down, Jules and Edith loved to go to Berlin's clubs. They were both very stylish. Jules was handsome, with big, bright eyes set in a heart-shaped face. Edith was thin and graceful, with gray eyes and short dark hair with a marcel wave.

They won ballroom dance competitions, tap dancing, fox-trotting, waltzing—and, their favorite, Argentinian tangoing—their way to top prizes. They went to concerts together, too, including those performed at the New Synagogue on Oranienburger Strasse, with its big golden dome and its Moorish Alhambra–like design, the center of the city's Jewish community. Their fellow Berliner Albert Einstein, who was not only one of the greatest minds of his generation but was a pretty decent violinist, played a charity concert there one late January evening in 1930. He and his violin—which he nicknamed Lina (short for *die Violine*)—played to a packed house, the genius dressed in black tie, tails, and a matching yarmulke. Lina's melancholy, soaring notes from Bach's two violin concertos drifted over the crowd of three thousand.

Jules and Edith would also spend hours at the nearby movie houses, including the Biograph Theater just a couple doors down from his sister Mollie's fur shop, and the Babylon cinema just around the corner. Its curved Bauhaus facade—sleek, spare, and elegant—was painted a golden hue, its name running in bold vertical neon on the building's side and in the shape of a ziggurat atop its marquee. The theater took its name from the plot of *Metropolis*, director Fritz Lang's 1927 retelling of the story of the Tower of Babel. The groundbreaking sci-fi dystopian tale told of an evil industrialist who uses technology to keep the masses down by enslaving them at the bottom of a giant skyscraper complex. Its Communist lesson of class struggle and capitalism left unchecked was a technological wonder, touting the latest in special effects. The movie's futuristic style—including robots and big explosions amid vast architectural models of Art Deco buildings and Gothic cathedrals—had been inspired by Fritz Lang's first trip to New York City in 1924. It cost more than $2 million to produce and had rocked the world—and Jules.

Enveloped in darkness, Jules and Edith watched the German

and American silent films, reading the intertitles as the music from the orchestra pit and house organ washed over them. Jules collected autographed film cards like American boys would collect baseball cards, each one featuring a sepia-toned glamour shot of a famous actor or actress of the day, women with blond permanent waves and men decked out in white tuxedo jackets.

Weimar Berlin was a thoroughly modern metropolis—Europe's first really—its cafés filled with people like Josephine Baker, W. H. Auden, and Christopher Isherwood, there to write his Berlin novels that would later become the stage play *Cabaret*. A left-wing stronghold, the city of four million was on the forefront of liberal thinking, nightclubs like the Eldorado and Silhouette accepting of homosexuals, bisexuals, and transgender people. As a result, it was at the center of Europe's culture wars, with the new Nazi Party declaring it "decadent," and citing rampant drug use and prostitution as the endgame of liberal thought. Jules had heard all about the Nazis and their leader, a rising political star named Adolf Hitler, whose rousing speeches convinced many young, disaffected Germans to join the burgeoning party's ranks. When Wall Street collapsed in October 1929, Hitler's audience began to grow. Nervous American investors pulled billions of marks in loans from Germany, sending that economy into free fall as well. Frightened and anxious, the general public in Germany started to seriously listen to Hitler, who blamed the Jews for the nation's economic hardships.

It was already well known in the Jewish quarter, where Jules lived, that Hitler hated the Jews and wanted them removed from Europe. He had made that clear not only in those speeches but in his 1925 book, *Mein Kampf*. Under Hitler's Berlin district leader, Joseph Goebbels, Nazi Party members violently clashed with Communists, Socialists, trade unionists, and Trotskyites in marches and riots in the streets and in meeting halls throughout the city. Rocks were thrown, knives were drawn, beer mugs and wooden chairs were smashed over heads.

But Jules avoided all that. He had heard the news surrounding *All Quiet on the Western Front*, the pacifist film that emotionally dramatized Germany's loss in World War I. Protests erupted outside theaters, while inside, young Nazis unleashed mice, snakes, and stink bombs to force audiences out. Though a huge fan of American cinema, Hitler slammed the film for "endangering Germany's reputation." A veteran of the Great War, Hitler was bitterly angry about Germany's defeat, blamed the kaiser, and longed to return the lost empire to its former glory.

In his lighter moments, Hitler loved Laurel and Hardy and Clark Gable and Jean Harlow. (Later, as Führer, he would often screen two films a night and sometimes one over lunch in his private screening room.) One of his favorite films was 1924's *Die Nibelungen*, a retelling of the thirteenth-century poem upon which Richard Wagner's operatic Ring cycle was also based. Hitler would see *Die Nibelungen* at least twenty times, drawing a correlation between current events and his favorite movie. To Hitler, the revenge fantasy of *Die Nibelungen* symbolized Germany's strength and rise from the humiliations of World War I. He loved the story's heroic character, Siegfried, even though the film was directed by a Jew, Fritz Lang, the genius behind *Metropolis*.

When he wasn't being entertained, Jules was busy entertaining those around him. He loved to be the center of attention, telling stories and making people laugh. As the youngest in his family, he had always entertained his five older siblings, particularly his sister Golda, the oldest. She was a bit of a rebel, quiet but headstrong with a steely determination to claim her own place in the world. Golda resembled Jules the most with her big eyes, fine nose, and light hair. Fourteen years older than Jules, Golda had moved to Amsterdam for a while, had married, and had a son. When her husband died in the influenza pandemic, Golda moved back to Berlin in 1918 with her baby boy, Don. Being alone in a foreign land with a baby was too much tragedy for a twenty-year-old to handle on her own. She came back to heal, but wound up helping to heal the rest of the Schulzbach family as well. Their father, a decorated Austrian soldier from the Great War, would soon die of complications from his injuries. Acting as a second mother to both Jules and Cilly, the youngest girl in the Schulzbach family, Golda would throw her sturdy arms around them and hug them tight. And Jules would make sure that she laughed.

Dressing up from time to time as Charlie Chaplin's Little Tramp, he put on the mustache and the hat, and waddled along with a cane, cracking everyone up. When he got a bit older, Jules pretended to play his girlfriend, Edith, like an upright bass, sitting her on his lap and plucking out imaginary notes on her stomach, popping his lips to imitate the sound. Edith was still in high school when he met her, a serious girl, who, like Golda, was not quick to smile. But his bass routine made her, and everyone around them, laugh. Jules's relentless optimism and high spirits could sometimes be exhausting, but Edith loved him for it. And loved him as much as he loved her.

To earn money for their nights on the town, Jules got his first job working for Mollie, his second-oldest sister, and her husband, David, in their fur shop on Münzstrasse in the Mitte district in central Berlin. It was a sprawling, two-story place with mirrors along the walls, chandeliers above, and leopard skin rugs below. Paintings of a roaring tiger and a lion head flanked David's last name on the sign outside the shop. It was called Schmerz, which means "pain" in German, which was fitting for a furrier, if you were an animal or an animal lover. A row of sewing machines lined the back room, manned by a large staff of white-coated furriers, both male and female, including young Jules, his hair parted in the center in the style of the day. Stuffed minks squatted on the shelves up front, and a live German shepherd was kept as a watchdog and pet.

Mollie, who was a decade older than Jules, would become the benevolent head of the family, proudest of them all to be a Berliner. Since their father had been laid to rest in the nearby Weissensee Cemetery, Mollie had taken charge of the finances, helping her mother support the family, then—as her siblings came of age—providing them work through David's fur business. Mollie even helped her older sister, Golda, find love again, setting her up in 1920 with David's handsome brother, Simon, a tailor in Berlin. Brothers marrying sisters. It made the family even stronger. Jules's sister Sara also married a tailor and ran her own fur shop in the upscale Moabit section of the city with their brother Max, a hunchback.

When it came to his needlework and design, Jules was an artist. But he was also developing into quite a salesman, catering to both wives of bankers with traditional tastes and the more stylish customers looking for versions of the slope-shouldered, fur-trimmed wrap recently made famous by Coco Chanel, which boasted cuffs as big as muffs and a collar so huge it resembled a sleeping dog. Jules was witty and loved to tell a good story, two characteristics that endeared him to his lady customers. He spoke Hochdeutsch, High German, with an upper-class accent, but was also fluent in Berliner Schnauze—Berlin lip—the sarcastic sense of humor special to the city's inhabitants. Jules was proud to be German and even more proud to be from Berlin, the only one in his family born there—a place where everyone seemed to be from someplace else. The Schulzbachs' original hometown of Kolomyia in Galicia had a strong Jewish community—half of the city's population—and was a center of Ukrainian culture with thirty synagogues and scores of publishing houses, newspapers, and magazines, and a public library that was one of the first in the region. But in 1910, two years before

Jules was born, the city officially began to turn against the Jews, voting to prohibit them from the local trades.

So here they were in Berlin. Here, the Schulzbachs made their living freely, as tailors and furriers. But fur—and the money to be made from it—were not Jules's passion. Edith Friedmann was.

Jules did his best to enjoy the good life with Edith, but couldn't ignore the danger that was threatening their carefree nights dancing and their long cool days at the Wannsee beach. As the sailboats drifted into their field of vision, Jules and Edith would admire the mansions across the lake. Right across from the lido where they always sunbathed was a cream-colored stone villa tucked into the wooded shoreline. Before the London plane trees were fully bloomed, Jules could just make out the three-story building if he squinted hard enough from his striped beach chair. For now, it was just another mansion on the far shore, with manicured lawns and hedges and a colorful garden surrounded by classical statues.

Jules, of course, could not foresee what would soon take place in that elegant Wannsee villa. That over a buffet lunch, with fine cognac and imported cigars, fifteen German bureaucrats and military officers would gather to discuss the murder of all of Europe's Jews, Jules's and Edith's families included.

HARRY DONENFELD

CHAPTER 2

SMOOSHES AND BOOZE

NEW YORK, CIRCA 1929

ON PAPER, HARRY DONENFELD WAS A PRINTER. HE AND HIS three brothers ran the Martin Printing Company in Lower Manhattan in the shadow of the Brooklyn Bridge. The nine-floor building was filled with printers, whose heavy machinery, mixed with the trolleys crossing the bridge, made the whole place rattle and shake.

It wasn't the prettiest spot in town, but was a vast improvement over where the four brothers grew up. Harry had worked his way out of poverty on the Lower East Side, having come at the turn of the century at age eight with his family from Jassy, the cultural capital of Romania, just as the government there decided to bar Jewish students from its public schools and colleges. The Donenfeld kids all slept in one bed together in a vermin-infested cold-water flat on Stanton Street. Each of the brothers now lived in the Bronx in neat, respectable houses. But the trip from the Lower East Side had been a long one. Harry had been a newsboy, a teenage gang member, and a garment worker. Now as a printer, he felt he had finally arrived. He was making good money. But there was so much more for the taking in New York City.

Bootlegging was in full swing in America. And Harry Donenfeld was about to get a taste. Harry was short—only five foot two—with a reedy voice and a thick New York City accent. But he was the boldest of his brothers, the middle of five children. He was also incredibly dapper and charming, with a high forehead, a slight slope to his nose, and a flinty spark in his dark eyes that meant he could cause trouble when he wanted.

On the Lower East Side, Harry had been in all the local gangs. There were the Allen Street Cadets, the Henry Street gang, the McDonald Street gang, the Five Pointers, and the Boys of the Avenue, the local Jewish gang filled with Yiddish-speaking shtarkers (tough guys) like Harry. Some gang members learned to pick pockets, gambling with that "found" money on horses, cards, and fights; running numbers; and rumbling with the rival gangs. The numbers Harry ran were called the policy racket, involving penny bets and steep odds at 999 to 1. Policy took its name from the insurance industry. The payoff was usually 600 to 1.

Some of Harry's childhood troublemaker friends were now grown-up gangsters. To make extra money, real money, Harry started running Canadian whiskey and Molson ale down to New York for his old buddies. The illegal liquor was stored amid Harry's giant paper rolls in his trucks and at the printing company.

Bribing the cops so they wouldn't look too hard in the weighed-down paper trucks, Harry's Mob friends would pick up the booze, Gillette it (slang for cut it), and deliver it throughout the city. Drivers would drop their crates at stores with painted windows, basement brownstone apartments, and the back rooms of restaurants—the speakeasies of New York. Harry was a regular customer at many of those "speaks." When Prohibition began in 1920, the city was home to fifteen thousand saloons, clubs, and bars. By the mid-twenties, the number had more than doubled.

The Broadway Mob, Harry's connection, supplied booze to many of the high-end speakeasies, like the Stork Club and the 21 Club, as well as the Cloud Club high atop the Chrysler Building. Harry developed a close bond with Francesco Castiglia, a fellow Broadway Mob bootlegger whose wife happened to be Jewish.

Francesco, originally from Southern Italy, would change his name to Frank Costello. It was through Costello that Harry met the gangster's Chicago associate, Moe Annenberg—publisher of the *Daily Racing Form* and other newspapers. He chose Harry to print six million promotional brochures as inserts for Hearst, the huge national newspaper chain, for whom Moe handled distribution. It was Harry's first big score—aside from the booze.

The Donenfelds' other printing clients included city hall, the International Ladies' Garment Workers' Union ("Look for the union label!"), and proto-feminist Margaret Sanger, who had them run off her illegal family-planning pamphlets and her newsletter—the *Birth Control Review*—promoting contraception. Under the Comstock Act passed by Congress in 1873, it was still against the law to distribute, sell, or possess contraceptives or any information discussing them, but Sanger, the founder of what would later become Planned Parenthood, preached that reproductive freedom was the key to women's equality. Sexual pleasure without procreation was not immoral, she argued. And Harry wholeheartedly agreed.

Most printers regarded Sanger's pamphlets "a Sing Sing job"—printing them would send you straight to prison. But Harry was happy to oblige. Anything for a buck, and to shake things up. He would not only print Sanger's material but would store her boxes of illegal diaphragms behind his big rolls of paper, right next to the booze.

Not surprisingly, Harry developed a strong taste for liquor—an occupational hazard—and would barely make it back to his home in the Bronx every night after tying one on. He loved to knock back a good highball (or two or three), but his favorite drink was a Heineken. His wife, Gussie, hardly ever saw him anymore. And she missed him.

The two had met at the Seward Park public library branch and worked together at the Great Eastern Waist Company on Twenty-Seventh Street, selling tailored women's blouses to wholesalers. Harry—with his thin mustache and black, slicked-back hair—cut quite a figure in his suit and vest and his fresh white starched shirt and collar. When young Harry met teenage Gussie, three years his junior, he took her around to all his favorite restaurants and cafés in the city. But what Gussie loved best about Harry was how he made her laugh. Harry was a practical joker and once gave a hotfoot to the up-and-coming heavyweight boxer Jack Dempsey, lighting his laces on fire. Dempsey, known for his powerful punches, turned around and playfully jabbed Harry, accidentally breaking his arm. But the two would stay good friends.

Harry and Gussie had been best friends back then, not just working together but protesting the Great War and the draft, attending Socialist rallies on Second Avenue, near their thirty-dollar-a-month newlywed apartment in the East Village. The cafés and bohemian bars were filled with young writers, artists, anarchists, and proponents of free love drawn to the area for its low rents. He and Gussie worked as Socialist poll watchers together during the 1918 elections and had attended what the radicals called Second Avenue University. At the intersection outside their railroad apartment, Socialist candidates set up small wooden platforms, giving speeches and lectures late into the night. All sorts of people attended those revival meetings—men, women, immigrants, Americans, Black, white—listening to talks not just on politics, but philosophy, history, and economics, the traffic stopping to avoid the huge crowds.

Though Harry and Gussie didn't go to college, they got an education on that street corner. They had become adults together there, holding hands under the stars and feeling they could change the world. Instead, Harry had changed. Ever since they had moved up to the Bronx, it was as if a light switch had been flipped. Gussie wasn't sure if it was the heavy drinking or the reality of starting his own family staring him in the face. Or maybe Harry had always been a bastard and she just hadn't noticed.

In 1925, Harry began running around Brooklyn with a married woman from Manhattan Beach. For people who had grown up in working-class and poor neighborhoods like Harry and Gussie, free love had a different name: cheating. Gussie filed for divorce and got a boyfriend of her own. But it was just so Harry could get a taste of his own medicine. Harry, it turned out, was immune.

There was the nurse he had the long affair with, and the woman he was dating whom he fought with at a bar and grill on the corner of West Twentieth and Seventh Avenue. The woman had grabbed a carving knife and stabbed Harry. But Harry's immunity stuck: He survived. And Gussie stayed.

Harry's shenanigans—the cheating, the drinking, the hanging with mobsters—did not sit well with his brothers, who were growing to dislike Harry as much as Gussie did. There was the time, years later, that a printing client, a mobster with a very bad stutter, came in to do business. Harry, always the joker, told him to wait a moment. He then ran and grabbed his youngest brother, Irving, who also had a stutter, and told him to wait on the guy. Moments later, the client stormed off—sure he was being made fun of—and Irving appeared, his face pale. "W-w-w-what are you t-t-t-trying to do?" Irving said. "He's going to k-k-k-kill me." Harry thought it was hilarious. His brother did not.

Harry broke with his two older brothers and started his own company on West Twenty-Second Street, printing *Screenland*, a successful Hollywood fan magazine. Irving decided to join him in the new business venture. Harry told Gussie it was a fresh start for them both and she foolishly believed him. She hoped the man she had fallen in love with under the stars on Second Avenue was still inside there somewhere, hidden beneath the fancy suits and the pinkie ring. Before she knew it, Gussie was pregnant. The following year, Harry shamelessly formed Irwin Publishing—named for his newborn son—printing a series of sex pulp magazines called *Snappy Stories*, *Spicy Stories*, and *Pep!*, which was filled with topless girls and gags.

Nothing was sacred to Harry, not even his firstborn son's name, as long as there was a buck to be made. And besides, he would argue, if it wasn't for sex, little Irwin wouldn't even exist, now would he? Fatherhood, however, did not cure Harry's wandering eye. He slept with the pulps' female editor, Merle Williams Hersey, adding her to his long list of mistresses. And editors.

The girlie magazines were called smooshes and were incredibly profitable. Their stories—accompanied by erotic photos and illustrations inside, and even brazenly on the cover—were said to revolve around one plot:

> *Boy meets girl.*
> *Girl gets boy into pickle.*
> *Boy gets pickle into girl.*

They involved deep kisses and heavy petting of "alabaster orbs" and "snowy white globes," with lots of trembling and throbbing and quivering. The writers always cut away before any serious action, hardly living up to the promise of the topless cover girls luring readers in. But no one came for the prose. It was all about the occasional "art" photos and line drawings: topless women shaking cocktail shakers over their heads, topless women kissing pilots in cockpits, topless women cavorting with the devil, topless chorus girls, housewives, farmers' daughters climbing into haystacks or into bed.

When the stock market crashed in 1929, Harry's sex pulps not only didn't feel the shock but increased profits, selling cheap thrills to the masses for twenty-five cents at newsstands. Business was so good that Harry hired a new accountant, Jack Liebowitz, whose stepfather, Julius, had been a union steward for the International Ladies' Garment Workers' Union (ILGWU). Harry and Julius had played cards together.

Jack, a full head taller than Harry at five foot eight—but with much less personality—had come from Ukraine with his family when he was ten years old, settling on the Lower East Side. Back in Ukraine, he had watched his older brother die from diphtheria after drinking tainted water from a barrel outside their house. A few years younger than Harry, Jack had also worked as a newsboy and remembered watching from the roof of his tenement apartment as smoke billowed from the Triangle Shirtwaist Factory fire. He had a head for numbers and very good handwriting, so good that when he was a boy his teachers would have him help write out the report cards for the whole class. Crafty even at a young age, Jack stole a few and, one year, wrote out a fake report card for himself so he could skip a grade.

His refuge was the newly built Seward Park public library, the place where Harry had first encountered Gussie. It had a beautiful roof garden, where Jack and the other smart neighborhood kids would gather at wooden tables and do their homework or simply read for pleasure. Jack would borrow books—fairy tales, Westerns, and the novels of James Fenimore Cooper—and devour them at home each night near the cast-iron stove in the kitchen, banging a big stick every now and then to keep the rats away. As in Harry's tenement apartment, there was never enough food to eat and he never had a coat, just a sweater in winter. Jack and his three brothers shared a small cot, which was incentive enough to study, cheat, or do anything he needed to do to get out into the world on his own. To say he and Harry were self-made men was a gross understatement. They were survivors.

After dabbling in Socialism and studying at New York University, Jack got his accounting degree and landed a job with the ILGWU, managing the union's strike fund, the money set aside for when and if its members walked off a job. Jack invested that money in the stock market, but after the Wall Street crash, the funds took a dive, and so did Jack. With very few clients, Jack wound up working for Harry.

With Jack at the helm, Harry expanded his distribution business. Jack explained that distribution was where the real profit was. For news vendors, the contact for the magazine was the distributor, who would visit the newsstands and take orders for the publisher. The distributor would then deliver the magazines and push for good placement, then collect on sales made. Depending on the distributor's deal, they would take a certain cut of the profit, maybe slightly less than half. But newsstands paid the distributors directly for what was sold, so until all the unsold copies were returned and the distributor showed his hand, there was no way for the magazine to know how much money they were owed.

The covers of the returns were ripped off or a hole was punched in them. Those damaged copies would then be sent by the publisher overseas or to magazine dumps, who would sell them at a discount. In the gap time, a distributor could invest the money, lend it out, or simply hold on to it. Sometimes if you held on to it long enough, the magazine would go out of business, and then Harry and Jack could step in and take it over.

The yin to Harry's yang, Jack Liebowitz was the tight-assed, detail-oriented numbers man to Harry's rambling, backslapping, hotfoot-giving guy. Though he looked like a comic villain with his skinny mustache, Jack played by the rules that Harry often trampled: he avoided doing anything outright illegal, but morals and ethics were definitely off the table. The little boy with the doctored report card was still alive and well in Jack's soul. If Jack even had a soul. He would one day become known as the Eraser by all the people he screwed over and made disappear—not through Mob hits, but through contracts and court cases. Jack was, like Harry, a *goniff*—Yiddish for a dishonest son of a bitch. Their coming together was like earth meeting sky, like Bergdorf meeting Goodman, Astaire meeting Rogers. Or Sundance meeting Butch. History— business, entertainment, and criminal—was about to be made.

CHAPTER 3

DAREDEVIL REPORTER

BERLIN, 1926

BILLIE WILDER (RIGHT, hands in pockets)
WITH PAUL WHITEMAN AND HIS BAND

BILLIE WILDER SAT AT A SMALL ROUND TABLE AT THE Romanisches Café, a cavernous hangout for musicians, artists, and intellectuals at the start of the two-mile-long Kurfürstendamm, the Fifth Avenue of Berlin. Occasionally, the smell of the nearby zoo elephants wafted over to the café's canopied outdoor tables or in through its Romanesque doorway. A tall, wiry redhead, Billie had recently moved to Berlin and liked the café because he could read all the newspapers—attached to long wooden sticks—for free. Close to fainting from hunger, Wilder used the change in his pockets to buy the cheapest meal on the menu, a soft-boiled egg, which the café served in an elegant, rounded coupe glass, a tall saltshaker placed beside it by a bow-tied, white-aproned waiter. The service and surroundings at the Romanisches made you feel like a prince, even if you were broke. And no one ever asked you to leave, no matter how long you loitered there.

The Romanisches had a long, vaulted arcade supported by tall marble columns stretching to its lofty ceiling. Coatracks were filled to tumbling with fedoras and fancy furs, moth-eaten cloaks, and overcoats. Both rich and poor, young and old, Jew and Aryan congregated here, arguing, writing, and reading, their newspapers spread like bedsheets before them. The chess players silently battled it out in the gallery above, while below sat the fashionable ladies in cloche hats over rebelliously short haircuts smoking their cigarettes. Already established artists sat in cliques, just tables away from the undiscovered, like Billie. Through the café windows Billie could glimpse the gargantuan Kaiser Wilhelm Memorial Church— built by the same architect who had designed the Romanisches. The church—a monument to imperial prewar Germany—loomed over everything, its spire rising like a sharp canine tooth, piercing the blue sky above it.

To Billie, Berlin was a revelation, its streets and cafés filled with smart-talking wiseasses like himself. Jews were not second-class citizens as they had been in his home in Vienna. Billie, a free-lance reporter, had come to Berlin to make a name for himself in 1926, though he wasn't sure exactly how to go about that or what his name should be. The city he found was filled with pastry shops, gourmet food shops, and restaurants, but Billie had no money to even pay rent. He slept in the railway stations, eventually renting a place on the Viktoria-Luise-Platz, a pretty park with a fountain that he unfortunately could not see from his tiny back room. The park had been named long ago for the daughter of the now-deposed kaiser.

After losing the Great War, to make up for the carnage they'd inflicted, Germany was ordered to pay billions in reparations to their French and English enemies as part of the Treaty of Versailles. The German economy was now in a tailspin, though the worst was yet to come. Families who would never have considered taking in boarders were now taking in several, breaking up once grand homes into small compartments. Billie's room was next to the hall bathroom, whose running toilet he would pretend was a beautiful waterfall in order to fall asleep each night. Unable to afford heat, he would, in more than one freelance story, describe his fingers turning blue. He cut his cigarettes in half to ration them and bought wine from one of the only store owners who would give him credit—just so he could dump out the contents and get the deposits on the bottles. He'd pay his debt to the wine merchant when he finally made a score. If he ever made a score.

Though the city's glamour had not rubbed off on Billie yet, he was thrilled just to be here, amid the colors and movement, the bright lights and nonstop life. The spark in the city's air even had its own name—*Berliner luft.*

Billie's mother, Eugenia, was from Neumark, Prussia—which later became Poland, thanks to Eastern Europe's shifting borders. Eugenia was smart and more sophisticated than most people they knew, encouraging her son to want more out of life. She had spent five years in New York City when she was an adolescent, living with an uncle who owned a jewelry store on Madison Avenue on the Upper East Side.

Eugenia—known as Gitla to her friends and family—begged her mother, the owner of a small hotel in Poland, to let her stay in New York permanently. But she was forced to return home, where she married and had her own children. Though Eugenia named her second son Samuel after her dead father, her nickname for him came from the American rodeo showman Buffalo Bill Cody, whom she saw during his Wild West tour of New York City in the 1890s.

Eugenia never lost her passion for New York and would tell Billie stories about how wonderful America had been in the Gilded Age, not just Buffalo Bill and his cast of cowboys and Indians, but the gaslit streets and stately mansions of Manhattan, the tamed wilderness that was Central Park, and the cat's cradle majesty of the Brooklyn Bridge. The neighborhood she had lived in was full of German-speaking Prussians like them, the streets dotted with bright bakeries selling strudel, and dark saloons pouring steins of lager.

Billie inherited her fascination with America and also her sharp sense of humor. Eugenia was a tough audience, so Billie knew New York must have been truly extraordinary to have wowed her.

Billie's father, Max, opened and operated railroad station cafés, moving the family from the small town of Sucha Beskidzka in Galicia to Kraków and eventually to Vienna. But in Austria, Max was denied citizenship because he was a Jew. A dreamer who wasn't sure exactly what to dream about, Max had high hopes for Billie. He wanted him to become a lawyer. And Billie was smart, but was not the best student, preferring billiards, soccer, and movies—particularly those of Buster Keaton, Chaplin, and Douglas Fairbanks, the King of Hollywood—to going to class. Eventually his mother sent him to a school for problem boys. Though he passed the *matura*, the exit exam from high school, he opted out of college and became a newspaperman in Vienna instead. He had seen too many American movies with men in raincoats and press cards stuck in their hat bands. Billie dreamed of becoming a foreign correspondent and moving to America. Never mind that he didn't speak English.

At the Viennese newspaper *Die Stunde*, Billie made crossword puzzles—a wildly popular new craze—before moving on to entertainment writing. Each morning, Eugenia woke him, saying, "Get up and write some anecdotes." And what anecdotes they were. Billie interviewed the composer Richard Strauss and a sixteen-member women's dance company, a Swiss clown, a Mexican escape artist, an Austrian card magician, a Russian opera singer, and a working witch who placed spells on the enemies of bankers and businessmen. He wrote about plays, movies, and jazz music, one of his loves, whose lyrics provided his only knowledge of English. As a reporter, he was collecting a cast of characters—and an ear for dialogue.

But he soon found himself enmeshed in a breaking scandal. Editors and advertising executives at *Die Stunde* had been extorting money from businesses: if you didn't pay a kickback, you got bad press. Billie was paid extra by his bosses for writing positive café reviews. They were his weakest pieces. "And the specialty coffee!" he wrote. "Praise be to the cook, praise to her heartwarming approach. . . . I have found my favorite café."

After writing positively about the orchestra leader Paul Whiteman, whom he genuinely admired and who had recently commissioned and played on George Gershwin's classical jazz masterpiece *Rhapsody in Blue*, Billie decided to follow Whiteman's band to Berlin in 1926. But when he got there, he decided he wasn't going back to Vienna. *Die Stunde* would soon fold, and Billie knew getting another newspaper job in light of the scandal would not be easy.

So here he was. In Berlin. His dream city. Or at least a close second.

To pay his landlady, a retired circus performer with a gray mustache, he took a job as a hired dancer, spinning rich old women on the floor of the Eden Hotel's grand Pavillon restaurant, located right near the Romanisches. Women in gowns with thick legs and even thicker waists waited for Billie and his fellow gigolos to approach their large round tables covered in crisp white tablecloths. As the cigarette boy glided past, murmuring, "*Zigarren, Zigarette,*" a small orchestra played on a raised platform. Rich husbands sat and watched, drinking and smoking as Billie and his fellow dancers waltzed about with their wives.

"I wasn't the best dancer," Billie would say, "but I had the best dialogue." He danced himself to exhaustion each night, sometimes falling asleep in his bed still wearing his secondhand tuxedo. One night, he dreamed a man had come to collect on back rent. Instead of garnishing his wages, he garnishes Billie's knees. When he tries to chase the man, he falls over, naturally, since he has no knees.

While working as a dance gigolo, Billie took copious notes, parlaying the job into a series of newspaper articles titled "Waiter, a Dancer, Please!" His writing was sharp and mean: the woman with hair the color of egg yolks, the husbands studying the prices on the wine list through monocles. The series caused quite a stir and landed him better freelance work as a newspaperman in Berlin, which had dozens of papers, more than any other city. He eventually made enough money to buy a used Chrysler, which he drove from anecdote to anecdote.

Billie met other writers at the café who were working for the German film industry, which was second only to Hollywood. So in his spare time, between his newspaper and magazine stories, he began to ghostwrite short silent film screenplays. At the Romanisches, he wrote a piece about the silent film director Erich von Stroheim, met a young actress named Marlene Dietrich and a producer named Joe Pasternak, who ran the Berlin office for Carl Laemmle's Universal Pictures in Hollywood. Pasternak hired Billie to write his own script in exchange for the thousand marks he owed him from losing at poker. The film, *The Daredevil Reporter*, drew on Billie's own experience as a newspaperman and was his first screen credit. Though it was a box office flop.

His next picture, written on napkins and random slips of paper and shot on a shoestring budget, was called *People on Sunday*. The 1930 silent film follows five nonactors as they go about their life in Berlin on their day off—couples meeting near the golden clock outside the zoo train station, and then swimming, picnicking, and sunbathing at Wannsee Lake. The film was a sensation.

It was around this time that Billie's father, Max, came to visit him in Berlin. But his trip would not last long. Max died of an abdominal rupture in Billie's arms in the back of an ambulance. He was buried in Weissensee Jewish cemetery in Berlin, not far from where Jules's father lay.

THE PORTICO AT THE JEWISH BOYS SCHOOL ON GROSSE HAMBURGER STRASSE

CHAPTER 4

STONE BOYS AND BEASTS

BERLIN, 1930

TURNING ONTO QUIET KREFELDER STRASSE, JULES PULLED his Model A up to Edith's six-story upscale apartment building. He patted down his hair, grabbed the bouquet of flowers lying next to him on the pleated leather seat, then nervously rang the doorbell. Though still a baby-faced eighteen-year-old, Jules was here to propose marriage. Albert, Edith's father, buzzed Jules past the frosted-glass front door and into the posh hallway, which was decorated in the German Art Nouveau style called Jugendstil. Shiny green tiles with embossed fleur-de-lis lined the entryway, while elaborate plaster gargoyles and beasts stared down at young Jules, making him even more nervous than he already was.

He climbed the carpeted hallway stairs two at a time, running his free hand along the polished wooden banister, stopping on Edith's landing and taking a deep breath before tapping the Art Deco brass knocker. Edith turned the elaborately decorated door handle and, suddenly, there she was. His love. She smiled, gave him a small peck on the cheek, and happily ushered him through the hallway and into the family study with its plush armchairs and tall grandfather clock. The sprawling apartment was well-appointed with antique furniture, imported carpets, and a balcony overlooking the street. Martha, Edith's mother, kissed Jules on each cheek, and offered to get him a beer. Edith's father vigorously shook

Jules's hand and told him to sit down. Edith, knowing why Jules was there, took the bouquet of flowers and left to place them in a cut-crystal vase.

Albert adored Jules, but he was worried the boy couldn't support Edith well enough. Jules still lived with his mother and several of his siblings in their cramped apartment across town on Anklamer Strasse in the Jewish quarter. Their busy, noisy court-yard was filled with empty baby carriages, bicycles, and wagons, and echoed the sounds in the other flats—children crying, fathers laughing, mothers praying, domestic spats building and then dying off each morning, noon, and night. The smells—garbage mixed with cooking cabbage and sauerkraut—drifted in through the windows as well.

Though his family was not well off, Jules had attended one of the best schools in the city, the free Jewish Boys School on Grosse Hamburger Strasse. The arched doorway over his school was decorated with two stone boys staring down into a stone book. He would gaze up at those stone boys each day as he made his way through the curved wooden doors of the school, and some days it seemed as if they looked away from their stone pages and stared right back at him. Jules liked to regale the family—and especially Edith's kid sister, Ursula, whom they called Ushi—with tales of his schoolboy days, which were barely over. He told stories of his soccer victories, about being a good and reliable student (so reliable he was named crayon monitor). Ushi loved Jules's stories. Everyone did.

The Friedmanns owned their own textile company in Berlin. Their apartment on Krefelder Strasse was in the well-off Moabit neighborhood just a short stroll from the flowering banks of the River Spree. A proud and decorated Great War veteran—a *Krieg-steilnehmer*—Albert was part of the establishment in Germany. And he loved his two daughters dearly. Edith was his oldest, and Ushi, six years younger.

Albert was thin and bald, with a mustache and big ears that stuck out from his head. His wife, Martha, was a brunette with full lips and large, melancholy eyes. She was well traveled, having even gone to Cairo solo to tour the pyramids. She had come from an intellectual, cultured family of bookstore owners in Posen, Prussia, and was much more outgoing than Albert, who was three years older than she was. Martha loved to dance and had passed that love on to Edith and Ushi.

Their daughters, somehow, had each gotten a different mix of their best features and were better looking than either of them. Edith, slim with a long face, had inherited her mother's dark hair, sad eyes, and perfect Kewpie doll lips, and her father's strong, angular nose, which looked like it belonged in a Picasso painting. Ushi looked nothing like Edith, with curly red hair, freckles on her round face, and a short pug nose. She actually looked Irish, a throwback to some long-lost relative. Their personalities were just as different as their looks—Edith, reserved and serious, and Ushi the chatty, outgoing one. But both sisters were well educated and incredibly smart, kind, and generous.

After taking a seat in the family study, Jules got down to business. Alone with Albert for a moment, he announced he had come to ask for his daughter's hand in marriage. Jules explained he would soon be opening his own fur shop with help from his sister Mollie and her husband, David, and swore he would dedicate his life to taking care of Edith. Albert, unable to resist Jules's good nature and charms, gave him his blessing.

Jules set out to prove he could provide Edith with the life she'd grown accustomed to. But it was a difficult time to make a go of it alone, especially in a high-end industry like furs. Times were not good for everyone in Berlin. With unemployment reaching nearly 30 percent by 1932, there were tent cities in the forests just outside town and long lines at the pawnshops. People were in search of a savior, but also for someone to blame for their poverty. Street clashes between Nazis and Communists became more frequent, exploding nearly every day, as the groups marched defiantly against one another, bottles and bricks in hand.

Fearful of a Communist threat—which Hitler featured in his speeches—leaders in Germany's business community began to join the Nazi Party. In the July 1932 elections, the party was triumphant, winning 230 seats in the German parliament. Usually, the chancellor would be appointed from the party with the most seats in the Reichstag. But Germany's president, Paul von Hindenburg, was hesitant to make Hitler chancellor. After back-room negotiations and pressure from politicians and wealthy industrialists, Hindenburg finally gave in.

Some politicians and critics failed to take Hitler seriously. They were certain that somehow they could control this fool. But plenty of people took him seriously. Just as Jules was proposing marriage, many of the city's intellectuals and artists began leaving Berlin; Marlene Dietrich and Albert Einstein, for example, headed to California, the scientist taking his beloved violin, Lina, with him. Fritz Lang, when told by Goebbels that the new chancellor wanted him to head the Nazi Party's film industry, left for Paris immediately.

"Concentration camps"—for now simply factory cellars and warehouses—cropped up all over Berlin, places where the Sturmabteilung, the Nazi paramilitary wing known as the Brownshirts, took those they didn't like and beat them, sometimes to death.

Still, the Friedmanns planned a beautiful wedding for Edith and Jules at a banquet hall on the Kurfürstendamm. As the date drew closer, they invited some of the younger members of the large wedding party over to their apartment for dance rehearsals. The young cousins waltzed and laughed and stepped on each other's toes, trying their best to ignore the evil unfolding outside their windows.

Ushi led the lessons. Mollie and David's young sons, Bob and Fred, were there, as well as Golda's son, Don, and his half brother, Paul. At nine years old, Paul was dark and wiry like his father, Simon, with a hesitant smile and big ears. Simon sported the short, cropped mustache of the day, like the one Charlie Chaplin wore, but that would fall out of favor quite soon in the Jewish community. He and Golda ran a clothing company in the center of Berlin near Mollie's fur shop.

Don, who had come with his mother as a baby from Amsterdam, looked nothing like his half brother, with light hair and a round face like Golda's. He attended a specialized high school for engineering, but he and his four fellow Jewish students were regularly abused by the other students. And sometimes by the teachers.

"Who are the thieves in Germany?" one teacher would ask each day.

"The filthy Jews!" the class would reply.

"Who are the rapists of German women?" she would ask.

"The filthy Jews!" they would shout again.

When the teacher was done with his verbal abuse, the Aryan boys would throw ink and books at them. When Don came home one day with ink all over his face, Golda called the school's director, who was sympathetic but helpless against the emboldened Hitler Youth on his rolls. During school soccer practice, Don and his fellow Jewish players were literally beaten on the field by their teammates. One day he stayed home from school and never went back.

Don, sixteen, got a job in the Berlin branch of Ford Motor Company, tending to tractors and cars, and while there, developed an attachment that could convert alcohol or kerosene into high-octane fuel. He was such a brilliant engineer that he was offered a spot by a Jewish organization to work in Palestine, which had opened its doors wide, accepting sixty thousand German Jews throughout the 1930s as part of a transfer agreement with Germany. He asked if his parents and brother could go with him, and the visas were granted. But his stepfather refused to even discuss leaving Berlin. Golda wouldn't go against her husband, but tried gentle persuasion.

"A window has opened," Golda said to Simon, "and we should go." But he wouldn't move to Palestine. He didn't like the hot weather, he said, and more important, he had built his men's clothing business here in Germany and felt he couldn't leave it behind. But it wasn't just about the money. A religious man, Simon believed that God would save them all from Adolf Hitler.

And so they all stayed, Don included.

Jules was at temple with his family on a quiet Saturday morning on the first day of April 1933. As they prayed together, mobs of their fellow Germans were busy paying visits to many of Berlin's closed storefront businesses in the early-morning light. When Jules went to open Mollie's fur shop for the day, he found a gold and black Star of David painted on the door. The newly elected Nazi Party had launched its first nationwide boycott, its first official attack on the Jewish community. The Brownshirts defaced the fronts of thousands of Jewish-owned businesses in Berlin and beyond.

Jules was enraged. He thought he might vomit right there on the sidewalk, which he always kept impeccably clean, sweeping it several times each day. Part of him wanted to break something, or someone, but he was much too civilized. He simply stared at the star, not knowing whether to scrape it off or display it proudly. It was the Star of David after all—part of his identity.

But it was the words scrawled beside the star, across the shop windows, that made the decision for him.

Geh nach Palästina!

"Go to Palestine!" was painted in black. Next door were the words "The Jews Are Our Misfortune," and across the street, "Don't buy from Jews." Jules, David, and his neighbors got to work with their paint scrapers and scrub brushes, but within the hour, a crowd of Brownshirts showed up. In pairs, they menacingly stood outside David's shop and all the shops on the street, blocking customers from entering. Some wore sandwich boards that read: *Germans, defend yourselves against Jewish atrocity propaganda*. Others chanted from the backs of trucks, "Germans, free yourselves of the tyranny of the Jews!" Local police were instructed not to interfere with the boycott. Some customers would defy the Brownshirts, but most turned and walked quickly away, not wanting any trouble.

Not wanting a fight, either, Jules and his siblings closed up shop for the day. It was the Sabbath, after all.

THE SA (STURMABTEILUNG), ALSO KNOWN AS BROWNSHIRTS, PICKETING JEWISH-OWNED SHOPS. THEIR SIGNS READ, "GERMANS, DEFEND YOURSELVES AGAINST THE JEWISH ATROCITY PROPAGANDA, BUY ONLY AT GERMAN SHOPS!" AND "GERMANS! DEFEND YOURSELVES! DON'T BUY FROM JEWS!"

HARRY'S FRIEND, MOB BOSS FRANK COSTELLO,
TESTIFYING AT A SENATE COMMITTEE HEARING

CHAPTER 5

PULP NONFICTION

NEW YORK, 1931

EVERY TWO WEEKS HARRY DONENFELD MET HIS BOOTLEG-
ging pal, Frank Costello, for overpriced cuts, shaves, and mani-
cures at the Art Deco barbershop inside the new Waldorf Astoria
Hotel. The barbershop—men only—was one floor above the
street and was filled with shining nickel-brass fixtures, inlaid mirrors, polished marble counters, and two rows of twelve chairs each.
A small army of white-coated barbers and nineteen manicurists
worked the giant room, which was decorated with small palm
trees. Those waiting their turn sat in deep leather armchairs. If
you got your hair cut here, it meant you'd made it in New York
City, and in America.

Costello, the consigliere of the Luciano crime family upon
whom the character of the Godfather would one day be based, was
around the same size as Harry and had come up in the city around
the same time and in the same way, through neighborhood gangs
as a teenager. He was known as the Prime Minister of the Un-
derworld and—despite his short stature—had grown his business
from bootlegging to prostitution rings and illegal gambling, with
some extortion thrown in for good measure. Within four years, he
would be running the Luciano crime family, with access to the press
through his pal and apartment building neighbor Walter Winchell,
the Hearst newspaper columnist and radio broadcaster.

The city around Costello and Harry was growing as fast as their wealth, what with the brand-new, shining Empire State Building—the tallest in the world at 102 floors—casting its long shadow over them and all New Yorkers, and the newly minted George Washington Bridge, its single span the longest on the planet, stretching west to the rest of America.

Sitting in their barber chairs side by side for their fortnightly chats, Harry and Costello discussed not only business but the news of the day, everything from the rising unemployment rate and dust storms in the Midwest to Prohibition agent Eliot Ness and his attacks on their Chicago friends. They talked about Nevada, which had just legalized all forms of gambling, and worried over a rising politician named Hitler, who was causing trouble over in Germany. Hitler would make friends with Mussolini, who until then Costello and many Italians thought was doing a pretty good job, literally draining the swamps, reclaiming land, and building schools and railroads. Costello's associate, Vito Genovese, happened to be friends with Il Duce. But Hitler was another story. Walter Winchell, who was Jewish, didn't like Hitler, either, and let it be known, not just to his friends, but in countless columns and broadcasts.

Harry was nowhere near the mobster that Costello was. Some people said that Costello and his cohorts were so ruthless they would stab their mother in the back and take bets on which way she would fall. Harry wasn't that bad, and as far as anyone knew, he had never been arrested for murder. (When his mother had passed in 1927 at the age of sixty-four, no one accused him of killing her or making any wagers.) For Harry, the late twenties had been spent trying to keep out of the clutches of the New York Society for the Suppression of Vice and the FBI. It wasn't easy. They created a dossier on him running more than two hundred pages. He was the focus of investigations not only in New York but also in Chicago, Milwaukee, Detroit, Buffalo, Cincinnati, Louisville, and Denver. They eventually caught up with Harry, who was finally arrested in May of 1930 for publishing obscenity. But he got off with a fine.

Business was booming, and by 1931, Harry formed Donny Press, leasing space at the spectacular Grand Central Palace. The thirteen-story building filled a whole city block at Lexington Avenue and Forty-Seventh Street and featured an indoor golf course stretched across the top floor and the country's largest dance hall, Clover Gardens, which filled the entire seventh. Harry's neighbors in the building would eventually include the IRS and the Selective Service, the agency in charge of the draft. Harry would joke that he was keeping a close eye on his enemies.

Using four different addresses, one for each of the four city streets the Grand Central Palace occupied, Harry formed company after company. The shell game helped him avoid paying his bills and also confused the feds. Among Harry's companies—all within a decade and most headquartered within the same building—were:

Donenfeld Magazines
DM Publishing
Deane Publishing
Detineur Publishing Co.
Tilsam
Culture Publications
Trojan Publishing Corporation (named after the birth
   control ads in his pages)
Forward Publications
Modern Publications
Arrow Publications
National Publications

National Allied Publications
Super Magazines
Detective Comics and
Leader News

Some of these he started himself, but others he edged his way into. Plotting with Jack Liebowitz, Harry would often swindle a company out of the hands of its owner. For instance, he would agree to distribute a magazine, but as part of his contract he would become a partner, and when the magazine couldn't pay its inflated printing or distribution bills, he would take it over. He would then fail to pay his creditors and writers, declare bankruptcy, and form an entirely new company. Play and repeat. That's exactly what happened in 1932, when the publisher of *Pep Stories* and *Spicy Stories*, facing distribution issues and debt, sold out, making Harry the undisputed king of the sex pulps. The unpaid writers would complain, but eventually would work for whatever new publication Harry created, since work was scarce and Harry did get around to paying every now and then.

Another key to his success was that Harry traveled cross-country, schmoozing drugstore and newsstand owners, plying them with "booze and broads," he bragged. Most distributors carried on their relationships by mail or phone, but with Harry, it was personal. He made each of them feel like family, giving them gifts, taking them drinking. Then if things didn't go as planned, there would be a visit from one of his old pals from the Lower East Side to strong-arm the dealers to do as he asked. Pretty please.

Prohibition ended in December 1933, the thirst for liquor quickly replaced by a growing hunger as more and more New Yorkers found themselves without work. One out of every four men was unemployed, but Harry expanded. With the profits from the smooshes, Harry formed Independent News, which distributed more respectable magazines like the *Saturday Evening Post* and *Family Circle*. When Jewish friends and family members came to Harry, he gave them jobs, and gave their kids jobs, too. He was not just a mensch, but a macher—a mover and shaker taking charge and getting things done. Your son Jake needs work? "He can sweep my office until something better comes along," Harry would say. And with Harry, something better always came along.

WILDER IN BERLIN AT THE BRANDENBURG GATE

CHAPTER 6

DIRECT TRANSMISSIONS

BERLIN, CIRCA 1933

THOUGH IT WAS PUBLISHED SEVERAL YEARS EARLIER, BILLIE Wilder finally got around to reading *Mein Kampf.* He could barely believe his eyes when reading lines like "If the Jews were the only people in the world they would be wallowing in filth and mire and would exploit one another and try to exterminate one another in a bitter struggle. . . . He is and remains a parasite, a sponger who, like a pernicious bacillus, spreads over wider and wider areas. . . . The effect produced by his presence is also like that of the vampire. . . ."

If they weren't so dangerous, Hitler's words could be taken as ridiculous. But now Hitler's speeches and writings on mass annihilation were being translated into action. When the elevator boy at Germany's UFA film studios showed up in a storm trooper uniform, Billie started to worry. Since the success of *People on Sunday*, Billie had been very busy in the German film industry, writing ten more films. But then one evening in late February 1933, Billie looked on, helplessly, as the SS marked up the windows of some Jewish shops and beat an old Jewish man in the street. The following night, Billie and his girlfriend had a front-row seat as flames tore through the Reichstag, the fire set by the Nazis, who then blamed the Communists. They watched the smoke billow from the glass parliamentary dome as they ate dinner at a nearby restaurant. "It's time to go," said Billie. His girlfriend insisted on coffee and dessert.

Years later, Billie would say that leaving Berlin wasn't his idea—"It was Hitler's."

The Nazis used the fire to declare a state of emergency and outlaw all other political parties. Hitler made speeches blaming the "elite" Jews for the Depression that had spread after the collapse of Wall Street, riling up his crowds, whom he pretended to sympathize with in their victimhood. Billie listened closely to his speeches, the hate regularly bleeding from cheap, government-issued radios. Because of those radios, which had a limited bandwidth and marked only German stations on their dials, the dictator was able to circumvent journalists and block out international transmissions. Hitler had a direct channel to his followers, feeding them a steady stream of lies and propaganda. Listening to foreign stations would soon become illegal and punishable by death. The rest of the world was lying, insisted Hitler, who called foreign journalists *Lügenpresse*—or lying press. Only *he* was telling the truth. Like the evil villain of *Metropolis*, Hitler had turned technology against the people.

When Billie's fourteenth film, *What Women Dream*, premiered on Hitler's birthday that April, his name was scrubbed from the credits. Jews were no longer wanted. But Billie was already gone by then.

Selling everything he had, he moved to Paris with $1,000 in cash, living for about eight months at the Hotel Ansonia, which would become a refuge for other Jews escaping Germany, including the actor Peter Lorre, who had starred in *What Women Dream*. In Paris, Billie directed his first film, *Mauvaise Graine* (*Bad Seed*), about a rich playboy who gets mixed up with car thieves, but by the time it premiered, he'd already left for Hollywood. He and Lorre both sailed to America in 1934, eventually rooming together at the

Chateau Marmont on Sunset Boulevard, eating Campbell's soup to survive. They fell in love with the constant sunshine, the smell of orange blossoms, the wide-open vistas, and the commotion of the busy Hollywood studios, whose owners, like them, were Jews. Being Jewish was no longer a crime.

With the help of director Joe May, whom he had met at Germany's UFA studios, Billie was hired at $150 a week to write the script *Pam-Pam* for Hollywood's Columbia Pictures, and was granted a six-month visa. Columbia was flush with cash due to the success of the Clark Gable film *It Happened One Night*. Gable was currently all the rage, inheriting the King of Hollywood title from Douglas Fairbanks. Billie's *Pam-Pam* screenplay had to be translated from German, and perhaps losing something along the way, was rejected by the studio.

When his six-month visa was through, Billie had to quickly come up with a plan. Because the Nazis required them to surrender most of their assets before emigrating, many Jews arrived on the shores of America penniless. To stop the flow, the US government required that immigrants provide paperwork from a well-off financial sponsor who would, if needed, help support the person once they came to the country.

Because he had no sponsor in America, Billie had to travel to Mexico and then reenter the United States to try and secure a permanent visa. Getting out of Berlin, it turned out, was not the hard part. The problem now was that no one else would let you in if you were Jewish. Though Hollywood's establishment was filled with members of the tribe, federal immigration quotas set up in 1924 were still in place. Billie wired Berlin to get the papers he needed—tax records and a police certificate proving he had no criminal record—but he was ignored. All he had were his birth certificate and his passport, which were not enough for a visa application.

At the Mexicali border, he and an American vice-consul, who looked a lot like the folksy humorist Will Rogers, just stared at each other for a while in a standoff. Billie started joking and tried to make small talk.

"What do you do for a living?" humorless Will Rogers asked.

"I'm a writer."

"What do you write?"

"I write movies," Billie told him, sweating profusely. Not from the heat. Billie was scared to death.

Will Rogers paced back and forth for a while. Billie sweated some more. The man picked up Billie's passport, took his rubber stamp, and pounded his approval. "Write some good ones," he told Billie.

One of the first things Billie learned in Hollywood was that his first name was spelled wrong. Billie—as in Billie Holiday—was for girls. He immediately changed it to Billy. By listening to the radio and playing Scrabble in the studio commissary, he learned to speak proper English and landed work at Fox with Joe May. His screenplay for the operatic film *Music in the Air* featured silent film star Gloria Swanson in her first talkie.

With two more screenplays sold, Billy traveled back to Europe in 1935—already a death-defying act—to try and convince his widowed mother and his grandmother to come back to America with him. He reminded Eugenia of the stories she had told him of living on the Upper East Side during the Gilded Age. The walks along Fifth Avenue. The horse and buggies drifting through wooded Central Park. Buffalo Bill's Wild West show. But she refused to leave. She was in her fifties and set in her ways. More important, she had met a new man, a Polish Jew named Bernard who worked as a *Flaschenverschlussezeuger*—a manufacturer of bottle stoppers. Eugenia was in love.

So Billy headed back to America alone, where he would start

writing *Bluebeard's Eighth Wife*, a mean-spirited romantic comedy starring Claudette Colbert and Gary Cooper. Directed by Ernst Lubitsch, a Jew who had left Berlin way back in 1922, the film would be viewed on a summer night soon after its release at a double feature private screening by one, Adolf Hitler.

APRIL 25¢

Spicy DETECTIVE STORIES

The LOVE NEST MURDER
by Jon LeBaron

SPICY DETECTIVE, APRIL 1934 ISSUE, ONE OF THE MANY SPICY HYBRIDS

CHAPTER 7

ALWAYS SUNNY

NEW YORK, CIRCA 1933

THE WOMAN WITH AUBURN HAIR WAS DRESSED IN DUSTY pink heels with her dress blowing up over her head, her hands pushing down at the billowing gold and scarlet fabric. She was smiling and was only half-heartedly pushing back against the wind, her frilled white panties showing, her bare back bent over, her left breast peeking out from her halter top dress. The woman was not real, but a version of her lived in the memories of New Yorkers from Harry's generation, who as teenagers had spent their afternoons loitering outside the Flatiron Building on Twenty-Third and Fifth, waiting for the ladies' dresses to blow up. Because of the wind at that unusual corner, women's ankles and legs, sometimes even a thigh, could be seen. That is until the police shooed the gawkers away. The old 23 skidoo.

Now, with the help of an illustrator, the woman was living and breathing on the March 1933 cover of *Spicy Stories*. Harry could make any dress blow up at will. And share it with his reading public, whose appetite was insatiable. There seemed to be no end to the girlie pulps on the newsstands. As a result, they were becoming more and more of a target.

J. Edgar Hoover tried to nab Harry again and again for interstate transportation of his obscene materials, but with Harry's legal connections and his shell games—switching business addresses and company names—Hoover could barely pin him down. When he did, the US Attorney and courts repeatedly ruled that the material in Harry's magazines was not even obscene. Though she no longer worked for Harry, his former sex pulp editor/lover Merle Williams Hersey was kept on his payroll so she wouldn't spill any secrets to Hoover.

With the election of reformer Fiorello LaGuardia to mayor in 1933, the New York City landscape started to change. LaGuardia cracked down on Costello's slot machines, arrested Lucky Luciano, and instructed the newly christened sanitation department to take the smooshes from the newsstands and throw them directly in the trash.

Most garbagemen probably weren't so conscientious. LaGuardia would have to take matters into his own hands. And so, the second week of March 1934, his commissioner of licenses made a sweep of one hundred newsstands, removing fifty-nine different publications and arresting shopkeepers and dealers. Featured inside Harry's January issue of *Pep Stories* on page 21 was a black-and-white photo of a willowy beauty holding a vase and wearing a pair of high-heeled pumps—and nothing else. It was an artsy shot, the naked woman standing in an arched doorway, glancing down at a checkered floor, a dark triangle of pubic hair showing just below the vase's base. Something Vermeer might have painted had he been a smoosh artist. Harry was promptly arrested. The magistrate claimed to be so horrified by the publications that he came in on his day off to handle the case. "The stories not only tend to arouse lecherous desires," said the magistrate, Alfred Lindau, "but are intended to do so."

The magazines were banned from newsstands in New York City, and though Harry and his competitors fought the order on First Amendment rights, they lost. The smooshes were still permitted in cigar stores, since they were less visible there, just not out on the street for young, impressionable eyes to see. But Harry changed gears and moved to mostly express-mail subscriptions.

After losing his fight against the city, Harry pleaded guilty and was sentenced to sixty days in jail. Luckily Harry still had some pull left over from his bootlegging days dealing with Tammany Hall, so he paid a hefty $950 fine—the equivalent of $18,000 today—and was given a suspended sentence. But that April, Harry was also brought up on state obscenity charges. Thankfully, his pull extended all the way to Albany. He was hit with a $250 fine and a six-month suspended sentence in exchange for his promise to tone down the content of his magazines. A third strike, the judge told him, would land him behind bars. So Harry took his name off all of the unsavory magazines in his stable and formed Culture Publications, incorporating in Wilmington, Delaware, far from the prying eyes of the New York Society for the Suppression of Vice—even though his offices would remain in NYC in the Grand Central Palace. Harry placed one of his financial department employees, Herbert Myron Siegel, a fellow Romanian Jew, in charge of the sex pulps. But in name only.

To stay alive in the past, Harry had incorporated under Gussie's name, friends' names, Merle's name, and other people's wives' and mothers' names. Now, under the watchful eyes of the censors, Harry began removing bared breasts from the covers of the pulps and toning down the already tame sex stories. But Harry instinctively knew how to survive. That April, he combined the typical pulp detective magazine with the girlie magazine, launching *Spicy Detective Stories*. The new magazine paid a penny a word to its writers, who were encouraged to create "rapid fire, two-fisted detective stories with a strong sex angle."

For example, from "Brunette Bump-Off":

From an open window beyond the bed, a roscoe coughed, "Kachow!" . . . I said, "What the hell—!" and hit the floor with my smeller. . . . A brunette jane was lying there, half out of the mussed covers. . . . She was dead as vaudeville.

Harry's new hybrid—sex paired with badly written detective tales—took Dashiell Hammett's hard-boiled literary concept and tossed it, fresh and bloody and three-quarters naked, to the masses. The illustrated covers usually featured a barely dressed woman being attacked by a man with a gun—or in Harry's parlance, a roscoe. *Kachow!*

Still shell-shocked from the violence of the Great War, and now reeling from the trauma of the Depression, Americans in the early 1930s found a strange comfort in detective stories. Crime was exploding on city streets, with the national homicide rate hitting an all-time high for the century in 1933. But the chaos in a detective story was controlled, with a guaranteed tidy resolution. With the added value of nearly naked women, *Spicy Detective* provided the perfect escape.

Spicy Detective was also the first of Harry's publications to feature an actual comic strip, *Sally the Sleuth*. Sally was a sexy blond dish who becomes a crime fighter; with her appearance, sales skyrocketed. After that, every one of Harry's pulps would carry a comic strip inside.

The new magazine was so successful it spawned a series of other *Spicy* fusions, including *Spicy Western*, *Spicy Adventure*, and *Spicy Mystery*. To keep ahead of the vice team, Harry would run two versions of each issue, a relatively "clean" version, which included nearly naked women, marked on the cover and the spine by a star; and the dirtier version, which was always kept below the counter at cigar stores and other fine establishments. These included racier stories and more nudity as well as exciting details like whispers of pubic hair and whip marks on the bodies of the S&M characters.

If you wanted it extra spicy, you had to ask for it.

Thanks to the spicy pulps, Harry was wealthy enough to move out of the Bronx and into a townhouse on Riverside Drive at Eighty-Second Street. Gussie readily agreed, thinking that maybe she would see more of Harry if his home was closer to his office. Their new neighborhood was still rough around the edges, but was being transformed under the West Side Improvement project by Robert Moses, the city's parks commissioner and master planner. For now, the waterfront was marred by rusted wire fences and tracks, whose smelly cattle and pig trains ran along the New York Central line. Riverside "Park" was just a big mudflat and ash heap where the city's sanitation department dumped garbage, hungry New Yorkers swarming around each new load to search for food for their families. Shantytowns—Hoovervilles—had sprung up all along the river's edge. There were river rats and still the occasional streetwalker. The car traffic on the West Side was also becoming a problem.

But Harry loved being back in Manhattan full-time, without that long commute to the Bronx. He also loved the fancy brick and limestone French Baroque and English Gothic houses that faced the river, some topped in copper, others edged like castles. Their views of rotting timber and tar-paper shacks would soon be replaced with a beautiful park and state-of-the-art highway, once Moses's $200 million construction was done in 1937. The neighborhood, like Harry, was on the rise.

Harry played the aristocrat, hiring a cook named Ethel, a young Bavarian housekeeper named Betty, a Polish nanny named Anna, and an Italian chauffer, Frank, who drove Gussie, their seven-year-old son, Irwin, and five-year-old daughter, Sonia—whom they called Peachy—wherever they wanted. Frank chauffeured young Irwin every morning to the exclusive Columbia Grammar & Preparatory School near Central Park West and went to all of his ball games. Harry only went to one of Irwin's baseball games and didn't even stay for the whole thing. He was always too busy traveling for business or out carousing. Now Harry was just a short stumble away from the Midtown bars he loved, which were now legal.

Occasionally he would sing his children to sleep, because, well, Harry loved to sing, especially when he'd been drinking. But he also made sure the kids got the music lessons his parents could never afford. Peachy played piano, Irwin the ear-piercing trumpet, which blended in with all that horn honking on Riverside Drive. Harry had only his voice. When the children were very young, he sang them Yiddish lullabies. But he preferred the completely inappropriate "Mama Don't Want No Peas an' Rice":

Mama don't want no peas an' rice
Mama don't want no coconut oil
Just a bottle of brandy handy all the day! . . .

Mama don't want no glass o'gin
Because it's bound to make her sin
Says it keeps her hot and bothered all the day!

The kids loved it, though it annoyed their mama, who was not a heavy drinker like Harry. By this time, Gussie had lost any sense of humor she had had when Harry first met her. Her children would remember her as grumpy and disagreeable. She didn't get along with Harry or anyone, really. But Harry had only himself—and his many infidelities—to blame.

Gussie no longer spoke of divorce, exchanging her anger for a role as a major stockholder of Trojan Publishing in 1934—and a juicy cut of Harry's business dealings. But she knew he was cheating. Everyone knew. The sales ladies at all the department store perfume counters in town knew because Harry was always buying a new girl-friend a new bottle. Even his own son, years later, said that Harry had a wife, a lover, and a mistress and cheated on all three of them.

But his favorite of all his lovers was Sunny.

Sunny Paley had been born Sonya Paley in the spring of 1911. She was also born in the autumn of 1909, depending on what story you believed. Or maybe 1907. Whatever the year, Sonya was born in Minsk to a barber, coincidentally or not, named Harry and his wife, Gussie. (The fact that Sunny's name was Sonya may have been the reason Harry renamed his daughter Peachy. It was all a big fat Freudian knot no one wanted to untie.)

Sunny and her three siblings grew up on Cherry Street on the Lower East Side in the shadow of the anchorage of the newly built Manhattan Bridge. All of Cherry Street was awful, but the area where the Paleys set up house—across from a horse stable, near a lumberyard and scrap metal dump—was particularly grim. Cherry Street had once been one of the premier addresses in New York City, with curved cobblestone paths, a view of the East River, and, of course, a grove of cherry trees. It got its name from the seven-acre orchard that stood there until houses were built, including the presidential mansion of George Washington.

By the time Sunny arrived, Cherry Street was full of dark, dirty alleys and the worst tenements in the city. To get out of the neighborhood, nineteen-year-old Sunny married a thirty-six-year-old raincoat manufacturer, sailing off to Cuba for a two-day honeymoon. The marriage was over nearly as quickly as the honeymoon. When Harry met Sunny, she was living a few buildings away from him, divorced and sharing an apartment with her brother Charlie, a musician.

Maybe Sunny bumped into Harry on Riverside Drive, the sad New Jersey skyline wincing in the distance, the baby black cherry trees and American elms newly planted in Riverside Park. However they met, Sunny soon became a fixture on Harry's arm. She had a tiny waist, unlike Gussie, and tiny feet—she wore a size 5 shoe. Sunny always smelled of Bal à Versailles perfume and she smoked, but only socially, and kept her cigarette in a cigarette holder. She drank scotch and quite a bit of it, maybe to forget, sometimes, that dirty street where she came from. It was one of the things Harry loved about her. But not the only one.

Sunny was stylish, swathed in fur wraps, with expensive alligator handbags draped on her slender arm even before she met Harry, gifts from her many admirers. Harry loved to give her presents, minks from the Upper West Side furriers and expensive jewelry dripping with diamonds. Her favorite possession was a ring with her full name—SUNNY PALEY—written in chunky diamonds all the way around the gold band in big block letters like a name flashing in bulbs on a Hollywood movie marquee.

She and Harry traveled to Hawaii and Florida regularly, though their favorite spot was Cuba, where they would stay at the National Hotel in Havana. Set on a rocky hill, the sand-colored National looked out onto the impossibly blue sea, its two red-tiled towers climbing higher than the palm trees leading to its balconied, Corinthian-columned portico. Financed by the National City Bank of New York and built for the gringo tourists who flocked there, the hotel was a monument to capitalism on an island fighting for its political soul. In 1933, student activists teamed up with enlisted soldiers to overthrow the government. After a coup d'état by Sergeant Fulgencio Batista, a bloody battle even unfolded in the hotel, leaving bullet holes in the walls and forty rebels dead. Of course, the trouble was just beginning for Cuba, its government precarious and its political divisions deep. But Harry and his Mob friends—like Lucky Luciano—considered it a second home. Occasional gunfire was a small price to pay for gambling in paradise.

With his love of the National, Harry had officially left his Socialist past behind. He would spend his days laying bets in the Mob-run casino there, and Sunny would, well, sun herself by the pool and on the beach. The two of them would stay together for more than twenty-five years.

Gussie no longer seemed to mind. She had the money, the Riverside apartment, the chauffer and cook. The mistress came along with the deal. She and Harry—and Sunny—were living the dream.

JULES AND EDITH ON THEIR WEDDING DAY

CHAPTER 8

IN THE GARDEN

BERLIN, 1934

JULES AND EDITH STOOD BENEATH THE CHUPPAH, THE STAR of David etched above their heads in gold embroidered thread. The rabbi delivered the seven benedictions, to represent the seven chuppahs that God and his angels set up for the first couple, Adam and Eve, at their wedding in the Garden of Eden. He spoke of how living in Eden was not enough to bring Adam and Eve joy throughout their life. They needed one another to be happy. They needed companionship. And so Edith and Jules would be companions to one another, just as Adam and Eve had been, thousands of years before.

Jules and Edith looked like they belonged on one of Jules's glamorous film cards—the striking bride in a floor-length veil of lace, the handsome groom with hair slicked back, dressed in a tux and white tie. Jules resembled Fred Astaire from the new smash hit *Dancing Lady*, a romantic musical with Joan Crawford starring as a stripper who falls in love with a Broadway director played by Clark Gable. Though Jules and Edith looked like movie stars, there was a tension—almost a hesitation—in their smiles.

It was September 2, 1934. In the formal family photos taken with the bride and groom at the Kurfürstendamm banquet hall that day, half the family is missing, driven out by the Nazis. Months earlier, Jules's sister Cilly had decided it was time to go. She and her boyfriend, David Zauderer, would marry in a quick ceremony in Berlin and leave on their wedding day for Paris, a permanent honeymoon. Jules could barely look at Cilly as he said his goodbye, for fear she would unpack her suitcase and stay to protect him. They were the closest in age in the family, and had bonded while their father was in the war and just after he died. But they were also closest in personality, funny and quick-witted.

Through letters, Jules would learn that Cilly and David were stopped at the French border. After serving time in prison, Cilly would finally make it to Paris and get a job working in an orphanage for Jewish children. She pleaded with Jules to leave Berlin, to come and join them in Paris. Or flee to Palestine. Or America.

Jules's sister Sara and brother, Max, took Cilly's—and the Nazis'—advice. Because Max was a hunchback, he would become a special target of the Brownshirts. They left Berlin after witnessing a Nazi march through the streets and eventually settled in Tel Aviv. They encouraged the rest of the family to follow. But Golda's husband, Simon, still refused to leave. He thought Hitler was simply riling his base supporters up. "Why should we run?" said Simon. "God will protect us."

Anti-Semitism was nothing new in Berlin, but now it was government sanctioned. It was no secret to the German people when they voted for him that Hitler planned on removing the Jews from Europe by "fire and sword." Jews were being systematically erased from public life, barred from restaurants and swimming pools.

All good sense told Jules that he and Edith should leave as well, but his in-laws were against it; they felt certain that the Nazis wouldn't harm people as well-off as they were. And besides, Hitler's popularity could not possibly last. Their fellow Germans, no doubt, would eventually see him for the fool and liar he was and turn against him. They just had to. People couldn't be that stupid.

Fellow Berliners who were once friendly refused to speak to Jules. All greetings were replaced with "Heil Hitler." Jules had to grit his teeth every time he said it, reluctantly raising his hand in salute. But by 1935, Jews were forbidden from using the "Heil Hitler" greeting. Though it was another law curtailing his freedom, Jules was relieved. The first of the Nuremberg Laws were passed, stripping Jews of their citizenship and forbidding marriages between Jews and non-Jews.

As he had promised Albert, Jules worked hard at the fur business, staying on top of the latest fashions, sewing into the night and honing his sales pitch, showing the Friedmanns he would not just live in Berlin, but thrive. Edith moved into Jules's family's apartment with his mother, Hanne, on Anklamer Strasse not far from Mollie's fur shop. But a few months later, Hanne died, leaving Jules an orphan. Edith's family loved him like a son, adopting him as their own. And he was as dedicated to them as he had been to his own parents.

With Mollie and David's help, and with that relentless optimism, Jules opened a shop of his own in 1935 in the Moabit neighborhood, just a short walk to his in-laws' place, filling the hole left from Sara and Max's shop when they left for Palestine. Edith was eager to learn the trade and took easily to designing and sewing the furs they would both sell. Jules and Edith set up an apartment there as well, on Waldstrasse. The neighborhood was a step up for Jules, a typical evolution for hardworking Jews struggling to get out of the Jewish quarter. Their building wasn't quite as fancy as the Friedmanns' but featured modern stained-glass windows and hallway banisters decorated with sea serpent heads. Most important, it had a retail space downstairs with a big display window. There was also a large cobblestone courtyard with a full garden and ivy climbing the back brick wall—not the noisy, smelly courtyard Jules was used to. A few steps from the busy foot traffic of Turmstrasse,

Waldstrasse (Forest Street) featured a line of trees down its center. Up the block was a small park where Edith hoped to bring their baby when the time finally came. But Jules and Edith could only sit on benches painted yellow, reserved especially for them and their fellow Jews so as not to contaminate the Aryan citizens of Berlin.

Jules and Edith's first child was born in 1936. They named her Hannelore after his mother. Jules would fall as hard for his daughter as he had for Edith. And for a while his love for his daughter distracted him from what was unfolding around them. The following autumn, Hannelore took some of her first baby steps in the fading garden in their courtyard.

Jews like Jules who thought they could stick it out in Berlin formed youth leagues and cultural organizations so the community could still see movies, attend operas, play sports, and enjoy life like they had before, except separate from the Gentile community. But nothing was like it had been before. Little by little, Jules's dignity and freedom were slowly chipped away, with more than four hundred anti-Semitic laws passed from 1933 to 1939. He was forced to place a yellow star in his shop window to show that it was owned by a Jew. Some pharmacies and grocery stores refused to cater to him and Edith. People's hatred, once masked behind a fake civility, was now raw and out in the open. Jules was cursed at, spat at, not just by his enemies but by his former friends.

Hitler Youth dressed in brown shirts and carrying daggers imprinted with the German eagle and swastika were blocking the entrance of Jewish children into public schools, linking hands and forming human chains to stop them from entering. Young Jews packed the classrooms to overflowing in Jewish schools like the one Jules had attended on Grosse Hamburger Strasse, the place with the stone boys over its arched doorway. Jules wondered when the hating would end. Or maybe it would never end here in Germany. It was one thing to be abused, but the thought of his daughter being abused was another matter altogether. While sitting on one of those yellow benches in the park one day, watching his daughter play, it suddenly occurred to Jules that Hannelore had no future there.

Jules decided he was ready to go. And so was his sister Mollie.

But Edith's father, Albert, insisted that his fellow Germans wouldn't dare harm him or his family. The Jewish community had not only assimilated in Berlin but had thrived, helping run the government, the banks, newspapers, department stores, and textile companies like the one Albert owned. Which, of course, was part of the problem.

Hitler argued that the Jews were overtaking the economy and were intent on world domination. To punish them, and to stop them from taking their money with them to other countries, Hitler had imposed a 25 percent flight tax in 1933 when taking office. The tax, plus transfer fees for moving what money was left, meant that Jews leaving Germany would have to leave three-quarters of their wealth behind. Albert called it government-sanctioned robbery and refused to submit to Hitler's bullying.

Germany was Albert's home. He had fought valiantly for it. And he refused to surrender the hard-earned money from his business just to settle in some far-off place where he didn't even want to live and where he didn't speak the language. Ushi was still a teenager, and Albert and his wife, Martha, refused to pull her out of her private high school and disrupt her life.

When he proposed, Jules had promised to take good care of Edith in Berlin. But that was becoming harder and harder to do. Even the lido at Wannsee where they had swum as a young couple was now off-limits to Jews, who would be beaten by a uniformed surveillance team. Jules and Edith pleaded with the Friedmanns to leave. "It's too dangerous for us here," Jules said, again and again. "This Hitler is a madman. He will kill us all."

Jules had not only seen the Führer in person but had seen how his fellow Germans reacted to him. When Hitler hosted the 1936 Olympics in Berlin, Jules decided to attend. A huge soccer fan who still played on weekends in a Jewish league, Jules was thrilled that the Olympics had come to Berlin and was excited to watch the competition. Though Hitler built a new stadium in the city, he barred Jewish athletes from the home team. Decades before, Hitler's favorite philosopher, Nietzsche, had written about his *Übermensch*; now Germany's athletes would prove themselves supermen before the entire planet. The games would be the first ever televised, transmitted live to special theaters set up around Berlin.

The crowd at the stadium truly frightened Jules: tens of thousands of his fellow citizens tossed their arms in the air like swords, screaming, "*Sieg heil!*"—Hail to victory!—as Hitler watched from the stands, the red swastika banners hanging all around them. Though he couldn't do much to fight the growing army of Nazis in his city, Jules cheered on Black track star Jesse Owens, who won four gold medals at the games, dashing Hitler's theories on Aryan supremacy. On his return to America, Owens was enthusiastically greeted by New York City mayor Fiorello LaGuardia and given a ticker-tape parade down Broadway.

But there would be no invitation from President Roosevelt to join the white Olympic winners at a reception at the aptly named White House. Owens wasn't surprised. "I'd spent my whole life," he would say, "watching my father and mother and older brothers and sisters trying to escape their own kind of Hitler, first in Alabama and then in Cleveland."

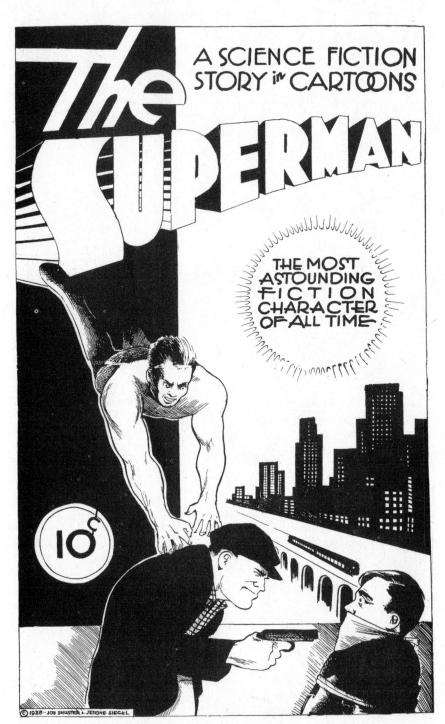

THE SUPERMAN, VERSION 2.0

CHAPTER 9

THE TEN-BLOCK WALK, TAKE 2

CLEVELAND, 1935

IN A SMALL ATTIC BEDROOM IN CLEVELAND, IN THE JEWISH neighborhood of Glenville, Jerry Siegel tried to sleep. It wasn't the summer heat that was keeping him awake nor his snoring older brother Leo snoozing noisily beside him. Twisting and turning, Jerry had a new idea for a story in his head. It involved a character like Samson, Hercules, and Moses all rolled into one—a new character that was an amalgamation of everything he had ever written or read. And he had read a lot.

Jerry, a nerd with glasses, had had few friends at Glenville High—ignored not just by the girls but the boys, too. He had been bullied for years, kids taunting him with rhymes like "Siegel, Seagull, bird of an eagle. Fly, seagull! Let's see you fly!" He had actually tried to fly once, jumping off the garage, holding an umbrella. But the umbrella turned inside out, and Jerry hit the ground—hard.

Jerry's father, Mitchell, was a tailor who had come from Lithuania, fleeing anti-Semitism. He had run a secondhand clothing store in Cleveland. But three summers earlier, he had died of a heart attack after confronting a couple of shoplifters, leaving the family struggling in the midst of the Depression. He'd had $131 to his name when he died. Jerry's older brother Harry got a job as a mailman to support them all. Thanks to magazines like *Amazing*

Stories that Harry brought home, Jerry discovered a new genre called science fiction.

Amazing Stories, which made its debut in 1926, was the first American science fiction magazine, featuring such stories as "Armageddon 2419 A.D.," which would eventually morph into Buck Rogers. With its disintegrating death rays and futuristic airships, early science fiction was a reaction to the technology that was sweeping the world and the inventions that were changing everyday life. Science fiction magazines would change Jerry's life—though not for the better.

He became so obsessed with comic strips and pulp magazines that he ignored his actual schoolwork and was held back. One of his favorite books, *Gladiator*, told the tale of a man with superhuman strength who could run faster than a train and jump higher than a house. Another favorite character was Doc Savage, a pulp magazine hero whose first name was Clark and who was known as "The Man of Bronze." Jerry tried his hand at creating his own comic strip takeoff on Tarzan called *Goober the Mighty* for his high school paper, the *Torch*, and won second place in the paper's annual contest for a story called "Death of a Parallelogram." But his grades were so awful he was eventually kicked off the newspaper.

Now, on that summer night when he couldn't sleep, Jerry, twenty-one and unemployed, finally got up, put on his glasses, slipped into the bathroom so as not to wake his brother, and started writing. He went back to bed, then threw off the covers after a couple of hours and wrote some more. By dawn, he had a complete script. He got dressed and, story in hand, took the porch steps at a gallop.

Jerry ran ten blocks through his neighborhood, past the wooden houses with their neat lawns and big porches, over to the cracked sidewalks of his best friend Joe's street. Huffing and puffing, Jerry arrived at the dilapidated two-story Maple Apartments that Joe and the Shuster family called home. "Joe, you gotta draw this," he said, waking him up, thrusting the script beneath his blinking eyes.

Joe and Jerry shared the same origin story, their parents having escaped the pogroms of Europe to live free in America years before Hitler's rise to power. But Joe's parents were so poor they made Jerry's family look like the Rockefellers. Joe's father, Julius Shusterowitz, had come from Russia with so little money that he couldn't afford paper for his talented son to draw on. At four years old, Joe started drawing on the walls, then moved on to butcher paper and the backs of free calendars. Joe's apartment didn't have heat, so in the winter, he and Jerry often paced back and forth to keep warm while developing their fantastical ideas, whose creation was by far the best escape from poverty. Sometimes it was so cold Joe had to wear several sweaters, a jacket, and even gloves, which made it hard to draw.

With his thick glasses, Joe was even nerdier, somehow, than Jerry. He was a rail-thin five foot two to Jerry's chubby five foot six. The clichéd ninety-pound weakling who gets sand kicked in his face, Joe tried lifting weights and exercising, and even bought physical fitness magazines, but it was no use. He was invisible to the girls at Glenville High, just like Jerry. Joe, too, worked for the school paper and was into science fiction characters. Unlike Jerry, Joe could draw them. He had even won a drawing contest at the *Torch*. The boys had been introduced by Jerry's cousin at the local public library, "like the right chemicals coming together," Jerry would later say.

The first drawing of Joe's that Jerry saw was one that Joe had saved from 1928, inspired by the new Fritz Lang movie *Metropolis*, which had blown both of their young, nerdy minds. The movie's lesson—the worker being kept down by the demented, greedy capitalist—was perhaps lost on them, though it was a harbinger of things to come. They both loved the way *Metropolis* looked, its set designs and special effects, its vertical cityscapes and sky trains. Jerry instantly fell in love with Joe's style when he saw his drawing, one of the few he ever saved from his childhood, a collection of futuristic skyscrapers and rocket ships that he called *The City of the Future: 1980.*

Together, they started a fanzine called *Science Fiction: The Advance Guard of Future Civilization.* They typed it out on a regular typewriter and gave it a cover that looked like the first page of a high school term paper, copied on the school mimeograph machine and stapled together. The third issue of *Science Fiction*—dated January 1933—featured a story about a telepathic bald villain intent on world domination. It was called "The Reign of the Superman." Hardly anyone read it.

Jerry and Joe tried pitching comic strips to magazines and newspaper syndication editors, but were rejected again and again. They tried creating a new version of the Superman, a hero—with hair, this time—whose bulletproof physique and fantastic strength are bestowed upon him by a scientist. And that June of 1933, there was a glimmer of interest from Consolidated Book Publishers, a Chicago company known mostly for putting out encyclopedias and Bibles. But the editors at Consolidated changed their minds about the Superman by August.

The pair took inspiration from a new art form called comic books, particularly the ones that editor Max Gaines started putting together in 1933, repackaging previously published Sunday comic strips into a separate booklet with a colorful cover and saddle stitches. *Funnies on Parade* and *Famous Funnies* were given away as a promotion to buyers of Procter & Gamble products, who had to clip coupons and mail them in for a copy. The newly packaged funnies proved so popular that Gaines decided to sell them for ten cents apiece.

Jerry and Joe pitched the Superman to Gaines, but that didn't go so well, either.

That fateful morning when Jerry arrived with his fresh script, Joe rubbed the sleep out of his nearsighted eyes, put on his Coke-bottle glasses, then read all about the new-and-improved Superman. Joe got it immediately, smiled, and sat down to work. He drew as fast as he could as Jerry paced the wooden floor and narrated, describing the action using film lingo: close-up, long shot, overhead shot. Joe's eyes were very bad, even with his glasses, so he drew very slowly and meticulously, his nose just an inch or so from the paper. The two spent the whole day—without taking a break, eating sandwiches that Joe brought in—creating Superman. From time to time, Joe would pause and look in the mirror, striking a pose or screwing up his face he imagined a character would make, then go back to his paper and try to re-create it.

Jerry suggested Joe put an *S* on Superman's chest—not just for Superman's name, but for Shuster and Siegel—and a cape on his back that would whip around, one of the few ways for Joe to show dramatic motion.

Superman would be an alien with super strength whose real name was Kal-El ("Voice of God" in Hebrew). Kal-El came to Earth as an abandoned baby, much like Moses in the Old Testament, just as his planet, Krypton, was destroyed. Like Jerry, his father would die while he was still young. Kal-El would be adopted by a couple of Gentiles and renamed Clark Kent, a name Jerry took from Clark Gable and B-movie actor Kent Taylor. By day, Superman was a mild-mannered goy with glasses (just like Jerry's and Joe's). He would live, naturally, in a city called Metropolis.

Their new version of Superman was not a villain, but rather the ultimate champion of the oppressed, battling corrupt politicians, saving the falsely accused, and beating up wife beaters. Maybe he was operating out of survivor's guilt, having been the only one from his planet to make it out alive. But this Superman was pure, doing good in the world for goodness' sake, not for rewards or recognition. In fact, he didn't want anyone to know who he was and spent half his time tricking his newspaper pals about his identity. He would have a love interest, named Lois Lane, who was based on a teenager named Joanne, whom Jerry and Joe found through an ad she had placed in the *Plain Dealer* looking for modeling work. The ad, which stated that Joanne had no experience, attracted mostly men looking for love. But when Joe reached out to Joanne, he made it clear he was an artist looking for a model for a comic strip he was developing. Joanne happily took the bus to his Greenville neighborhood, and when Joe answered the door, the two briefly chatted. Finally, she asked for Mr. Shuster. Joe was just a boy. But, of course, she was just a girl. "I'm Mr. Shuster," Joe replied.

In the drawings he made, Joanne became Lois. But unlike the cynical Lois Lane in the comic strip, Joanne believed in the nerdy guy with glasses. "You're going to be famous," Joanne told him. "I can feel it." Joe even dated Joanne for a little while before she moved to New York to pursue her modeling career.

This new-and-improved Superman could hurtle a twenty-story building and run faster than an express train, but he wasn't bent on world domination like Hitler's model. Just the opposite. He was here to save us all.

Superman, an illegal alien, had come millions of miles not to be featured on the front page of the *Daily Star*, but to save mankind from itself, its ugly awful self. And by the looks of things in Europe, and the bleak Depression in America, the world could use some serious saving.

With their new version complete, Jerry started sending *Superman* out to newspapers. They didn't copyright the strip because they thought it had to be published first.

King Features Syndicate returned the strips.

NEA Services rejected them, too.

Bell Syndicate said no.

Publishers Syndicate of Chicago, nope.

Super Magazine, no dice.

Famous Funnies returned the package—tied so tightly in knotted string—unopened.

Max Gaines said no once again.

Esquire Features lectured Joe to pay more attention to his drawing and called his figures "crude and hurried." The Ledger Syndicate was just as harsh. "Frankly, we feel that the public have had their fill of superhuman subjects."

The boys were crushed. But they persisted.

They got their first bite after sending *Superman* to another publisher, who rejected it but said he might buy two of the other characters they'd pitched: a swashbuckler named Henri Duval and Doctor Occult, a detective who deals with the supernatural. Drawn on the back of some old butcher paper, the flying Doctor Occult donned a red cape like Superman's. Joe convinced his parents to lend him money for some real drawing paper, then used his mother's breadboard as a drawing table. Jerry submitted the final drawings to the publisher who'd nibbled, a man they'd never met, but who would change their future.

Everyone called him the Major.

MAJOR MALCOM WHEELER-NICHOLSON

CHAPTER 10

THE MAJOR AND THE MINORS

NEW YORK, 1935

MAJOR MALCOLM WHEELER-NICHOLSON WAS A SELF-MADE character right out of the adventure pulps. According to him, he had joined the United States Cavalry back before World War I, chasing bandits on the Mexican border, had led a battalion against the Bolsheviks in Siberia, and had commanded the American forces in the Rhine. In the Philippines, he had led a group of African American buffalo soldiers and battled the top brass over the racism they faced. His Black soldiers challenged their white counterparts in a contest of machine gun readiness and not only won but were written about in the press. The Major's military career ended abruptly when he dared to publicly criticize the army command of favoritism and unfair discipline in an open letter to President Harding in the *New York Times*. He was court-martialed and survived what he believed was a military-sanctioned assassination attempt. Discharged without benefits, the Major turned to writing pulp fiction, using his own experiences as material.

The Major wore spats, a beaver hat, smoked from a long cigarette holder just like Sunny, and liked to drape his coat over his back like a cape. He had seen Max Gaines's *Famous Funnies* and thought it was a brilliant idea, but decided to take the concept one step further. He created the first comic book with completely original material and advertising in February of 1935. Called *New Fun*, it was a full-color and oversize ten-by-fifteen-inch, thirty-six-page magazine with twenty-nine different comics.

The Major needed a printer and distributor with a wide network and the ability to handle a big job. Soon enough, he found one. And his name was Harry Donenfeld.

This would be one of dozens of publications he and Jack Liebowitz churned out every month. Though sales were not great at first, Jack saw the potential in these colorful magazines, whose audience was young and untapped. The Major's sequel to *New Fun* was *More Fun*, soon followed by *New Comics*, *New Adventure Comics*, and *Adventure Comics*.

The stories inside were aimed at everyone, silly stuff for the kids, cowboys and detectives for the dads, classic literary characters for the moms, and spacemen for science fiction geeks like Jerry and Joe. The boys' first published comic appeared in October 1935 in the Major's *New Fun* #6, its red cover filled with twelve panels of a character named Charley Fish, a photographer who was always getting into comic adventures. Inside was Siegel and Shuster's Henri Duval, Famed Soldier of Fortune, and Dr. Occult, the caped hero busy saving a victim from a vampire.

Like many creative geniuses, the Major was a terrible businessman. At best, he was late in paying his artists, who earned a mere $6 per page. Jerry and Joe, who were grossing $36 each per month from the Major, had never sold anything before this, so they had no idea whether or how much they should complain about bounced checks and withheld payments. Plus they had no leverage and couldn't go elsewhere, since no one else would have them.

When the Major's checks trickled to a stop, they resorted to selling empty milk bottles for pocket change to go to the movies at their local Crown Theater. But seeing their work finally in print made them euphoric and was nearly payment enough, so they kept working for the Major, creating two other comic stories, *Federal*

Men and *Spy*. They also continued to send Superman, still homeless, out to other publishers, hoping he would eventually land. He
was their favorite character and they believed in him, even if no
one else did.

In March of 1936, the Major wrote and told Joe and Jerry he was
developing a brand-new magazine and wanted them to fill between
four and six pages. Because of the Major's money troubles, Harry
became his partner in that magazine—*Detective Comics*—which was
a success partly thanks to Harry's ability to get good placement on
newsstands. Behind on his bills to Harry, the Major enthusiastically
welcomed him aboard. Harry, after all, was a charmer. But behind
the scenes, he and Jack Liebowitz were already plotting to take
over the company, which was also called Detective Comics.

Excited by his new comics venture, Harry told friends and
family about it, even encouraging one of his old neighbors from
the Bronx to invest some money with him. *Detective Comics'* first
issue featured a Fu Manchu character on a bright red cover. Inside
was a detective character named Slam Bradley, written and drawn
by Jerry Siegel and Joe Shuster.

Jerry and Joe were on a bit of a roll, appearing so frequently
they used different bylines—Leger and Reuths—if their comics appeared more than once in a single book. But they still weren't being
paid regularly by the Major. To confront him about the money he
owed them, the boys took a trip together to New York in February
1937, staying at the YMCA. They also planned to meet with some
other editors to try and sell their Superman character. Fearful of
pickpockets and gangsters, Jerry wore a money belt. But the thieves
he would eventually encounter wouldn't use a gun.

They met with a United Feature Syndicate editor and gave
him their long Superman spiel. He seemed interested, but when
they got back to Cleveland, they got a letter that United was passing, calling Superman "a rather immature piece of work." The

Major had promised that they would be paid, but when the check still didn't arrive, Jerry wrote to him, demanding their money yet again.

Harry sent the Major on a cruise to Cuba that April with several other creatives to think up new material for another joint venture that was to be called *Action Comics*. The following autumn, fishing around for original art for *Action Comics*, Harry and Jack talked to their friend and business associate Max Gaines and asked if he had any unpublished material lying around. Max found the Superman strips and sent a letter to Jerry in November saying there was some interest. He and Joe, who at this point had been shopping their Superman character around for five long, torturous years, were thrilled.

In early December, Jack Liebowitz wrote to Jerry, introducing himself somewhat suspiciously as half owner of Detective Comics, and proposing he and Harry pay any money that the Major owed them. Jack also urged Jerry and Joe to sign an agreement he had enclosed and send it back by collect telegram. ASAP.

The same day, the Major was filing his trademark for *Action Comics*, oblivious to Harry and Jack's plans.

Jerry, thrilled his Superman creation might finally be launched, excitedly headed to New York to the Grand Central Palace to meet with Harry, Jack, and Max. Riding the elevator up to the ninth floor, Jerry was greeted warmly by Harry's secretary, Gerda, and was then met by the publishers, who slapped his back and made him feel like he had finally arrived. Jerry gladly signed a two-year contract to create *Slam Bradley* and *Spy* for them. They might also want to run *Superman*, they said, but they would get back to him on that. ASAP.

A couple of weeks later, in late December, Harry sued the Major for the $5,878 he owed him in printing costs. When the Major couldn't pay, he was forced into bankruptcy. Harry and Jack, as they usually did in such situations, bought up all the Major's debts, fifty cents on the dollar, and completely took over the business. It was December 27.

Merry Christmas.

The Major, who always enjoyed an evening martini, hit the bottle pretty hard and fell into deep despair that winter. Perhaps to prove his fingerprints weren't all over the theft, or maybe to ensure he didn't bump into the Major on the street or in a bar, Harry left around Christmas on his own cruise aboard the SS *Statendam* to the West Indies, then headed to Cuba, where he stayed in an ocean-view room at the National Hotel, gambling at its casino long into the night.

From Cuba, Harry took a flight to Miami, where he stayed at the brand-new, oceanfront, Art Deco Dempsey-Vanderbilt Hotel, owned by his old hotfoot buddy, Jack Dempsey, whose sports magazine Harry was about to publish. Tanned and slightly hungover, Harry got back to New York in February.

That spring, Jerry and Joe sold the rights to *Superman* for $130—$10 a page for the thirteen-page story—nearly double what they had been paid for their other comics and just one dollar shy of Mitchell Siegel's total net worth when he died. They happily signed a contract on March 1, which gave Jack and Harry their character "to have and hold forever." Jack Liebowitz promptly sent them a check, misspelling both their names. When they signed on the back, they had to spell their own names wrong.

The publishers were in a rush and needed *Superman* redrawn from its original single newspaper strip submission to full-page comic book form. But Joe didn't bother making a new version; he simply cut out each strip and pasted them over thirteen pages, leaving some panels out, which made it slightly nonsensical. After a very brief introduction to Superman's origins, we see the superhero leaping to the governor's mansion with a captive woman who is bound and gagged with no explanation of who she is. Transitions are missing and the ending is abrupt, with no resolution or invitation to see what will happen in the next issue.

Joe's cover image was Superman holding a green car up over his head, a scene pulled from the story. But that cover would be redrawn by Harry's pulp studio artists to make it "pop" more. As always, just like in the girlie pulps, the cover was incredibly important. Harry was worried, even after the *Action Comics* cover was redone, that it wasn't right. "It's too ridiculous," Harry said. "No one will believe a character can lift a car over his head." But the presses were waiting, and Harry was overruled by Jack.

His rush into the comics industry wasn't just a financial move. It would also provide cover. While he was cruising the Caribbean, new obscenity charges were being drawn up against Harry for transporting his "obscene, lewd book"—*Snappy*—across state lines. The April issue, volume 17, number 4, hit newsstands in January and featured a story called "A Girl Named Gerry," who appeared both topless and bottomless in some sexy line drawings. In another story called "Young and Healthy," the main character, Kitty, is suffering from the summer humidity, dressed in "a pair of short, sheer and satin panties and high-heeled slippers. And that was all."

Maybe Harry was tipped off to what was coming his way. The federal charges landed that spring, just as *Superman* was hitting the newsstands. Harry may have figured that publishing *Action Comics* would make it look as though he had turned over a new leaf. Had they not been in such a hurry to print, he and Jack may not have even called Max Gaines for something to plug the hole—and Superman may have never taken flight.

Being a publisher of children's comic books was a good (though slightly creepy) front for the sex pulp publisher, but it probably wasn't enough to keep Harry out of jail. If convicted, Harry would end up behind bars. Strike three. He needed a bigger insurance policy. And its name was Herbie Siegel.

After strike two back in 1934, Herbie, Harry's fellow Romanian Jew, had started posing as the "publisher" of Harry's sex pulps. Now Herbie would take the fall for him, claiming he slipped the lewd images into *Snappy* without Harry's knowledge. He was fined and sentenced to sixty days in jail, but got out early on good behavior. In return Herbie was given a new lifetime job by Harry—sitting at his desk each day, reading the *Racing Form*.

Though he claimed, officially, to be done with the girlie magazines for good, Harry kept publishing them for another year or so, much to Jack's dismay. Jack wanted him to leave the smooshes behind once and for all.

As for Jerry and Joe, they were thrilled to have *Superman* finally in print. Years later, Jerry would lament the fact that they weren't more careful with their beloved character, that, in an effort to get him out into the world, they had fallen victim to bullies once again. "Superman of course represents what the plain ordinary, crushed-by-reality person would like to be but can only be in his wistful daydreams," wrote Jerry, "because we are what we are."

JULES ON THE *QUEEN MARY*

CHAPTER 11

THE WAIT

BERLIN, 1938

JULES'S FEET HURT. HE HAD BEEN POUNDING THE PAVEMENT for weeks, running from one city office to another in Berlin, gathering the many documents he needed to flee to America: two copies of each of their birth certificates, certificates of good conduct for both him and Edith from the German police. Jules visited the Jewish authorization office, the passport office, the tax office, the foreign exchange office, the public emigrant advisory office, and finally the American consulate, where he put his name on a waiting list for an interview. He, Edith, and Hannelore also had to undergo a physical examination to prove they were fit to enter America. He filled out medical clearance forms, tax documents from his fur shop, and a police certificate declaring he had no record. It seemed to Jules like a forest's worth of paperwork. Hitler's party wanted Jules and those like him to leave the country, so why make it so difficult?

And it wasn't only the Nazis. In 1938, the United States issued visas to a fraction of the Jews desperate to escape the Third Reich. Jules worried that they had waited too long.

His most difficult hurdle would be finding a financial sponsor in America, someone who would vouch for him, providing an affidavit promising to support him if he couldn't support himself. This was perhaps the most important document of all. Without a sponsor, Jules could not immigrate to America.

Jules knew where to start. He had a cousin in New York City, in a place called the Bronx. Her name was Faye. Her mother and Jules's mother had been sisters. He sent Faye a letter to enlist her help and got a response back saying she would do what she could, but maybe he should think about coming to America himself, just for a visit, to try and find a sponsor. Jules was his own best advocate: he was handsome, smart, and an experienced salesman.

Faye wasn't well-off enough to be Jules's sponsor. But she was smart and savvy and fairly well connected in New York. Born in Austria at the turn of the century, she came to America in 1924, when it was much easier to do so. When she first arrived in New York, Faye met her husband, Sam. They set up an apartment in Boerum Hill, Brooklyn, but while on their honeymoon in upstate New York, in a rowboat on Lily Lake, Sam had a heart attack and fell into the water. Faye, barely four foot ten, was unable to save him, and watched in horror as he went down amid the lily pads.

Somehow Faye rebounded and got a job working at Thomas Cook Travel Agency, where she would learn proper English. There was barely a trace of an accent by 1938. Faye was sophisticated and cool. And Murray, her new husband, was a mensch. Everyone loved them. The family—remember this was a family of furriers—jokingly called them May and Furry. (Murray had a dark mustache, though he was balding and not all that furry.)

Faye was a neatnik and a princess who never cooked and either ate out or ordered in Jewish deli. On weekends, they visited relatives for dinner. No one ever ate at Faye's. Well, hardly ever. She made spaghetti with ketchup for the kids, but it didn't go over so well.

Faye and Murray lived in the Norwood section of the Bronx, a great place to raise kids, with the newly constructed Williamsbridge Oval park built on top of the old Gun Hill reservoir, which had supplied drinking water to generations of Bronx residents. Whenever their Bronx apartment needed a paint job, Faye and Murray would simply move to a new apartment. They moved within the same Norwood neighborhood every three or four years.

Murray was doing well in the dental lab business in Manhattan, creating the crowns, bridges, and dentures used by dentists, probably making between $3,000 and $4,000 a year, a respectable sum for 1938. But he was not doing well enough to sponsor refugees from Germany. Though the State Department refused to say how much a sponsor had to make, a $5,000 annual salary was rumored to be the cutoff. Each case was different, with American bureaucrats weighing many factors: the refugee's skill set, earning potential, education, relation to the sponsor, and the willingness and sincerity of the sponsor to actually step up and support the immigrant and their family members if need be. In some cases, it was better to have a close family connection with some money rather than a distant millionaire "friend." But there were no hard-and-fast rules set down by the US government on what would get you through the golden door to America. No "open sesame" answers. No guaranteed formula. Refugees were forced to just guess and pray.

Scams and sponsors-for-hire were a problem. Some sponsors would claim to have set aside a special fund for the refugee to help support them when they arrived on US soil. But the State Department soon discovered many cases of "revolving funds," where a sponsor would withdraw the money as soon as the immigrant arrived in the US, then place it in the name of another immigrant. And so on. For this reason, the State Department didn't give much weight to letters of credit or bank funds, since those trusts were often fake and fleeting. A rich family member was your best bet, though Jules had no rich family members in America.

Faye promised to help find a reliable sponsor not only for Jules but for Jules's sister Mollie and her furrier husband, David, as well, who were also ready to leave Berlin. Mollie tried to convince her sister Golda and her husband, Simon, to leave Berlin, too, but Simon was still depending on God for help and refused to talk about it.

And so it was that they all decided Jules would travel to New York in search of a hero.

He booked passage on the *Queen Mary* and got a transit visa to travel through England, then bought an expensive double-breasted pin-striped suit to impress anyone who might consider sponsoring him. Reserving a room at the grand Art Deco Piccadilly Hotel in Times Square to make it look like he was more well off than he actually was, Jules played the part of the young entrepreneur coming to America.

Jules left his small family behind in Berlin, with Edith running the fur shop on her own. It was a painful goodbye, but Jules tried not to make his anxiety known. He hugged them, kissed them, and said he would see them in a few weeks. Not to worry. But Jules secretly worried he might never make it back. So many things could go wrong.

In the harbor in Southampton, the *Queen Mary* sat with her three red and black raked funnels. It seemed impossible that something so large could actually float, but there she was, patiently waiting for him. Jules boarded the opulent Deco ocean liner and set sail. Over five days, Jules would visit her two indoor swimming pools, three-story high-columned dining room, and Jewish prayer room—built by the British ship designers to show their German competitors that they were not anti-Semitic. In one photo, Jules stands on deck in his double-breasted suit and a beret, a *Queen Mary* life preserver around his neck.

The day Jules sailed, Hitler returned triumphant to Berlin after having annexed Austria. Hitler had been born in Austria and long believed the two German-speaking countries should be united. More than a million fans swarmed the streets in Berlin, waving Nazi flags, climbing onto lampposts to get a better view, hanging out of windows, and screaming "Heil!" as the Führer led a motorcade of 150 cars from the Tempelhof military airfield to the Reich Chancellery. In a black Mercedes convertible sedan, Hitler waved at the frenzied crowd. A national holiday was declared, and the soldiers were out in force, trying to control the unruly but happy hordes. Giant red swastika flags draped the buildings en route. Edith stayed home with her sixteen-month-old daughter, listening to the horror unfold on the radio, not daring to go out, and secretly wondered, now that he had his chance, if maybe Jules would run away and never return. She cried at night, fearful he would not come back, even if he wanted to.

All week long, Edith followed the Nazi propaganda. Prominent Jewish businessmen as well as Catholic clergy opposing Hitler were arrested that week in Vienna. Though the German military had already occupied Austria and Hitler considered the countries united, the chancellor of Austria held a vote on independence. Hitler declared it would be subject to fraud, and said he would refuse to accept it. The referendum on whether to unite with Germany was held nonetheless, the YES circles large, the NO circles very small on the ballots, campaign workers watching which way their fellow Austrians voted. Turnout was 99.7 percent, with 4.4 million votes for the Anschluss—unification—versus fewer than 12,000 against it. After the vote, Austria's chancellor was arrested and sent to a concentration camp.

Jules stepped onto the cold streets on the West Side of Manhattan, the Empire State Building and the other skyscrapers looming so close, just like the ones he had seen years before in *Metropolis*. He was armed with a list of contacts, phone numbers, and addresses, all people he had never met, including Faye in that mysterious place, the Bronx.

Jules was no peasant from the hinterlands, but Times Square weakened his strong, twenty-five-year-old knees. The glittering signs advertising Camel cigarettes, Coca-Cola, and Planters, with the monocled Mr. Peanut bowing and removing his top hat, shone down upon him in glorious, pulsing neon. The zipper on the *New York Times* building shouted the latest headlines that week—Neville Chamberlain vowing to fight for France or Belgium if they're attacked, but making no such promises for Czechoslovakia. Mussolini declaring that Italy was primed for war. But Jules could not read English. He recognized the names, but the other words scrolled by in an electric blur.

He understood the marquees, though, and couldn't believe his tired eyes. Cab Calloway and his Cotton Club Orchestra performing at the Paramount and Count Basie stomping at the Savoy. Milton Berle was starring at the Globe, Deanna Durbin live at the Roxy, and Kitty Carlisle opening up at the Majestic. The Strand featured Edward G. Robinson, a Romanian Jew like Harry, who had escaped with his family to the Lower East Side at the turn of the century after his brother was hit in the head with a brick by an anti-Semitic mob.

The Piccadilly Hotel was on Forty-Fifth Street and Broadway in the heart of Times Square. It felt like Jules was staying at the center of the world, at the center of this miraculous, vertical city, the lights of the skyscrapers like diamonds sparkling in the cold air, the ice crunching beneath his wingtips. The hotel bar, the Piccadilly Circus Lounge, attracted actors and theatergoers alike. All week long, Jenö Bartal and his orchestra played in the hotel's Georgian ballroom with its crystal chandeliers and pine paneling decorated with Victorian-style portraits and still lifes. If only Edith were here, they would tango and fox-trot, he thought. If they ended up settling in New York—Lord willing—Jules promised himself he would take her here to dance every chance he got.

Every day he searched for a sponsor. He would travel up to the Bronx to meet Faye and Murray and go to temple with them, meeting their friends and making connections. When he met someone who might be a potential sponsor, a successful doctor or dentist or furrier, Jules would treat them to a cocktail at his fancy hotel or a beer at Jack Dempsey's new bar on Broadway and Forty-Ninth Street, trying his best to appear casual and confident and not the desperate man he actually was.

Though it was officially spring, it was snowing in New York. During his stay, Jules trudged through the slush and took the subway to the German neighborhood of Yorkville on the Upper East Side to chat up his fellow countrymen, not daring to tell them he was a Jew. Apartments, they told him, could be rented for $75 a month. His main activity, aside from looking for a savior, was checking out the city's many fur stores—his potential competition—and then meeting with a fur dealer downtown. At the Astor Place subway stop—named for the nineteenth-century fur baron and owner of the Waldorf Astoria, John Jacob Astor—Jules noticed the beaver plaques and tiles along the station walls. He laughed to himself. It was as if the beavers were calling him to his new home. Jules was thrilled when he learned that New York's official city seal featured beavers, a reference to the pelt trade that had been its first big business in the sixteenth and seventeenth centuries.

Until he arrived in New York, Jules had had no idea how stressed he had been on the streets of Berlin, worrying that any moment he could be beaten up or detained by police, his arrest or death a whisper away. In New York, there were no neighbors to curse him or spit at him or call him a dirty Jew. He didn't have to hear "Heil Hitler" every ten minutes. There was a sudden lightness in his step, a slight relaxation in his shoulders, and a feeling that he had a future, a feeling he had lost the last few years in Germany.

Jules tried to read the headlines in the *New York Times* and the other papers hawked by the newsboys on the city's corners until he finally tracked down a German newspaper in Yorkville. He was sorry he had. The lightness he had found in America was now clouded by the horror quickly growing in his home country. The panic crawled from the headlines into his head, where it took up permanent residence. Some Jews, despondent over financial ruin and unable to find passage out, were committing suicide. The situation in Berlin was growing more dire by the second. Jules's time— and that of his family—was indeed running out.

Fearful and yearning for Edith and Hannelore, Jules would visit the movie theaters in Times Square, ducking in for a night showing or a matinee. Jules sat in the darkened theaters alone, forgetting the headlines for two hours. Playing that week was *Bringing Up Baby* with Cary Grant at the RKO Palace, and over at the Loew's State, *A Yank at Oxford*, with Maureen O'Sullivan falling for Robert Taylor, "a two-fisted Yankee who takes England by storm."

Without subtitles, Jules didn't understand much of the new American releases, but they were a comfort nonetheless. Afterward, he would stroll through Central Park past horse-drawn carriages and crying babies, hungry pigeons and happy families, missing his own so deeply, he looked down to see if there was an actual hole in his chest.

FAYE AND NEIL STERNBERG

CHAPTER 12

THE SIGNATURE

NEW YORK, APRIL 1938

AFTER THEY WERE FIRST MARRIED AND SETTLED IN THE Bronx, Faye and Murray had lived next door to a printer, a small guy with a big mouth and boundless energy. His name was Harry. About a year earlier, Harry had told them he was starting a new business and wanted them to invest $500, but Murray didn't have that kind of money. "You need money to make money," Murray would complain.

Harry had told Murray that his new business was making books of stories with balloons in them, and in those balloons were words—the words the characters in the stories were speaking. He had made a small fortune on the smooshes and the bootlegging, and was likely earning five figures a year in the distribution and printing business. But his real wealth would come from the comics, which were just starting to take off. In years to come, Faye would remind Murray they had blown it. Comic books were about to become all the rage. "We could have been rich," Faye would say, sighing.

Faye and Murray were still good friends with Harry, even though he had moved to a new tax bracket and into upper Manhattan with a view of the Hudson River. So when Faye called and asked if she could come and pay him a visit, Harry said sure, of course. Faye brought along her son, Neil, who was only five years old that spring and not yet in kindergarten. Having Neil with her would help soften her pitch to her old pal. Harry was a master salesman, but she had no experience selling anything.

Faye combed Neil's dark hair that early April morning, smoothing his stubborn cowlick, and put on a pretty number herself. She hadn't told Jules about her plan to visit Harry for fear he would be devastated if it didn't work out.

Neither Faye nor Murray could drive, so Faye walked over to the bus stop with Neil. Or, as she would say, they slid over. Rain had followed a six-inch snowfall, so the city streets were a big, sloppy mess. And Faye always hated a mess. She held Neil's hand so he wouldn't slip in the gray slush or throw ice balls at passing cars. From the bus, they got the IRT into Manhattan. Neil was all bundled up, with an ear-flapped hat and a scarf across his face. Faye was wearing her cloth winter coat, which she was really quite sick of by now.

Faye's nails were freshly done, as were her makeup and hair, which she checked in the reflection of the subway's windows. A bottle blonde, with big eyes that made her look a little like Bette Davis, Faye was always well put together, dressing flamboyantly in bright colors and prints. But whenever she saw Harry she made a little extra effort. The truth was she liked to flirt with Harry. And Harry with her. That day, she made even more of an effort to turn his head. Harry was a ladies' man. Everyone knew it, even his wife, Gussie. He liked to get a look at a nice pair of legs whenever he could and frequented local strip clubs with his mobster pals. At thirty-two, Faye still had some moves left.

Dressed up as usual in a worsted wool suit with wide lapels, his dark hair slicked back from his deeply tanned face, which helped set off his hundred-watt smile, Harry stretched his arms wide when Faye walked through his door. As she stepped into his busy ninth-floor office, Harry came to the far side of his desk and hugged her. He planted a kiss on her rouged cheek and barely had to bend over to ruffle Neil's neatly combed hair.

While the adults talked, Neil thumbed through Harry's comic books. Already a bit precocious and a charmer like his mom, Neil would grow into a voracious reader, thanks, partially, to Harry's comic books. On the cover of Harry's latest magazine was a man in bright blue tights with a cherry-red cape and a golden chest shield, lifting a green sedan high up over his head. The sixty-four-page comic book was filled with all original material, including this new character named Superman, who filled the first thirteen pages. Above the cover drawing of Superman was the title in screaming red type: *Action Comics* #1. Copies exactly like this were about to land on newsstands across the country, on sale for a thin dime.

Harry glanced over every now and then at Neil, who was seated in a big armchair, riveted by his reading material. Harry's son, Irwin, now twelve, had told Harry he liked this Superman character. But Harry still wasn't so sure, and worried about having put him on the cover. Five-year-old Neil was Harry's one-man focus group.

After some small talk about Murray's dental lab, Superman, and the bad weather they'd been having, Faye prepared to make her move. Harry was a generous man, always willing to help, especially fellow members of the tribe. But this was a big ask, and Faye paused.

Harry was smart enough to know that Faye had not come here to make small talk. So he helped her out. "What can I do fa you, my lovely?" he asked, taking a seat behind his giant desk.

Faye explained that her cousin Jules had just arrived from Berlin. He had left his wife and daughter behind, but was trying to gather the paperwork to bring them over with him and stay for good. She paused and sighed. "But Jules needs a financial sponsor."

"And that's where I come in," said Harry, a statement more than a question.

Faye nodded and smiled.

Harry asked if Jules could be trusted. And Faye said of course, that he was a furrier with a successful shop in Berlin, who would open a new shop in New York the minute he got here. He had already met with suppliers downtown.

Harry nodded and said, "I'll see what I can do." When Harry moved to hug Faye goodbye, she stopped him, digging into her big purse. Like some secretarial magician, she pulled out an envelope containing the financial support papers, not just for Jules, but for his sister Mollie, her husband, David, and their two children as well. Faye handed the papers to Harry, who rifled through them, at first surprised, but then laughing as he saw there were two sets.

David is a furrier, too, Faye explained. And his wife, Mollie, was Jules's sister. Wonderful people. They were wealthy, but had to hide it from the authorities so the German government wouldn't confiscate their money. They needed a sponsor, too, someone to vouch for them. They would never ask Harry for a dime. And neither would Jules.

Harry laughed and put the papers on his desk. "I see a fur or two in Gussie's future," he said. Faye smiled and hugged him goodbye.

Later that day, Harry signed the letters of recommendation that Faye had already typed up; had his secretary, Gerda, secure two bank letters itemizing his income, savings, stocks, and real estate holdings; produced two copies of his tax returns; and signed two affidavits, witnessed by a notary public, vouching for Jules and David, even though he'd never met the guys. The affidavits were stamped with a round red seal. On the forms, Harry had to list his dependents, give his own immigrant background and his year of naturalization, and swear that he had never been arrested for a crime, which was a bit of a lie. But he assumed no one would check. He also had to list the reason for his "friends" coming over to America: religious persecution.

In bold red type that made it jump out from the other lines on the page, the affidavit declared:

I am willing and able to receive, maintain, support and be responsible for the alien(s) mentioned above while they remain in the United States, and hereby assume such obligations, guaranteeing that none of them will at any time become a burden on the United States or any State, County, City, Village or Municipality of the United States; and that any who are under sixteen years of age will be sent to day school until they are sixteen years old and will not be put to work unsuited to their years.

Harry's secretary made six copies of each of the signed affidavits, as required by law, then placed the papers in a manila envelope. When Faye returned later in the week, Harry slid them across his wide desk to her.

"Mum's the word," he said. "Next thing ya know, every refugee in Europe'll be on my doorstep."

CLARK GABLE, THE KING OF HOLLYWOOD

CHAPTER 13

THE WAY BACK

BERLIN, APRIL 1938

WITH THE PRECIOUS PAPERS IN HAND, JULES BOARDED A more modest liner for his return trip to Germany a few days later. He refused to mail the documents for fear they would be intercepted or simply be lost and never arrive. Jews were leaving by the thousands from Germany each day, desperate to escape, desperate for papers like these. The growing throng headed to America, Palestine, North Africa, Cuba, or other cities across Europe. But Jules was headed in the other direction. No chest shield. No X-ray vision. Jules's only superpowers were his wit, his ability to tell a good yarn, and his love for Edith and Hannelore. Jules had never been away from his wife and daughter for so long, so as his ship pulled close to the German shore, he anxiously prepared to disembark. With his gray fedora tilted at a jaunty angle, and his white scarf tied fashionably around his neck, Jules put on his overcoat and grabbed his suitcase.

He made his way down the long gangplank with dozens of other passengers—all nervous and well dressed like he was. One by one they were stopped at a series of long customs tables in the ship's terminal. Flanking the tables were unsmiling officers in green sloping helmets and uniforms holding rifles or MP40 submachine guns. Though they hadn't even been asked yet, passengers anxiously dug and fumbled through bags and pockets for their identification, while officials in uniforms and black caps sat waiting. A man approaching the next table over from Jules was a Jew, and the German official informed him, quite bluntly, that he couldn't come back into the country.

Jules suddenly realized that getting out of Germany was hard, but getting back in would be much harder. He was merely coming home, but Germany no longer considered itself his home.

He tugged at the brim of his fedora with a trembling hand and loosened the white scarf a bit, to give himself more air. When his turn came, Jules confidently placed his passport on the table. He wasn't sure if the man behind the table was a customs officer or Gestapo, but as he examined Jules and his passport, the man's eyes narrowed.

"You are a Jew? You are supposed to be traveling in the opposite direction, no?" the man said to Jules, pointing toward the ship and shaking his head. "You know you are not wanted here."

Jules thought of showing him Harry's papers, and explaining that he was simply returning to get his wife and child before leaving again, but it was too much of a gamble. What if the angry officer took the papers and never gave them back? The future of Edith and Hannelore, Mollie and David and their two sons depended on those papers.

He needed to think fast. Pausing for a moment, he looked down at the agent and, suddenly, Jules was someone else. Just like that. No disguise. No costume. No mask.

"I've just returned from a meeting with Clark Gable in Hollywood," Jules lied, his arrogance and Berliner Schnauze in full flower. "I'm his film agent. And if I don't come into the country, neither will Mr. Gable's next film." Jules sounded cool and slightly annoyed. He may have even shrugged, looked off into the distance, and yawned. And then the clincher: "Think of what the Führer will say when he finds you were the man who stopped Clark Gable's movies from entering the country." He smirked and waited, his knees secretly weakening.

Gable's next big film would be *Gone with the Wind*, which would become a favorite of Eva Braun, Hitler's paramour. But, of course, Jules couldn't have known that yet; no one did. He was just working on what he had read in the papers and movie magazines. Knowing Hitler and most Germans were big fans of Clark Gable, Jules decided to become the actor's agent.

The official got up and walked over to a uniformed officer, this one with a pistol on his hip, to whisper about Jules's situation. They spoke tensely for a moment, the first man nodding in Jules's direction. Jules strained to hear what they were saying, all the while appearing aloof and slightly annoyed. His hands, though, were still shaking and were slick with sweat, his striped oxford shirt soaking through in the warm mid-April day. It wasn't possible that either of these men knew Clark Gable's real agent, was it?

But what if they did? Would Jules be arrested? And what would he do if they simply wouldn't let him in? Maybe he could just leave the country again and mail Harry's documents to the rest of his family. He wondered how long Edith would wait for him near the dock before giving up and taking that long drive back to Berlin. His beloved, horrible Berlin. He worried she wouldn't have the courage to stand up to her parents and leave on her own. Or maybe she would run into trouble with the Nazis while trying to escape. Would he ever see her again?

The man sauntered back over to his table and sat down. Without saying a word, he stamped Jules's passport, folded it closed, and handed it back to him. Jules had to stop himself from reacting to this miracle, from jumping up and down and giving a shout of thanksgiving, from kissing this dour man before him. All those idle hours spent in darkened movie houses had suddenly paid off. Jules barely smiled, and nodded his head. As he walked past the table, the official stopped him. Jules inwardly winced and prepared himself. But when he turned, the man was smiling.

"Give our regards to Mr. Gable," the man said, equal parts impressed and intimidated by Jules's phony identity. Jules smiled wider and nodded again. "I certainly will."

Edith was waiting for him patiently, though worriedly, outside the terminal in their Model A with her father, Albert. Their reunion at the dock was like something out of a Hollywood movie, the two overjoyed to be in one another's arms again. But on their return to Berlin, life for them and their fellow Jews quickly deteriorated even more. Starting that April, many Jewish business owners were forced to sell out to Aryan Germans at below-market prices. Jules began looking for a buyer for the fur shop. Germany passed a new law demanding that Jews provide a detailed inventory list of all their property, down to the cups and saucers in Edith's kitchen cabinets, on which they would have to pay an exorbitant tax. Jules sold many of those belongings and hid the cash. By October, Jews were made to surrender their passports and were issued replacements, with a giant red *J* stamped on the first page.

Jules secured transit visas from the countries he and Edith would pass through, both the Netherlands and England. When his appointment with the American consulate finally rolled around, he sat in the waiting room, a clock ticking on one wall and the American flag on the other with its forty-eight stars idly shining down on him. He patiently waited, repeatedly counting the stars in their neat six-by-eight rows, beads of sweat forming on his forehead and freshly shaved upper lip. He took out the white folded handkerchief he always carried in his suit pocket, a stack of which Edith lovingly ironed after every wash, and dabbed the sweat away.

Finally, he was led into his meeting with the vice-consul, Halleck Rose. Jules coolly chatted about his well-off relatives in America, his cousin Faye and her husband, Murray Sternberg, and his "good friend" Harry Donenfeld in New York City. He spoke enthusiastically of his plan to open a fur shop there, describing the competition he had just studied on the streets of Manhattan. A fur coat retailed for around $3,000 in New York, he excitedly told the vice-consul. He already had a supplier all set up and ready to go, whom he had met with on the Lower East Side. Jules laughed and mentioned Astor Place and all those beavers. Rose smiled and gladly stamped Jules's transit visas, shook his hand, and wished him good luck. "You will need it," he said in German.

Now all they needed was their exit visa.

In August 1938, the German government revoked the residence permits of foreigners living in the country, including those, like Jules, who were German-born. Even if you were a Jew born there, the German government considered you a citizen of the country where your father was born. In Jules's case, Poland. Mollie and David, with Harry's sponsorship, had already fled, first to Palestine to visit Sara and Max, and then to New York. Hiding rolls of money in dining room table legs that they would send overseas ahead of them, Mollie and David handed their shops over to two female employees with an agreement that they would send them profits when things returned to normal in Berlin. By that summer, only nine thousand shops out of the fifty-five thousand owned by Jews would still be in Jewish hands.

Poland announced a plan to revoke the passports of all Polish Jews living abroad that October, sending those like Golda's husband, Simon, scrambling back to their homeland. Simon, the man who had refused to leave for Palestine with his family, was forced to travel back to his home city of Bielsko in the country's south. Golda's twenty-one-year-old son, Don, who was Dutch-born, but who also had a Polish passport because of his parents' nationality, would soon follow his stepfather. They would both be trapped for

several days in the no-man's-land between Germany and Poland—
the military on both sides of the border trying to keep the Jews out.
Don would finally be allowed into Poland, though he wouldn't stay
for long.

That October, Golda and Simon reached out to a friend of the
family in New York, who wrote a letter to the American consul in
Berlin offering to sponsor them. But his offer was denied.

Golda would stay behind for now in Berlin with her younger
son, Paul, and try to sell their men's clothing business. Then she
and Paul could join her husband and Don in Bielsko. By late October, the Nazis were forcibly deporting all male Polish Jews back to
Poland. Jules would have to make a move soon.

All through the summer and fall, the Friedmanns begged Jules
and Edith not to leave and take their only grandchild away from
them. So Jules and Edith stalled. But at the end of October, the
couple finally went to get their travel visa. The line was unbearably
long, everyone on it frazzled.

While waiting, Jules held Hannelore in his arms, her chubby
legs around his waist. A half hour went by and the line hadn't moved
more than a few feet. Jules suddenly pinched the toddler's bottom.
Hannelore let out a surprised wail. Edith looked at him and said,
"What on earth are you doing?" as their daughter cried. But then
the couple in front of them insisted Jules move ahead of them. He
looked at Edith and winked. Jules then offered his daughter a lollipop, only to pull it away. More wails followed. Edith had to stop
herself from comforting her daughter and instead looked away as
she screamed. One by one, up the line, the others insisted that Jules
move ahead. No one could stand a shrieking baby.

Just after they got their visas, the window closed for the day.

The following Tuesday, a few days after Hannelore's second
birthday, Jules was stopped by one of his neighbors in their apartment building—a member of the Gestapo. He liked Jules; maybe

Jules was his exception, the one Jew that he felt was decent. Hating a group was much easier than hating an individual whom you passed on the carpeted stairs every day.

"Julius," he said, talking low so his words wouldn't echo in the tiled hallway of their six-story building. "A major sweep is coming. You need to leave."

Jules started to explain, telling him how they were preparing to go, but that he hadn't sold his shop and that Edith didn't want to leave her parents and sister behind. The neighbor cut him off mid-sentence, taking him by the shoulders of his wool coat with its fur collar. "Listen to me. You have to get out. Right now. Not tomorrow. Not next week. Now. Do you understand me?"

Jules nodded, his mouth dry and slightly agape, his eyes dazed. He headed back upstairs to tell Edith to pack their bags. They were leaving. Now.

Not tomorrow.

Not next week.

Today.

Edith stared at her husband for a moment and then started to argue, but when she saw the look on Jules's face, she knew. Jules was not a bossy man. He was not a bully. He always listened to her and never argued. But this time was different. All he had to say was "Please, Edith."

Jules and Edith closed up their shop. Not for the day. But forever. They packed three suitcases, one for each of them, mostly clothes, but also Jules's Leica camera and a few family photos. They left behind furniture, dishes, carpets, a piano, and most of their clothing. No furs. No gold. The only jewelry they took were their wedding rings. They headed over to Edith's parents to warn them of what their neighbor said was coming. And to say goodbye.

Edith's father, Albert, fifty-three, was set in his ways and convinced no harm would come to people of means like them. At least that's what he said. But the truth was he was unable to muster the fight to make it across the vast ocean—his life, his home, everything he had worked for was here. How do you begin again at age fifty-three? But he said none of this. What he did say was "How can I just up and leave?" Jules nodded his head and said he understood. But Jules was young. His whole life was ahead of him. Jules didn't care if the Nazis stripped him of all his wealth and belongings before he left. He would start again in America. And he could not really imagine being too tired to run for his life.

"But you understand that we must go?" Jules asked him. "We can't wait any longer." Albert nodded his knobby head. He hugged his son-in-law and then his daughter and granddaughter as tightly as he could. Martha held them close, one by one, her tears falling on their faces and mixing with their tears. As Ushi embraced her big sister, she quietly whispered, "I wish I could go with you." But her parents wouldn't let her go. They were convinced they could make it through this crisis.

Jews emigrating had to hand over most of their money before leaving the country. Those caught with large sums of cash would be arrested for smuggling. So Jules left most of their money and the furs from the store to Albert.

For the first time in his life, Jules was glad that his parents were dead. They could not have lived through these times, this goodbye. It was a blessing they were already gone and buried in the Weissensee Cemetery.

Jules's brother and sister, Max and Sara, had already moved to Israel. Cilly was in Paris. Mollie and David had settled on the Upper West Side. The only one left in Berlin from his own family to say goodbye to was Golda, his second mother. She would stay here with her teenage son, Paul, to guard her business. Paul, because he was still a teenager, hadn't been forced out of the country. He was tall, dark, and skinny like his father, Simon, who was now safe in

Poland with Don, waiting for Golda and him to arrive. Forty-year-old Golda, stout and sturdy, could certainly take care of herself and Paul here in Berlin. At least for a little while longer.

Golda told Jules that once she managed to sell or lease the company, she and Paul would head to Poland to meet Simon. Jules told her again what his Gestapo neighbor had said, that the Nazis were planning some sort of a coordinated attack on the Jews in Berlin. "You can't stay here."

"No need to worry about me," she said, trying to smile and hugging her baby brother so hard she nearly broke a rib. "I can take care of myself." Jules shook his head, climbed into his Model A, and headed due west toward Rotterdam with his own small family, waving to Golda and Paul as he pulled away.

The date was November 8, 1938.

A STOREFRONT WINDOW DESTROYED DURING KRISTALLNACHT

CHAPTER 14

BROKEN GLASS

BERLIN, NOVEMBER 9, 1938

THE NAZI STORM TROOPERS MARCHED ONTO THE DARK streets of Berlin, their swastika armbands hard to make out in the gloaming on Wednesday night, November 9. But with clubs and bats, they made their presence known, systematically smashing all the windows in the Jewish shopping district, and then in every neighborhood where Jews lived and worked. Jewish families watched silently from apartment windows, afraid to go out, but soon their homes were invaded as well, fathers and brothers dragged into the streets and beaten. The storm troopers were not alone in their organized attack. Mobs of Berliners joined in the beatings and the looting of businesses—furniture, leather goods, groceries, and clothing now exposed to the cool autumn air. The windows and mirrors of David's and Jules's fur shops were smashed with bricks and sledgehammers by their former friends and customers.

Jules's Gestapo neighbor had been right. This had been planned, not just in Berlin, but all throughout Germany, Austria, and Czechoslovakia.

Tombstones were uprooted and graves violated, dozens of hospitals and schools destroyed. The New Synagogue, where Albert Einstein had once played the violin, was invaded by the Nazi mob, its Torah ark opened and desecrated, furniture smashed and piled up to start a fire, which, thankfully, was put out before the whole building and its golden dome burned.

But there were very few sirens that night amid the shouts and screams and the sounds of glass shattering. Police and firemen were ordered by the Gestapo to let the synagogues burn, to allow the storm troopers to pour their gasoline and light their matches. The flames lit the dark streets like holy bonfires, the smoke billowing for hours and clouding the city's air. As night turned to day, the attacks continued. The window of an art supply store was smashed, its paints and brushes taken to help mark the walls of the destroyed shops with the words *Jewish Pigs*. A Jewish man in a black coat was stopped by a group of laughing storm troopers, who painted a white Star of David on his back and then punched him repeatedly, leaving him lying, bleeding in the street. He was just one of hundreds that night who were kicked to the curb and left for dead.

As the sun rose, Jewish men were made to line up in the streets and were marched off to God knows where, the first man in line forced to hold a large cardboard Star of David sign, wives and children shouting and crying after them, passersby laughing and jeering. Thousands, dressed in topcoats and hats, would be sent to the concentration camps Dachau, Buchenwald, and Sachsenhausen, which was conveniently located just outside the city in a quiet suburb, tucked behind neatly kept houses. It was a short train ride away. Those Jews who remained in Berlin—including Edith's parents— were forced to pay for the cleanup of the mess the Nazis had made.

Jules's sister Golda and her son Paul were thrown into the street by their housekeeper, a young German farm girl, and her SS officer boyfriend, who looted their house of its jewelry, clothing, furs, and furniture. They smashed what they couldn't take and broke all the windows. Golda's business was looted and destroyed as well, the men's suits stolen and distributed among the young Nazis. Escaping without even her purse, Golda stayed with one of her kinder employees until she and Paul could make it to Poland to meet Simon and Don, to what she assumed was safety.

Jules, Edith, and Hannelore drove all day to Rotterdam, where they stayed for a few days in a small hotel. They heard the news of Kristallnacht and talked about whether to turn around and go back to Berlin. But getting to America—and then sending for their family from there—seemed like the better plan.

They drove to the waterfront and left their car at the dock. It pained Jules to abandon his beloved Model A, but really, it was the least of his worries. On November 12, the day they left for America, the German government issued a decree barring Jews from operating retail stores. What would this mean for Edith's family, and for Golda back in Berlin? Did Albert have enough money to keep the Nazis bribed and at bay?

Nauseous with worry, Jules and Edith hastily boarded the SS *Veendam*. The Holland America liner had partially sunk at the Hoboken docks ten years earlier after being rammed by another boat on a foggy night. But the *Veendam* was quickly repaired and its interior redesigned, eliminating many of its first-class cabins to transport a new surge of fleeing refugees. It was a far cry from the triple-stacked, Art Deco glory of the *Queen Mary*. That luxury had been reserved for Clark Gable's agent.

Jules and Edith, her young daughter in her arms, stood at the railing and watched as the tugs push-pulled their ship out into the dark water of the harbor, the dock full of waving strangers growing smaller and smaller. Hannelore pressed her small face into her crying mother's neck. Neither she nor Jules nor Edith waved to the crowd, since there was no one there they knew.

Their family members had already said their goodbyes.

On the *Veendam*'s previous voyage to America, a Jewish refugee from Austria had disappeared in the middle of the night after being despondent over leaving all her worldly possessions and a family member behind in a concentration camp. She had jumped overboard. In a photo taken at sea by Jules on his beloved Leica, Hannelore is smiling widely, but Edith looks depressed, no doubt thinking of all she, too, had left in her wake.

The *Veendam*, a third the size of the *Queen Mary* (four decks compared to the *Queen*'s twelve) and nowhere near as luxurious, was a sign of what was to come for Jules and Edith in their new, more Spartan life in America. Once in New York City, they crowded in with the Sternbergs for a few months until they could find an apartment of their own. Jules would take his wife and daughter from the Bronx down to Manhattan to Central Park, show them the bright lights of Broadway, and as he promised himself, would take Edith dancing at the Piccadilly ballroom once they were settled. But dancing was no longer as joyous as it once had been for Edith and Jules.

Mollie and David had settled on the Upper West Side in September, opening up their own fur shop, one of twenty-two furriers along Broadway between West Seventy-Second and Ninety-Sixth Streets. David eventually changed his last name to Payne—a loose translation of *Schmerz*. Pain. Payne. To break out from the pack and establish his own clientele, Jules headed crosstown to the Upper East Side to live and open his business. For Passover and the other holidays, they would go west to Mollie's place. But the Upper East Side was now Jules's domain. Their new neighborhood, Yorkville, was filled with Germans. It was so German, in fact, that a stretch of East Eighty-Sixth Street was known as "Sauerkraut Boulevard" and would be the scene of a Nazi parade in 1939.

Though his fellow Germans wanted him dead, Jules still identified strongly as a Berliner. He continued to read copies of the German American newspaper *New Yorker Staats-Zeitung*, which was sold at corner newsstands, and ate at German restaurants like the Heidelberg, which served schnitzel, sauerbraten, and Dinkelacker.

Yorkville was the very same neighborhood where Billy Wilder's mother, Eugenia, had lived three decades before as a young woman. It's where she had stayed with her jeweler uncle and his wife, strolling its gaslit streets at night and eating at those very same German restaurants, where she had dreamed of a permanent life in New York City.

Jules was reinventing himself yet again on those streets. His first shop—and railroad apartment—was tiny compared to their sprawling place in Berlin, on the second floor of a building on Lexington and Ninety-First, above a French dry cleaner and next to the Ninety-Second Street YMHA, the biggest Jewish community center in the country. Jules, Edith, and the baby lived in a couple of cramped rooms behind the shop, making the "commute" easy for them. The place was so narrow it resembled a bowling alley. They were so poor Edith would buy day-old bread from the bakery. But Jules and Edith worked hard, sewing furs into the night. They worked twelve hours a day, not just to make their business succeed, but to forget what and whom they had abandoned in Berlin.

What Jules missed most, besides his siblings, was having a car. He and Edith couldn't afford one, so he bought Hannelore a toy car, a green metal windup Kommando Anno 2000. It wasn't just any car but an exact double of the green car on the cover of the first issue of *Action Comics*, the car Superman had held up over his head. No one knows if Jules bought it because of the celebrated cover published by the man who had helped save them, or if it was just one of life's strange coincidences, one that you would miss if you weren't paying close enough attention. Jules showed Hannelore how to use the small key to wind the car up and send it on its way across the worn wooden floorboards of their new home. In America.

SUPERMAN FLOATS ABOVE THE MACY'S THANKSGIVING DAY PARADE, NYC

CHAPTER 15

A JOB FOR SUPERMAN

SOMEWHERE IN AMERICA, 1940

JOE DiMAGGIO WAS ANXIOUS. THE NEW SUPERMAN COMIC was on the newsstands already, but his roommate, Lefty Gomez, was giving him a hard time. Every month, as soon as the comic book hit the stands, it was Lefty's job to buy a copy for DiMaggio when the Yankees were traveling on the road. Lefty was six years older than Joe and had originally been paired up with him on their trips to help the young player adjust to the majors, to joke around with him and keep him happy. Comics were for kids, and DiMaggio, a grown-up comic geek, didn't want to be recognized buying his favorite magazine, which he would read over and over until its pages were dog-eared. If anyone saw DiMaggio buying a comic book, it would be in the press in no time. Lefty was a great pitcher, but was not a celebrity like Joe. He had a face no one would recognize or remember.

At the newsstand, DiMaggio subtly pointed out the comic book to Lefty. "Is this the one you want?" Lefty asked, teasing DiMaggio, who got so mad he walked away from the newsstand. But Lefty would finally buy it and hand it over. Leading the American League with a .352 batting average and thirty-one home runs, DiMaggio was America's hero that summer of 1940.

But Joe DiMaggio's hero was Superman.

The Man of Steel, to Harry's surprise, had taken flight the summer of 1938. The comics business was still new to Harry—new to the rest of the world as well—so to increase his chances, he had printed up twenty thousand promotional posters for drugstores, newsstands, and corner stores hawking his new magazine. The returns trickled in, so it would take weeks before Harry knew whether or not *Action Comics* was a success and if Superman had taken flight into American popular culture. Well, not flight exactly. At that point, Superman leapt tall buildings in a single bound. The flying would come a little later.

Harry printed 202,000 copies of *Action Comics* and left them on store shelves and racks starting April 18 for six weeks rather than the usual four, to give the comic book a little time to percolate. The date on the cover read June 1938. He was so doubtful about this Superman that he planned to run another image on the cover of *Action Comics* #2, to mix things up a bit.

The first issue sold 130,000 copies, more than anyone had anticipated. Anything over 50 percent of a print run meant you were making money. Though they didn't realize right away that the Superman character was to thank for *Action Comics'* success, Harry and Jack conducted a reader survey in the fourth issue asking kids to list their favorite stories in the magazine. Out of 542 responses, 404 chose Superman as number one. That September issue would sell 190,000 copies, causing newsstand vendors to beg for a bigger press run. Even after the survey, Harry was still skeptical, and it wasn't until he was at a newsstand one day that he became convinced of Superman's popularity. A boy approached and said to the news vendor, "Give me the one with Superman in it."

The money from the pulps and bootlegging would be like pocket change compared to what was about to roll in for Harry and Jack. By the following winter, Jerry Siegel and Joe Shuster started getting inquiries into syndicating the character from the very newspaper editors who had turned them down. When they wrote to DC about it, Harry invited them to come to New York to discuss it.

Jerry arrived and was reminded by Harry and Jack that he no longer owned the rights to his character. To drive the point home, Jack sent him a letter that read:

"Our company has very little to gain in a monetary sense from the syndication of this material. Also bear in mind, that we own the feature, 'Superman,' and that we can at any time replace you in the drawing of the feature and that without our consent this feature would not be syndicated and therefore, you would be the loser in the entire transaction."

Once Jack put them in their place, he and Harry proceeded to sell the rights to Gaines's McClure Syndicate, then offered Jerry and Joe a ten-year deal for around $100 a month to produce the syndicated comic strip. Take it or leave it. Not knowing what else to do, they signed. Superman flew into syndication first in the Cleveland *Plain Dealer* in January 1939 and into 230 papers across America. That same year, Superman got his very own quarterly comic book, which would sell a million copies a pop.

Superman would still star in *Action Comics*, where sales continued to rise. The September 1939 issue included a story Harry must have loved called "Superman and the Numbers Racket," featuring a thief with a gambling problem. It was a winner, selling 625,000 copies.

By 1940, the world's first superhero was everywhere, flying onto the airwaves in *The Adventures of Superman*. The radio show was produced by Bob Maxwell, who had been one of Harry's best spicy pulp scribes. Maxwell and a team of radio writers—not Jerry—were cranking out scripts week to week, bringing in an additional $75,000 a year for Harry and Jack. The most difficult hurdle for Maxwell was creating the sound of Superman flying, eventually created by mixing a fifty-mile-per-hour wind with the sound of a bomb falling during the Spanish Civil War. The program was an instant sensation, eventually appearing on 218 stations nationwide and driving Harry's newsstand sales and merchandising profits high into the stratosphere. There were Superman games, toy ray guns, dolls, puppets, greeting cards, puzzles, jeans, coloring books, shaving cream, bread, milk, bubble gum cards, and even high-octane gasoline.

Superman made his debut at the Macy's Thanksgiving Day Parade that November as a giant balloon that bore very little resemblance to the actual comic book character but did have a twenty-three-foot chest and an eight-foot smile. Supermania even spread to the New York World's Fair, which held a Superman Day, with a special comic book featuring the superhero given to thirty-six thousand kids, including Faye's son, Neil. It was the first time a man would dress in a Superman costume. Harry was there for the festivities and rode a live elephant for the occasion.

Because of DC's success, the comics industry exploded overnight, with a legion of new characters riding on Superman's coattails (or at the edge of his cape). The first on the scene was Wonder Man, drawn by artist Will Eisner after publisher Victor Fox stumbled upon the early sales numbers for *Action Comics*. Fox opened an office in the same building as DC in the winter of 1939 and churned out his first issue, prompting Harry and Jack to immediately—and successfully—sue for copyright infringement. But the copycats kept on coming.

Later that year, Fawcett Comics dreamed up Captain Marvel, aka Shazam, while Timely Comics—eventually called Marvel—published the Human Torch and, later, Captain America. MLJ Comics, which would become famous for its *Archie* comics, debuted the patriotic superhero the Shield, and the now-forgotten Rang-a-Tang the Wonder Dog. Crestwood Publications followed in 1940 with the awkwardly named K the Unknown, who, by the second issue, morphed into the Black Owl. Crestwood would also publish *The New Adventures of Frankenstein*, kicking off the horror comics trend. Joining the crowded field of superheroes in 1941 was Harvey Comics' Captain Freedom and Standard Comics' American Crusader.

But Superman reigned supreme. With the radio buzz and a new telescoping 3D logo refined by DC artist Ira Schnapp, the Superman comics reached out and grabbed every kid in America—and Joe DiMaggio, .352 batting average—selling over six hundred thousand copies a month and grossing nearly $1 million in 1940. Harry and Jack made an extra $100,000 on newspaper syndication, which reached 4.5 million readers each day.

By 1941, "Superman enterprises" were grossing $5 million a year. But Harry kept all the finances from Jerry and Joe, who were on salary, plotting out Superman's future, week to week. Jerry and Joe together made a total of $75,000 that year ($1.4 million by modern standards)—more than they ever had in their lives, and quite a tidy sum at the time—but just a fraction of what DC was raking in.

Harry lied and told them the radio show was actually losing money. To keep them happy, Harry leaned on his connections at the *Saturday Evening Post*—which he distributed—to do a seven-page spread on the dynamic duo. The article—titled "Up, Up and Awa-ay!"—told the boys' origin story, describing them as "the puniest kids in school," who were constantly bullied. It told of their years-long struggle to get their character out into the world, mentioned a new character, "Superboy," that they were working on, and included photos of their improved lives at home in Cleveland.

Except for a conference that Jerry attended in New York every two or three months with the editors and publishers of DC, he and Joe didn't leave their hometown. Harry and Jack, wanting more control over their content, convinced them to move to New York in early 1939, but the boys hated it and hightailed it back to Cleveland.

Joe moved out of his family's shabby apartment and took his

mother, father, brother, and sister with him, renting a ten-room house in a much better neighborhood for $75 a month. With his newfound riches, he bought a radio phonograph console, a camera, a car, lots of detective novels, and lifts for his shoes. He even hired a maid to clean the house twice a week, though his mother continued to cook all their meals, including a daily T-bone steak to help bulk up her skinny son. Joe now weighed a whopping 128 pounds. Still slightly in shock about their success, Joe and Jerry told the *Saturday Evening Post* reporter that they had to keep pinching themselves.

And it wasn't just about the money and the real estate. With success, Jerry finally found love. In 1939, he married a girl who lived across the street from him, Bella Lifshitz, a plumber's daughter who was six years younger than Jerry. As soon as she graduated high school, Jerry planted a big diamond engagement ring on her finger. His brother Leo—the snoring brother with whom he shared a bed—stepped in as best man.

Jerry lavished Bella with a mink coat and a diamond bracelet, all thanks to Superman. He finally moved out of his parents' house and bought a $15,000 home in Cleveland with air-conditioning, a radio in every room, a chrome-gadget-filled kitchen, and a basement playroom with a Ping-Pong table, a dartboard, and a bar, even though he and Bella didn't know how to mix a drink. The most important room in the house, though, was Jerry's study. To the sound of Benny Goodman on the record player, Jerry would write three or four Superman stories at a time, which he would then send to New York for edits. The stories often came back marked in red with grammar and tense corrections.

With a final draft in hand, Jerry would head over to the small office he and Joe rented for $30 a month, to meet with the five-member art staff they'd hired for $16,000 a year to help with their ever-increasing workload—a thirteen-page story for the monthly comic book, six daily strips a week for syndication, and one Sunday comic. The phone was pulled out and the frosted door kept blank to avoid distractions from their growing legion of fans. Weekdays from 9:30 a.m. to 5:00 p.m., the staff—including Joe's brother Fred—would come in and pencil and letter the panels that Joe mapped out. Joe, the only artist on staff allowed to draw Superman's facial features, would then come up with a color scheme and send it all off to New York, where Harry's staff would color it in.

With the money rolling in from Superman cartoons, comics, radio, and merchandising, all of Harry's girlie sex pulps folded, except for the *Spicy* hybrid line. The National Organization for Decent Literature, founded by a group of Catholic bishops in 1938, had placed new roadblocks in the industry's way, drawing up lists of forbidden magazines and books and canvassing stores to put pressure on pulp publishers like Harry. But the reality was, Harry no longer needed the sex pulps. He had Jerry and Joe's brainchild.

With a staff of 250 people employed in Superman enterprises, Harry was now rich beyond his wildest fantasies. He moved from Riverside Drive to a giant duplex on the nineteenth floor of the twenty-two-story Beresford, one of Manhattan's most exclusive buildings. One of 175 apartments in the Italian Renaissance–style Beresford—with its distinctive three towers—Harry's place had a terrace overlooking Central Park West and was just a ten-minute walk from his buddy Frank Costello. The Mob boss lived in a nine-room apartment also on Central Park West, in the Art Deco Majestic. Costello's living room featured a gold-plated grand piano and a set of slot machines that were always set to pay out for all his guests, including Harry.

To promote the Superman radio show, Harry paid $100 to his pulp fiction cover artist H. J. Ward to paint a full-color, life-size portrait of the superhero, hands on his hips, red cape blowing in the wind, blue skies behind him, staring straight into the future. The painting ended up hanging on the wall of Harry's office, greeting visitors as they walked in. Harry also started wearing a Superman T-shirt under his dress shirt, and whenever he had had a few too many, in a business meeting or in a bar (sometimes both simultaneously), he would rip open the buttons and say, "This looks like a job for Superman!"

While strolling the beach in Miami that December of 1940, a little boy came up to him and asked him if he was Superman. "Yes, son, I am," Harry said. The kid looked doubtful. "Let's see you pull that palm tree up by its roots," he said. Harry laughed, though he probably wanted to give the kid a swift kick in the pants.

In some ways, Harry *was* Superman. Certainly to the families he saved. And to the Jews whose lives he was trying to help in other ways. Harry may not have made an honest living most of his life, but he was about to make up for it. Superman's penchant for social justice was as strong as Harry's once was back in the twenties. His comic hero was fighting the good fight in Jerry's socially conscious plotlines—fighting corporate evil, political corruption, and gangsters, like the ones who had helped Harry build his fortune.

"Superman in the Slums," featured in *Action Comics* #8, paid homage to Harry's lowly Lower East Side upbringing. Though he wasn't writing the plotlines, Harry—and Jack and the other editors—maintained control over the stories, ensuring Superman never used a weapon, and destroyed property only when absolutely necessary. In the "Slums" story, Clark Kent covers a court hearing where a neighborhood gang member—much like young Harry—appears before a judge. The boy's distraught mother makes a desperate plea to keep her son out of jail, but he's sentenced to two years in a reformatory. Superman then intervenes as the other gang members attempt a series of robberies and gives them a lecture: "It's not entirely your fault that you're a delinquent—it's these slums." Superman destroys the slums, and a spanking new housing project is built in their place. Fighting for affordable housing was just one of Superman's—and Harry and Jerry's—many causes: they fought against war profiteers, financial fraud, unsafe labor practices, and for prison reform.

But that wasn't all.

Nearly two years before the United States declared war, Harry's stable of Jewish artists was doing its best to try and convince President Roosevelt to join the fight. Comic artists and writers were mostly Jews who had been kept out of the mainstream literary establishment in New York City.

Superman's comic villains were suddenly Axis spies and dictators. In 1940, *Look* magazine featured a strip called "How Superman Would End the War," with the Man of Steel dressed in white, twisting German cannons and smashing plane propellers, then busting through the roof of Hitler's retreat. Superman lifts Hitler by the neck, saying, "I'd like to land a strictly non-Aryan sock on your jaw but there's no time for that." The dictator begs to be put down. But Superman carries Hitler with him to Moscow, where he swoops onto a balcony and grabs Stalin. He then drops the two in Geneva at the League of Nations, where they stand trial and are found guilty of "unprovoked aggression against defenseless countries."

If only it were that simple.

DON WITH MOLLIE'S SONS, BOB AND FRED,
AND HIS BROTHER, PAUL, IN BERLIN

CHAPTER 16

TAKING SIDES

ROMANIA, JUNE 1941

THE ROMANIAN SOLDIERS IN THEIR SAND-COLORED UNI-
forms and large sloping helmets came together with the plainly
dressed civilians on a warm summer weekend in the midst of World
War II. They gathered on the streets of Jassy, Harry's Romanian
hometown, in late June 1941, not to celebrate or to protest or to
even shoot at the Russian bombers intermittently attacking their
city. They were there for one reason: to kill the Jews living among
them.

The pogrom had been planned days before, maybe even weeks
or months before, the tension hanging over the city like a dark
storm cloud. The fascist Romanian government, which had joined
the Axis in 1940, claimed they were worried the Jews would conspire
with their enemies, the Communists, and so ordered their deaths.
Over three days, Romanian and German forces fired machine guns
at all Jews found walking on the streets. Some soldiers laughingly
tossed hand grenades into basements where Jewish families hid
huddled together in darkness. Though the Nazis were there to help
cleanse Jassy of its Jewish population, the anti-Semitism had run
deep for centuries. It was the reason Harry and his family had left
long ago.

Using rifle butts to knock their neighbors' doors in, the Romanian police invaded home after home after home, shooting those

inside. As men, women, and children tried to flee, their fellow citizens stabbed and beat them to death with clubs and crowbars, their blood staining the walls of the city and running onto the cobblestones in large puddles. The victims were people their murderers had seen every day, the baker, the grocer, the tailor, and had said hello to in passing for years. Their bodies now lay dead in the streets, stripped of jewelry, watches, and, in some cases, their clothes.

Local police officers, once the purveyors of law and order, forced hundreds of Jewish residents into their headquarters' courtyard at gunpoint, and then shot them all to death, their bodies moved to large piles in the local churchyard. It took two days to remove all the bodies. Some were buried and others were thrown into the Bahlui River.

On Sunday and Monday, thousands of massacre survivors were crowded onto two trains, like the ones that had once passed Harry's apartment on Riverside Drive. Instead of pigs and cows, they were full of humans, headed for a concentration camp. But the trains moved so slowly and stopped for so long in the intense summer heat that most of the passengers, denied water or air, suffocated to death.

Perhaps news of the twelve thousand massacred that week reached Harry in New York through relatives and neighbors that he and his family had left behind.

Similar purges were taking place throughout Europe. All but two hundred of the Jews from the Schulzbachs' native city of Kolomyia were murdered. Jules's sister Golda, who had been thrown out of her apartment on Kristallnacht, tried to flee Poland once she got there, but quotas in the United States were tightened. She was placed on a six-year waiting list. Regretting their decision not to leave for Palestine when given the chance, she and her husband, Simon, tried to arrange escape through Cuba, but it was too late.

In March of 1941, they, along with thousands of other Polish Jews, were sent to the Kraków ghetto, along with their younger son, Paul.

Golda's older son, Don, the teenage engineer who had had to quit high school in Berlin because of the Nazis, was not with them. He had left Poland long ago. His story, like all the stories of Jewish refugees, was more dramatic than any Hollywood screenplay Billy Wilder could ever dream up.

Don, like Jules, was intent on leaving for America. Because of his Dutch birth, quotas were still open to him in 1939. However, he had no copy of his Dutch birth certificate, only his Polish passport. He visited the American embassy in Warsaw, where they assured him his papers were on their way from Berlin. He returned again and again, but was finally told by the American consul that the United States didn't need people like him.

After waiting for weeks for his Dutch papers to arrive, he returned to Berlin to retrieve a copy of his birth certificate. But it had been sent to Warsaw weeks before. Halleck Rose, the American vice-consul in Berlin who had helped Jules, was sure it had been stolen and sold by the corrupt anti-Semitic American diplomats in Warsaw. Rose issued Don an exit visa. But the next day, Germany declared war on Poland. Don, a Jew with a Polish passport, was trapped in enemy territory.

Scrambling for a way to escape, in mid-September Don boarded a train in Berlin to Sassnitz, Germany, where he hoped to catch a ferry to neutral Sweden. As soon as he got on the train, he surveyed the car to see if there was any way he could blend in with the other Aryan passengers. If the Germans discovered he was a Polish Jew, he would be arrested.

In one compartment, he noticed an old German farm woman with baskets of fruit and potatoes at her feet. She also had a bottle of vodka and was already feeling no pain. Don, very handsome and blond, sat down next to her and asked if he could have a sip.

After a while, he pretended to be drunk as well, and started singing German songs with her. Don made sure she kept drinking and put his arm around her, swaying back and forth to the music they were making. At one stop, the compartment doors opened and a member of the Gestapo, dressed in black leather, entered.

Don sang louder. The farmer by this time was soused, swinging her bottle as they sang together. When the Gestapo asked for her ID, she didn't even hear him. Don, only pretending to be drunk, heard him quite clearly but ignored him. When the Gestapo officer asked again, the conductor stepped up and tried to help.

"These two are drunken pigs," the conductor said to the Gestapo agent, shaking his head. "Let's just move on to the next compartment." And miraculously, they did.

The train approached the German coast, and Don disembarked a few stops later to catch the ferry to Sweden. He showed the border guard his visa. But when he saw Don's Polish passport, the guard jailed him in a small blockhouse near the railroad tracks. Don tried to convince him that the Germans wanted him to simply leave the country, but the border guard insisted on calling Berlin.

While he waited, Don noticed an old German railroad worker walking past the jail. "Pssst," he called out through the bars. "Pssst." The railroad worker was afraid to approach at first, but slowly made his way over.

"What are you doing in there?" he asked Don.

"You know these young guys, they don't know what they're doing," said Don, shrugging. Many older Germans were resentful of the young Nazis among them. "They're checking on my papers, but I'm going to miss my ferry."

The railroad man shook his head in sympathy.

"Can't you unlock the door for me?" Don asked.

But the man shook his head again and walked away.

Ten minutes later, he was back. Don heard him turn the key

in the door to the blockhouse. But he quietly told Don not to leave yet, since the guard was sure to see him. He whispered that a freight train would be passing by soon and not to open the blockhouse door until it was there. He instructed Don to jump onto the moving freight train and ride it just around the bend to where the ferry was waiting. The freight train would be his cover.

When the train came into the station, Don threw open the blockhouse door and made a run for it, jumped aboard, and hid between two cars. As he approached the ferry terminal, Don leapt from the train and ran toward the waiting boat. He snuck into the storage hold, where he waited in the dark until he heard the ferry doors close.

But there was a long delay. Don cautiously made his way to the upper deck. Some of the passengers had been on his original train and had seen that he'd been stopped by the German guard. They had implored the captain to hold the ferry for him. And now here he was. They were happy Don had made it. The captain welcomed him aboard. And set sail for Sweden.

With the help of a Jewish aid group, Don made it to Gothenburg, Sweden, and then to New York at the end of September 1939 on the SS *Drottningholm*, living with Mollie and David on the Upper West Side until he joined the war.

The news drifting over to America—from people like Don who had barely escaped the Nazis' clutches—made Harry step up Superman's game. The December 1941 issue of *Action Comics*—which went on the stands a month earlier—featured Superman battling a Nazi paratrooper midair. The *Washington Post* did a front-page story on Harry headlined "Superman to Sweep World for Democracy, His Boss Says." Harry boasted that his comic book character was traveling to Germany and Italy "to clean them up."

In return, Mussolini banned Superman comics from Italy. The

pro-Nazi German American Bund protested outside DC's offices and teamed up with the Ku Klux Klan for a rally in New Jersey. The Nazi weekly paper, *Das Schwarze Korps*, ridiculed Superman's writer, calling him Jerry "Israel" Siegel, and making fun of his creation. (By this time, the Nazis had made Jews with non-Jewish-sounding names adopt the middle name Israel or Sarah to make it easier to identify them for persecution.) "We see Superman, lacking all strategic sense and tactical ability, storming the West Wall in shorts," the Nazis wrote. "Woe to the American youth, who must live in such a poisoned atmosphere and don't even notice the poison they swallow daily."

Harry wasn't the only big shot trying to make a difference in the prewar effort against the fascists. His old pal Margaret Sanger helped Jews escape from Italy, Germany, and Czechoslovakia. Her former husband, William Sanger, was a Jew from Berlin who had left decades before. Sanger spoke out against Hitler as early as 1933, and he returned the favor, burning her books publicly in the vast bonfire of anti-Nazi and subversive literature that year. But in 1938, she took more direct action, signing affidavits for twenty Jews, most of them doctors, to come to America and work with her.

"We can scarcely stand by and have the opportunity to save a life from torture and not do it," she wrote. But Sanger didn't publicize her actions, worried the American public, still full of anti-Semites, would attack her. "The sudden antagonism in Germany against the Jews and the vitriolic hatred of them is spreading underground here."

Another high-profile American working to save Jewish refugees was Universal Pictures founder Carl Laemmle, the man who had helped Billy Wilder get his start as a screenwriter. Laemmle retired from Hollywood in 1936 to devote his time to helping fellow German Jews escape. He had had Hitler's number early on when his *All Quiet on the Western Front* was banned from German theaters in 1930. In the buildup to World War II, Laemmle urged both William Randolph Hearst and President Roosevelt to take a stand against Hitler—though by the time they did, it was too late for millions of Jewish families.

Laemmle sponsored more than three hundred refugees and urged his friends to do the same, helping to finance the Anti-Nazi League for the Defense of American Democracy in 1936. Co-founded by *New Yorker* writer Dorothy Parker, the league's five thousand members held rallies, worked to promote anti-Nazi content in movies, and boycotted Hitler's propagandist filmmaker Leni Riefenstahl when she visited Hollywood in 1938 to network with industry leaders. That same year, the European Film Fund was cofounded by Ernst Lubitsch, collecting 1 percent of members' salaries to provide money for refugees and help them find work in Hollywood. Two years later, Lubitsch also formed a Hollywood committee with Marlene Dietrich and Billy Wilder to gather money and send it to Europe, hoping to liberate Jews from camps and bring them over. Edward G. Robinson, Harry's old neighbor from the Lower East Side who had become famous playing tough guys and gangsters, personally donated more than a quarter million dollars to political organizations to fight Hitler.

Director Charlie Chaplin also bravely took up the anti-Hitler rallying cry. Chaplin had always felt an unfortunate connection to Hitler: they were born four days apart, and of course, the Führer had stolen his signature mustache. But the Nazis had hated Chaplin for years, thinking he was a Jew, calling him a "disgusting Jewish acrobat"—even though only his half brother was part Jewish. Chaplin knew from his Jewish friends in Europe the extent of the Nazis' hatred toward them. After seeing Leni Riefenstahl's *Triumph of the Will*, which featured the Führer whipping his Hitler Youth into a frenzy, Chaplin decided to do something about it.

Chaplin started filming *The Great Dictator*, his first talkie, in the autumn of 1939, just after Hitler invaded Poland, and released it in 1940, making it the first feature to directly criticize the Führer. (The Three Stooges poked fun at Hitler in a short earlier that year.)

Chaplin played dual roles—the dictator and a Jewish barber/World War I vet who was a talking version of Jules's beloved Little Tramp. The film climaxes with the barber being mistaken for the dictator and thrust onto the world stage to make a speech on the radio. Greed, he tells the crowd, has poisoned men's souls, and technology seems to be pushing us further apart. But he pleads with the world to join together.

"Dictators free themselves, but they enslave the people!" his character proclaimed. "Let us fight to free the world—to do away with national barriers—to do away with greed, with hate and intolerance. Let us fight for a world of reason, a world where science and progress will lead to all men's happiness. Soldiers! In the name of democracy, let us all unite!"

HARRY DONENFELD WITH ELEANOR ROOSEVELT AND HER SON JAMES

CHAPTER 17

COLLATERAL DAMAGE

NEW YORK, DECEMBER 1941

THOUGH IT WAS ONLY THIRTY-SIX DEGREES IN THE SUN, THE chilly stands at the Polo Grounds in upper Manhattan were packed with people watching the Giants and Dodgers football game. The gusty wind that early December Sunday made it feel more like it was in the teens; bundled up in coats, hats, and scarves, fans cheered and bounced up and down to keep warm. Just before 2:30 p.m., the football play-by-play was interrupted with a bulletin: "The Japanese have attacked Pearl Harbor, Hawaii, by air, President Roosevelt has just announced." The game stopped. The crowd went silent and still. There were murmurs. A few men in uniform pardoned their way through the crowd and moved toward the exits. The football game began again. But suddenly, it didn't seem to matter who won.

Concerts, movies, Broadway matinees, and religious services throughout the city were all interrupted in the same way to make the same announcement, the crowds stunned and quiet for a few moments, then slowly realizing that this meant war.

Despite the cold, editors and writers at the Time-Life Building threw open their Sixth Avenue office windows and tossed paper airplanes out, announcing the news in scrawled notes. As the afternoon wore on, large groups of people found warmth huddling together in Times Square, watching the news zipper for the latest developments. Their relatives and neighbors on leave quickly donned their uniforms and streamed through Grand Central Terminal, Penn Station, and the subways to hurry back to their military postings. Lines to the local recruiting stations grew by the minute, outraged young men wanting to get even with the Japanese.

Mayor Fiorello LaGuardia—who was half Jewish—sped to city hall in a police radio car to meet with his top commissioners to develop a defense strategy. Later in the day he took to the airwaves on WNYC to warn residents "not to feel entirely secure because you happen to be on the Atlantic Coast." He ordered the Empire State Building blacked out and Japanese nationals rounded up.

Jules and Edith—and even little Hannelore—sat and listened in their living room that night, heads bent toward the rounded Art Deco radio. For many Americans, the attack on Pearl Harbor left them angry and vengeful. But to mothers with sons already in the military, and immigrants with family still in Europe, the news was devastating. For the past few years, Jules and Edith had hoped that their beloved FDR would enter the fray and save their loved ones. But now that war was actually coming, they wondered if their German relatives would simply be part of the collateral damage.

Walter Winchell greeted Jules and his fellow New Yorkers that night on WJZ with an alarming broadcast. "Nothing matters anymore now except national security," he screeched. "The American population is electrified tonight with the knowledge that every corner of the globe will be at war by tomorrow night." Edith didn't even have to say anything, just had to give Jules a sorrowful look to express what was unfolding in her head: her sister, Ushi, and her parents, Martha and Albert. Jules gave Edith the same weary look: his sister Golda, wherever she was with her own family, and Cilly, his youngest sister, somewhere in Paris, all of them in the line of fire.

Jules joined the New York State Guard and the city's Civil Defense, searching for enemy aircraft and ready to guide people to bomb shelters if any bombs ever actually fell. Air-raid wardens and auxiliary fire departments stood by for emergency orders as hundreds of workers reported to the Brooklyn Navy Yard to guard the battleships that were under construction. The lights of Broadway, the Statue of Liberty's torch, Times Square, and all the lights in the city would be dimmed each night as a precaution against air raids; it was part of Jules's job to enforce the brownout.

He and Edith devoured several newspapers a day to improve their English and keep up on the war. They were distressed to read that the *Veendam*, the ship that had carried them to safety in America from Rotterdam, had been captured by the German navy and was now being used to house off-duty U-boat crews. Together, the family listened to *The Adventures of Superman* and to FDR's radio chats, hoping it wouldn't be too long before their loved ones were freed from Hitler's grip on Europe. Inspired by the president's speeches, Jules made him a fur pillow and mailed it to the White House, and to his amazement, received a letter of thanks in return.

For Harry, the declaration of war was a relief. He, too, still had relatives in Europe, though his immediate family had all come to America decades before. The cartoon Superman began hawking savings bonds and urging kids to organize drives for scrap metal and paper, which would be recycled to build armaments and make paper packaging for military supplies. After reading their Superman comics, they gladly gave them up for the war effort (which made them all the more rare in decades to come).

Harry got in on the action and hosted a number of rallies in Miami Beach, Florida, at the Versailles hotel, selling millions in war bonds. He also hosted groups of air force returnees at the hotel, treating them to cocktails, food, and dancing. Jack Liebowitz was still running the finances and growing the business back in New York, but Harry was the smiling face of the company, always traveling, entertaining the troops, and running corporate conventions and meetings with publishers, wholesalers, and anyone capable of holding a drink.

Along with a million other kids, Mayor LaGuardia's two children joined the Supermen of America club. The superhero was ubiquitous, flying across every strata of American culture. The Russian writer Vladimir Nabokov, who had escaped Berlin with his Jewish wife to France and then to America, wrote a poem about Superman, inspired by his son Dmitri's reading habits. Imagining Clark Kent walking through a park with Lois Lane, Nabokov comically explained the superhero's fake glasses: "Otherwise / when I caress her with my super-eyes / her lungs and liver are too plainly seen / throbbing."

No one loved Superman more than the troops, though. The 33rd Bombardment Squadron adopted Superman as their insignia, and the navy included copies of *Superman* in its ration kits. At FDR's request, Harry made comics specifically for the army, handing out one hundred thousand copies of the Overseas Service Edition of *Superman* every month to keep morale high and to help the troops pass the time between battles. Boring troop training manuals were also made into comic books to keep the young soldiers' attention and to add some levity. Harry and Gussie would become friendly with both Franklin and Eleanor Roosevelt, a picture of Harry and Eleanor together hanging in their apartment.

Even the Mob got in on the war effort. Costello and his buddy Lucky Luciano, from prison, orchestrated numbers runners, bartenders, and hatcheck girls to eavesdrop in Jules's German Yorkville neighborhood and work as informers from their own clubs and restaurants throughout the city.

Once the United States was in the war, Yorkville—where Jules had felt so comfortable when he first arrived—drastically changed. Once-proud German-owned businesses removed their German-language signs. "Liberty cabbage" replaced sauerkraut on menus. And *Aufbau*, the newsletter published by the German-Jewish Club on Ninety-First Street near Jules's apartment, urged all Germans to stop speaking their mother tongue in public. Hannelore was sent to kindergarten at the 92nd Street Y, where she learned English and helped teach it to her very German parents.

In 1940, Edith gave birth to their second child, Evelyn—whom they called Evy—making their cramped quarters seem even smaller. They left Yorkville altogether in 1941 to a new apartment in a reddish brownstone on Lexington and Sixty-First Street, its three front windows looking out onto a bus stop and its back bedroom view a tar roof where pigeons cooed in the afternoon. They moved the fur shop to a much more accessible first-floor storefront across the street.

The rooms were small and the apartment was modestly decorated. But the shop—more extravagant to attract upscale customers—was tastefully done with modern leather and chrome furniture, tall plants, and long mirrors. Edith had impeccable taste and was an equal partner in the business, working both in the back room designing furs and up front helping customers. The couple worked all the time, usually until 2:00 a.m. Once they were old enough, even Jules's daughters would help in the shop, especially with repairs, tearing out old linings or separating the seams on the furs with their nimble fingers. Jules would deliver his creations to the luxurious apartments of his wealthy customers on the Upper East Side, who would sometimes make passes at the handsome young furrier.

Jules encouraged his customers to visit nearby Bloomingdale's, pick out the style of fur they liked, and he would make it at half the price. Sometimes he even went to the department store with them to browse for what they wanted. Business was booming and Jules was able to hire another German refugee, Alice Limmer, to come and work with them in the shop. Alice lived way uptown in

Washington Heights and had met Jules through the Jewish Friends Society. They not only worked together but became close friends. Alice would bring pumpernickel bread from a great Jewish bakery in Washington Heights. Edith would bring the cheese and salami. And they all—the girls included—would have picnics in the shop during their lunch break. Alice doted on Hannelore and Evy and they loved her back.

Though they were making money, Jules and Edith were frugal, never spending much on themselves or the girls. Still traumatized from their flight from Berlin and having to leave all their possessions behind, they saved their money in hopes of bringing their remaining relatives to America. The apartment was decorated in leftover fur scraps: mink pillows, a zebra skin rug, a fur-covered chair. The smallest bits were made into hand muffs and earmuffs for Jules's girls. There were fur baby blankets and tiny white lambswool coats for them. A framed, signed letter from Albert Einstein hung on a wall in the living room, a reminder of their days in Berlin.

One extravagance the couple allowed themselves was a small piano, upon which Hannelore was given lessons. They loved music, particularly Lena Horne, and often attended the Yiddish theater downtown. To appear more American, Hannelore's name was changed to Helen; and their last name changed from Schulzbach to Schulback. Even Jules officially changed his name from Julius. New identities, all in an effort to appear more American.

CHAPTER 18

BLEEDING LETTERS

NEW YORK—THE THIRD REICH, 1940–1943

EDITH, MARTHA, AND USHI

SEVERAL TIMES A DAY, EDITH FAITHFULLY VISITED THEIR apartment building vestibule. Climbing down the two flights of stairs, hand on the wooden banister, she would check the dented metal mailbox. If she was at work, she would quickly run over between customers to have a look. Carefully turning the tiny key, she would peek inside the bronze-colored mailbox, saying a small prayer under her breath, hoping to see a letter tucked in with the bills. An airmail letter with foreign postage was like a drop of water in a desert that stretched between the Schulbacks and their loved ones in Europe.

Paper, like food, was scarce. Once every few weeks, Edith's mother and sister would write to her on onionskin stationery so thin that the words would bleed through to the other side. Enough space had to be left between sentences on the front page so there was room to write on the reverse side. The letters, written in painstaking, cramped script, were censored by the German government. Though the Nazi Party swastika stamp on the front of the envelope would send a shock of terror at first, Edith's heart flipped slightly in her chest with happiness whenever she opened a letter from her family: their Krefelder Strasse return address written on the envelope's front in her sister's or mother's hand meant they were still alive.

But the words inside were crushing. The letters were difficult to read, not just because of the sentences bleeding through.

In 1940, Edith's sister, Ushi, sent a letter from Berlin saying she was writing to them by candlelight. "We have all become indifferent and tired," she wrote. "I haven't danced in a long time. No radio. No gramophone. Nothing. Nothing at all." Jews were not allowed to keep radios, and they had sold many of their possessions to simply feed themselves. "Sad Papa," she said, had lost his company. "You can't escape your fate and you have to put up with it." Ushi asked how the baby was and wished she could take her for a long walk, then signed off by saying she wasn't sure what else to write. "What I want to write is not allowed," she said. Edith had to read between the bleeding lines, filling in the spaces with what she read in the news and heard on the radio or from her German neighbors in New York.

By 1941, Jews were beaten regularly in Berlin's streets. Bicycles, cameras, and typewriters were forbidden. Curfew was 8:00 p.m. Restrictions on food purchases—the types of bread or vegetables, for instance, and times to buy them—were enforced. Eggs and milk were forbidden. Jewish-owned companies, like theirs, were taken over by Aryan Germans. But the worst part was that friends and neighbors started disappearing. Whole families. Suddenly gone. The Nazis said they were taken to work camps and retirement homes in the east. In a letter in 1941, Edith's mother wrote that she was despondent. Though she couldn't say so in her letters, she and Albert and Ushi and all Jews in Berlin were forced that September to wear a yellow star on their clothing to set them apart from the rest of the population. Friends and neighbors had already turned against them, but now strangers had their sign to call them dirty Jews. Though she had been forced to pay, like all Jews, for the yellow star for the front of her clothing, Ushi made snaps for it and, instead of sewing it on, could remove it and blend in with the Gentile population, with her red hair and freckles.

Her mother, Martha, had once been a vibrant woman who had loved to dance and travel. Now she was confined to her apartment, sick with worry and a bad gallbladder for which she desperately needed surgery, her skin turning nearly as yellow as the star on her chest, her will to live waning.

"I can't bear life anymore," she wrote at one point, hinting at suicide. Tentative plans had been made for Jules to pay for their escape. Fixers could be hired to help smooth the immigration process, and sometimes clerks at certain US embassies would take bribes to move people up on the waiting list. But the arrangements Jules paid for, and the man behind them in New York, turned out to be a scam, not an uncommon occurrence as desperation grew to escape Europe. "I'm doing everything imaginable to emigrate as soon as possible," Martha wrote to her family in New York. "All would be good if only I could get out—please help me, I beg you again."

Once the United States joined the war, naturally all German immigration was completely halted, including German Jews who were under siege. But with war looming, the State Department had stopped most immigration as early as June 1940. Officials were advised to "put every obstacle in the way" and to "postpone and postpone and postpone" the granting of any visas.

Historians have debated what President Roosevelt knew about the murder of the Jews in Europe and when he knew it. His trusted adviser, a Viennese Jew named Felix Frankfurter, had received an avalanche of letters beginning as early as 1933 from fellow European Jews begging for help in escaping. But Frankfurter did not bring them to the president's attention, not even letters from his own family members, for fear it would give the impression he was receiving special treatment. Maybe he hoped FDR would even forget he was Jewish. When presented with a firsthand account of the extermination of the Jews in Poland, Frankfurter refused to believe it. It had to be an exaggeration, he thought.

But in January of 1942, fifteen top Nazi leaders and bureaucrats gathered at that elegant villa in Wannsee—the lake where Edith and Jules and the characters in Billy Wilder's film went on Sundays to swim. The Nazis were not there for recreation. The lake was frozen, the spruce and bare plane trees covered in a thick layer of snow. The Nazis were in Wannsee to discuss the Final Solution to the Jewish Question—"the expulsion of the Jews from every sphere of life of the German people."

The villa had once belonged to a Jewish pharmaceutical manufacturer but had since been taken over by the SS as a guesthouse.

That January day, the Nazis gathered around its long dining room table for a top secret meeting to decide what to do about the Jews, not just in Germany but in all of Europe. Over drinks and a light lunch, they discussed their agenda: how to handle those of half-Jewish blood and whether to "evacuate" them or simply sterilize them. Over cigars, they debated whether the Jews should be used for much-needed labor and simply die of "natural causes" or instead be "evacuated" immediately.

Already, thousands of Jews had been shot to death by Nazi death squads and by their own anti-Semitic neighbors throughout Europe. But soldiers were complaining of the stress of having to shoot such large groups of people, and ammunition was running low. There had to be a better—and faster—way to kill so many. In the ninety-minute meeting, the Nazis in attendance finalized their plan to systematically transport and murder eleven million of their fellow human beings.

Though Jules—and the rest of the world—knew nothing of the Wannsee conference and the Nazis' plans, he wrote to Ushi telling her they would do everything possible to bring her to the United States. They were praying hard, he said, but had also enlisted a Palestinian activist to try to help them immigrate there. "Another wind is blowing. We will leave no stone unturned, you can be sure of that," Jules wrote in German. But the letters from Edith's parents, and from Ushi, Cilly, and Golda, would eventually stop coming. Slowly, the blanks would be filled in and the family story jigsawed together.

Golda's life was now confined to the Kraków ghetto, located near the left bank of the winding Vistula River, cordoned off by a wall made to look like a series of Jewish tombstones. Some parts of the wall were made from actual uprooted tombstones. Those who tried to escape the ghetto were murdered. Food was scarce and any valuables were confiscated. In January of 1942, all Jews in the ghetto were ordered to hand over their furs. Some burned them, rather than surrender them to the Nazis. Around eight thousand furs were collected. But Golda had no furs to surrender or burn.

Golda, Simon, and their son Paul lived for over two years in the ghetto, crowded in with fifteen thousand other Jews in the suburb of Podgórze, confined to fifteen streets and a mere 320 houses. The ghetto, one of 1,100 set up by the Nazis throughout Eastern Europe, was guarded by both Germans and Poles, but was policed internally by fellow Jews, who participated in beatings and round-ups. Because the family had worked in the men's clothing business, the head of the Kraków security police placed them on a list of essential cobblers and tailors. Golda, Simon, and Paul worked inside the ghetto's uniform factory and were able to remain longer than most Jews, saved from "evacuation" for a time. White-collar workers were sent nearly two hundred miles away to Belzec to a camp set up as a killing center for Polish Jews.

Forced to clean the ghetto streets and the snow in winter, Golda's legs ached and her hands went numb, day after day. Paul, now a teenager, was made to scrub Nazi uniforms. It never entered Golda's mind that one day soon she would miss the ghetto. They huddled together with three other families in their one-room apartment inside a small house with a sloped red roof on an alley named after Jan Długosz, Poland's first historian from the fifteenth century. Two of Golda's fellow ghetto prisoners were a young boy named Roman Polanski, and Eugenia, Billy Wilder's mother.

Before the 9:00 p.m. curfew, they would sometimes gather at the local pharmacy to read the newspaper and discuss the war, or visit a corner café, where live music could still occasionally be heard. Whenever they left the apartment, for limited rations or to work, they had to wear a four-inch-wide white armband with a blue Star of David on it, which they had had to pay for themselves. In March 1941, both Golda and Eugenia Wilder registered as Jews and paid $5—a large sum back then—for an ID, certificate, and armband.

But by 1943, they would no longer need their armbands. Golda and her family were sent to Montelupich Prison in Kraków to sew and repair Nazi uniforms. Eugenia Wilder was moved to a concentration camp. The reason for their imprisonment, listed on their paperwork: they were simply Jews.

BILLY WILDER AND ERICH von STROHEIM
ON THE SET OF *FIVE GRAVES TO CAIRO*

CHAPTER 19

FAKE NAZIS

HOLLYWOOD, 1942

THE BRITISH ARMY TANK ROLLED SLOWLY OVER THE SEEM-
ingly infinite sand dunes of Egypt, its driver lifelessly hanging out
of the top, having been killed by the Germans. Tobruk, the Libyan
city near the Egyptian border, had fallen and General Erwin Rommel and his troops were now beating the British back toward the
Suez Canal. And director Billy Wilder was smack in the middle of
the action.

Except this wasn't really North Africa, and the "dead" British
soldier atop the tank was just an extra.

In the summer of 1942, Wilder began work on an elaborate,
complicated script about the lone British survivor of a brutal battle in Egypt who goes undercover to foil Rommel's Afrika Korps
campaign. When we meet Bramble, the British soldier, he's barely
alive, nearly asphyxiated by the gas fumes backing up from the exhaust inside that rolling tank.

From America, Wilder had been desperately trying to reach
his actual family in Poland, but there was only a dreadful silence
on Eugenia's end. Since he had left his mother and grandmother
in Europe in 1935, he knew that Eugenia had remarried. But he
knew little else. At some point, the letters had stopped coming.
Throughout the war, he had anxiously worried about his family
and guiltily wished he'd been able to convince them to come with

him to America. Frustrated and helpless, Wilder was doing what he could in Hollywood to stoke America's hatred for the Nazis and keep up the Allied troops' morale. At thirty-six, he was a young, ambitious director. And the Nazis were his target.

Until America joined the war, most studio heads in Hollywood were reluctant to attack Hitler. Though most of the movie moguls were Jewish (except for Darryl F. Zanuck and Howard Hughes), Germany was a secondary market and a huge moneymaker for them throughout the 1920s and '30s, with German audiences flocking to the Hollywood films released there. Some moguls had even allowed the Nazi government to edit scripts and quash projects that were critical of the Führer. America's neutrality toward Germany early on and its own vast anti-Semitism didn't exactly encourage the moguls to take a stand. But now that our boys were fighting overseas, Hollywood—like Superman—was all in. And that included Wilder and his writing partner, Charles Brackett. With his own family possibly the victims of the Nazis, Wilder took his latest writing assignment very personally.

The film was Wilder's sophomore effort as a Hollywood director. His directorial debut in America, *The Major and the Minor* starring Ginger Rogers as a woman masquerading as a little girl, was a box office hit. Now Wilder had to prove to the moguls—and his audience—that his success hadn't been a fluke. He went enthusiastically, though anxiously, into his new project with both guns blazing—and all tanks rolling.

The scene that played out in Wilder and Brackett's office each day resembled Jerry Siegel and Joe Shuster's writing process. Like Jerry, Wilder paced frantically back and forth, shouting out ideas and directions—but in his Austrian accent. Brackett, like Joe Shuster, was bent over his pad, but instead of drawing he was writing furiously in longhand. To keep the juices flowing and his own hands busy, Wilder waved a riding crop, a cane, or a big stick. "A pencil wasn't long enough," he would say. He often goaded Brackett and the two would argue, the sparks flying and landing somehow on the page.

Wilder's mean streak hardly ever fazed Brackett, who was more than a match for him. When his partner went too far, Brackett would strike back, hurling a telephone book or an ashtray at him. Just as tall as Wilder and fourteen years older, Brackett was from a blue-blooded Saratoga Springs family. After graduating from Harvard Law School, he turned to writing because, like Wilder, he was really good at it. Brackett published three novels and worked as the drama critic for the *New Yorker* before heading to Hollywood in the 1930s, where his first assignment was a project about Jack Dempsey—Harry's old hotfoot buddy. The script never got off the ground, but Brackett would write seven more films before meeting Wilder.

When Paramount Pictures teamed them up to write *Bluebeard's Eighth Wife* in 1936, they seemed a good fit—Brackett the even-keeled literary gentleman to Wilder's brash comedian. But they fought constantly, breaking up and getting back together like some doomed married couple. Every day they would write, argue, break for lunch, write some more, take a nap, write, play cribbage, and then have late-afternoon cocktails. By 1942, they had written ten films together, including *Ninotchka* and *The Major and the Minor*.

Wilder and Brackett's latest plot was pulled from the newspaper headlines as General Rommel—known as the Desert Fox—fought his way across North Africa. But their script involved a slightly ridiculous fictional backstory: Rommel goes undercover before the war as an archaeologist, secretly planting underground stores of gasoline in the desert to fuel German Panzer tanks once the war in North Africa begins. The main character, our British hero Bramble, goes undercover as a waiter at an Egyptian hotel where Rommel is staying. The female lead, Mouche, sleeps with the enemy, trying desperately to get her brother out of a Nazi concentration camp. The layers of secret identities, with triple agents, masked Nazis, and compromised women, were no accident, inspired by the harrowing experiences of Wilder and his friends and family trying to escape Europe.

Paramount Studios wanted to call the film *Rommel's Last Stand*, but Wilder and Brackett insisted on *Five Graves to Cairo*. In the real world, by the time filming began, recently promoted Field Marshal Rommel had begun to retreat in the North African desert because of the Allies' air attacks. But Hitler insisted he push on. Rommel, disobeying his orders, pulled back his Afrika Korps soldiers, handing British general Bernard "Monty" Montgomery a major victory. But the fate of North Africa was still unknown, not only on-screen but in real life.

Unable to shoot in war-torn North Africa, Wilder had to stay close to home. In an effort to make the film look authentic, he shot in both the desert near Yuma, Arizona, and near the Salton Sea in California. With the help of the army ground forces at Camp Young, he staged a battle at their Desert Training Center in nearby Indio, using American M2 tanks as stand-ins for German Panzers. When he first arrived, the sand was covered in army jeep tire tracks. Wilder rounded up as many brooms as he could find and got busy with his crew smoothing out the desert. A stickler for detail, he used photographs of Rommel's siege to plan the film's battle scenes and located actual uniforms for Edith Head's costume team to painstakingly reproduce.

To make the film *sound* authentic, he hired German actors to play the Nazis. The standout in the cast was Erich von Stroheim, Wilder's fellow Austrian Jew, who played Rommel, complete with a white field marshal's dress uniform and a riding crop. Most famous for playing a German ace World War I pilot in the 1937 French film *The Grand Illusion*, von Stroheim was also known as one of the greatest—but most difficult—silent film directors of the 1920s. He was one of Wilder's idols because of the unflinching realism of his films. Wilder had once sent von Stroheim a fan letter asking for an autographed photo, which he had framed. As a young journalist in Berlin, Wilder had also written a piece about him in 1929 called "Stroheim, the Man We Love to Hate." In the story, he revealed that von Stroheim was not from noble lineage (as the added "von" would suggest), but got his start in America as a flypaper salesman in Newark, New Jersey. He hadn't been back to Austria or Germany in years and was considered a traitor because of his portrayal of cruel German officers.

While von Stroheim was trying on German uniforms for *Five Graves to Cairo*, Wilder nervously went over to introduce himself, practically bowing down and saying what an honor it was to work with him. "You were always ten years ahead of your time," Wilder told him.

"Twenty, Mr. Wilder, twenty," von Stroheim quipped.

To help Wilder achieve the World War II realism he was after, von Stroheim ordered German binoculars and cameras for his character to use in the movie and even insisted on placing film in those cameras. When Wilder asked who will know whether the cameras have film in them, von Stroheim barked, "I will know!" Von Stroheim also instructed the film's makeup chief, Wally Westmore, to apply a deep tan to his face, but stop short of his upper forehead, knowing that Rommel never removed his cap in the hot desert sun.

Von Stroheim had immigrated to the United States back in 1909 at age twenty-four, so his accent wasn't quite as authentic as the more recent émigrés in the cast, his Austrian pronunciations littered with American *r*'s. When the film was released in 1943, audiences in the United States couldn't tell the difference. But Billy Wilder could.

Five Graves to Cairo did well at the box office, but the greatest response came from the British military. Inspired by the multiple secret identities in the plotline, the Brits got the idea to use an actor to double as General Montgomery, their top military leader. The actor, M. E. Clifton James, deceived the Germans in the weeks leading up to D-Day as part of Operation Copperhead. After being trained to mimic Monty's mannerisms and speech, James was planted on Winston Churchill's private plane and then sent on to public appearances in Algiers. British intelligence hoped James would confuse German intelligence and throw them off about the planned attack in Normandy. The thinking was that if General Montgomery was in Algiers, the invasion of Normandy wouldn't be happening anytime soon. In another nod to Wilder's film, James was secretly sent to Cairo to hide out until the invasion was successfully completed. The real Montgomery, of course, was leading the British ground forces on the beaches at Normandy, going head-to-head with Rommel. Truth, as always, was stranger than fiction.

At the end of *Five Graves to Cairo*, after exposing the underground gas dumps and abandoning the hotel, Bramble, our British hero, discovers that his leading lady has been killed by the Nazis, no doubt echoing the worries in Wilder's head about his mother. At her grave in the final scene, Bramble kneels and tells Mouche, "When you feel the earth shake, it'll be our tanks. . . . We're after them now, coming from all sides."

ALBERT, MARTHA, AND EDITH

CHAPTER 20

STOLEN BREAD

BERLIN, 1942

EDITH'S SISTER, USHI, ALWAYS HAD SMALL HANDS, FINE AND delicate. Just perfect for assembling radio parts. Under the Nazi regime, she was forced to work at Siemens electronics out near the Spandau neighborhood in Berlin. It took her an hour to get to her Wernerwerk F factory, where she stood at a lathe for ten hours a day dressed in coveralls. Around her, more than eight hundred other Jewish workers toiled here at the company's main location in Berlin, a five-hundred-acre industrial city called Siemensstadt. It resembled the city out of the film *Metropolis* and in its heyday was often referred to as the Electropolis by its fifty-five thousand workers. Siemensstadt had been built around the turn of the century in the swampy wilderness on the River Spree as a futuristic, forward-thinking development. But now its vast network of concrete high-rises and sprawling factories used forced laborers to crank out parts for Nazi radios, telephones, and armaments. Ushi's small "salary" was around $2 a day, which was heavily taxed by the Nazis and not nearly enough to feed her and her parents.

One Monday morning in June 1942, her father, Albert, went to a bakery in their Moabit neighborhood. Any excursion into the outside world was an invitation to disaster, the Nazis looking for any excuse to arrest and deport you "to the east," but there was nothing left in the house to eat. The Friedmanns had begun to hear terrible rumors and stories of how the Jews "evacuated east" were simply murdered. But how could that be? How could the Nazis kill so many? "It's impossible," Albert said, shaking his head.

Albert told his wife he would just buy some bread and hurry back. When he failed to return, Ushi went to the bakery and discovered that her father had been falsely arrested for stealing a loaf of bread. She hurried home to tell her mother the terrible news and the two argued over who should go to the police precinct to help him. Martha won the fight and went to plead Albert's case. But Martha never returned.

Ushi, sick with worry and guilt over letting her mother go alone, waited and waited, growing more and more panicked as the sun set. She wanted desperately to go and search for her parents, but was afraid to leave the Krefelder Strasse apartment building, which was now pitch-black, like the rest of the city, because of the Allied air raids. Unsure of what to do, Ushi packed a small bag and traveled crosstown to Charlottenburg to visit her friend Leja, who worked with her at the Siemensstadt factory. Ushi told Leja she wanted to go search for her parents, but Leja said it was too dangerous, that there was nothing she could do to help them now.

"You can't go back there," Leja told Ushi, shaking her head.

"But everything we own is in that apartment," Ushi said, wringing her small hands. She thought of the family heirlooms they hadn't sold yet and the furs Jules had given her parents, a $1,500 Persian wool men's coat for Albert and the $1,000 long mink marble coat for Martha. Ushi also longed for her comfortable bed and her books and her trousseau, filled with the embroidered tablecloths and napkins that had been made in Albert's textile company and set aside for her own home someday after she was married.

But Ushi didn't say any of this out loud. It seemed preposterous to worry about furs and embroidered linens when the world was ending around you and your parents were missing.

Leja hugged her friend tight. "When life returns to normal, you can go back and get your things," she said. But they both knew normal might never return to Berlin. That night, over a simple dinner, Leja and her mother convinced Ushi to move in with them in their apartment in a building filled with fellow Jews. The next night, against Leja's warnings, Ushi returned to her family apartment and hurriedly gathered a few personal belongings, some photographs, some more clothing, and her typewriter, whose vowel keys had umlauts on them. Typewriters had been outlawed for Jews for many months now and so openly owning one was a sign to the outside world that you were an Aryan.

A few weeks later, the Gestapo confiscated everything else in the Krefelder Strasse apartment: the beds, the dressers, the clothing, the sheets, the linens (including Ushi's trousseau), blankets, the dining room table and chairs, a sofa, armchairs, Albert's desk, bookcases and the books inside them, a mahogany and oak buffet with glass doors, the kitchenware, two grandfather clocks, the carpets, the furs (including the Persian wool and the long marble mink from Jules, as well as another coat with an otter collar, a silver fox cape, and a marten cape), paintings, lamps and light fixtures, towels, and even the curtains on the windows. Jewelry, including a pearl necklace, an aquamarine pin and pendant, several gold chains, two gold watches, diamond earrings and necklaces, a brooch, and Albert's gold pocket watch and chain were all taken, as well as Martha's diamond engagement ring and the couple's gold wedding bands. The Nazis took a silver setting for twelve, two silver candlesticks, and crystal glasses, bowls, and vases, including the one Edith had placed the flowers in the day that Jules had proposed to her.

Of course, Ushi would have traded it all for just a chance to say goodbye to her parents. Not that it was hers to trade anymore.

From Ushi's new Wielandstrasse apartment, the looming spire of the Kaiser Wilhelm Church could be seen nearby. They lived just steps from the Kurfürstendamm, still relatively lively despite the war. Ushi moved in with Leja and her mother that summer, waiting in vain for news of her parents, week after week after week. She and Leja slept in a twin bed together, running to the building's basement whenever the air-raid sirens rang out and the American and British bombers appeared.

One day that following February, on a short break at the Siemensstadt factory, one of Ushi and Leja's coworkers pulled them aside in the ladies' bathroom. It was here that the Jewish female laborers had all their meetings, discussions, and even celebrations—the only place away from the prying eyes of the Aryan foremen. One of those foremen—a secret Communist—had been drinking in a bar the night before and had overheard some SS officers talking about how all the remaining Jewish workers at Siemensstadt would be replaced with Christian refugees. To keep the SS talking, the Communist sent over some more drinks. The drunker the SS got, the more they talked.

"They say they will be transferring all the Jews from here to work camps outside Berlin in two days," their friend told them in hushed whispers in the Siemens ladies' room. Because of the Allied bombings, the company was in the process of moving their factories to hidden locations outside the city. Over the past several years, trucks had been pulling up to Berlin's factories, workers taken away and "sent east" to a vast network of forty-four thousand concentration camps, ghettos, and prisons throughout Europe. Forty-four thousand. Now the last of the Jewish workers would be deported. Forced labor would become slave labor, thousands of Jews transferred and worked literally to death at Ravensbrück and other concentration camps.

The rumors of the deportation drifted through the bathroom and then through the brick courtyard at the Wernerwerk factory. The next day, half the Jewish workforce failed to show up. Ushi walked away from Siemensstadt that afternoon and never returned.

Leja and her mother abandoned their apartment for fear the Nazis would come looking for the girls now that they hadn't shown up at Siemensstadt. But Ushi decided to stay awhile and take her chances on Wielandstrasse. A few nights later, the Gestapo came and banged at the door. In their deep, gruff voices, they demanded that Ushi open up. But she sat frozen in bed in the darkness. The banging wouldn't stop, and Ushi, so frightened, stayed perfectly silent and still, like a rabbit at the side of a country road that knows it has been spotted.

In her head, she sang songs from the musicals and operas she had loved, to try and stay calm. Closing her eyes, she silently prayed the Gestapo—still banging—wouldn't break the door down. She wondered where she could hide in the apartment if they did. Opening her eyes, she strained in the dark to survey the room. Under the bed? The wardrobe? Out a back window?

The banging finally subsided, but Ushi wasn't sure if the officers were just waiting for her to emerge in the hallway, only to reach out and grab her. So she stayed still for another hour.

Two hours.

Three, her limbs falling asleep, the pins and needles daring her to stomp her feet.

Eventually, Ushi had to pee. After gently tiptoeing to the bathroom, she went as quietly as she could, whispering a stream of pee into the toilet. As her bladder emptied, she kept repeating in her head over and over, *Don't flush, don't flush. Whatever you do, don't flush.*

The next morning, weary from not sleeping, she tried to crack the door open to see if the hallway was empty. But the door was stuck. Grabbing the doorknob with both hands, she pulled hard. The door gave way, but Ushi saw that yellow tape had been used to seal it shut.

The Gestapo had not broken the door down because the building's janitor had told them Ushi was still working nights at Siemensstadt.

She packed some clothes and her typewriter and moved in with a friend and fellow Siemens worker named Hildegard, an Aryan who took pity on Ushi. Not everyone in Berlin hated the Jews and some would show kindness, especially to those who didn't fit their stereotypical picture of what a Jew looked like. Dark, curly hair and a large nose were usually only a problem if you were already targeted as a Jew or were gathering with a large group of people who looked like you did. But Ushi looked Irish.

For two years she and Hildegard lived together in the tiny apartment near the Tempelhof airfield, fearful all the while that the Gestapo would knock at the door and take them both away. They slept head to foot in Hildegard's bed and shared her meager rations. All of Berlin was starving, some even resorting to eating the zoo animals that were killed during the air raids. The bombing over in Charlottenburg was now relentless because of the German anti-aircraft gun tower placed near the zoo. The November after Ushi moved out of Leja's apartment, an Allied attack destroyed much of the area, the spire of the Kaiser Wilhelm Church cracking wide open, its jagged edges giving it the nickname "the hollow tooth." The train station where Jules and Edith and Wilder's characters had once met on Sundays was badly damaged. But its golden clock under which they had once met miraculously survived.

Ushi returned only once to Leja's abandoned Wielandstrasse apartment, boldly breaking the new seal on the door to collect a few more possessions. But she otherwise avoided the ravaged neighborhood and stayed under cover.

Hiding just below the surface, Ushi was just one of seven thousand Jews secretly living in Berlin during the war, known as "U-boats," or "submarines." A half dozen other Jewish girlfriends, including Leja, were part of Ushi's network. Hildegard's brother,

Helmut, a German field officer, rented an illegal apartment for Leja and her mother, helping them to survive.

In small towns, it was nearly impossible to hide out as a Jew, since everyone knew your background. But Berlin was a big city. It was easier to move from place to place anonymously, especially if you had support. Some of Ushi's friends got jobs working for rich families whose Aryan maids had been forced to work in munitions factories, replacing the drafted soldiers and the many Jews who were murdered. For a while, Ushi got a job working as a milliner making ladies' hats.

Jewish spies called "catchers" were employed by the Nazis to identify fellow Jews, who would be captured and sent to concentration camps. Ushi worried about seeing someone she knew, someone who was aware of her Jewish background and might turn her in. Though she defiantly refused to look nervous around them, she avoided police and Gestapo officers, children in Hitler Youth uniforms, and Nazi Party members with their red circle swastika pins proudly displayed. While traveling illegally on buses and trains, her eyes were sharp and her body primed to get off at the next stop as soon as an obvious enemy climbed aboard.

Every day she lived, Ushi thought, was a day closer to the end of the war. When she went out during the day, she had to pretend she was confident, not scared for her life. Walking, never running. Smiling, never crying in public.

To pass the hours in hiding, she would crochet or knit, if she could find some yarn, or read, if she could get her hands on a book. Because the noise attracted too much attention, she stopped writing letters on her verboten typewriter. Fearing she would be found out, she stopped writing any letters at all to Edith, who assumed she was dead.

MARTHA AND ALBERT

CHAPTER 21

GROSSE HAMBURGER STRASSE

BERLIN TO MINSK, JUNE 1942

NEITHER JULES NOR USHI NOR EDITH EVER LEARNED THE fate of Albert and Martha Friedmann, who had disappeared after Albert's arrest for the "stolen" loaf of bread. Albert and Martha had treated Jules like their son when he married their daughter, and he mourned them in their absence, as he had his own parents. But it would be nearly eighty years before Jules's grandchildren would discover what had happened to them. The truth was as horrible as anyone could have ever imagined, a slow step-by-step journey into darkness, with each day worse than the one before.

Because of Albert's military service in World War I and his high standing in the Berlin community as the owner of a respected textile business, it seemed inconceivable to him and Martha that they could be mistreated.

The night that Martha went to the police station to help Albert, she was placed under arrest as well. They were both taken to Grosse Hamburger Strasse, where a Jewish home for the aged and a boys' school—the very same school Jules had attended when he was young—had been forcibly seized by the Gestapo. The buildings were converted into *Judenlager*, internment centers for Jews being deported.

The boys carved in stone over the school's arched doorway silently stared down as Albert and Martha were pushed inside with dozens of others who were scheduled for transport. Jews were tortured in the basements of the school and the old-age home, sometimes to death, their bodies buried on-site, their bones, including those of children, found decades later. Next door was the oldest Jewish cemetery in Berlin. Philosophers and physicians, silver traders and musicians had once been buried there. But the cemetery would be desecrated by the Nazis and turned into an air-raid shelter whose walls were fortified with Hebrew-etched gravestones.

In late June 1942, both Albert and Martha were taken from the internment center to a synagogue in the Tiergarten neighborhood, where scores of other Berliners were forced to register and hand over any jewelry and cash they had. But the Friedmanns had left the apartment with nothing but the clothes they were wearing. They were forced to sign documents transferring their real estate and all their belongings to the Nazis in exchange for an apartment outside Germany. To protect Ushi, Albert listed his address as the cemetery on Grosse Hamburger Strasse.

Albert and Martha slept on the floor on bags of straw overnight, or tried to sleep, anyway, and the next morning were forced onto a passenger train at Berlin's Grunewald station, just a ten-minute drive from where Ushi and Leja were staying. Their train headed for Königsberg, Germany's easternmost big city, known for its medieval Prussian castle. The deportation was called *Straftransport* (punishment transport), for those associated with the *Reichsvereinigung*, the group of Jewish leaders who were forced to work with the Nazis and had helped with emigration and running segregated Jewish schools. That same month, all Jewish schools were closed in Berlin. Those on the deportation list were being punished for simply being Jews.

Martha had loved to travel and even the sound of a train had once made her heart beat faster with anticipation. Boarding this train was much different, their impending journey filled with anxiety and dread.

Their only consolation was that the train was not a cattle car. The Friedmanns had heard about cattle cars being filled with Jewish prisoners and sent to work camps across Eastern Europe. Some of the rumors were far worse, that the Jews not young enough or physically fit enough to work were murdered. But no one wanted to believe that; Albert was fifty-seven and Martha, fifty-four. This was a passenger train, with seats. Third class. There were young, healthy people among them. They were simply being taken to a new apartment, or at worst to a Jewish ghetto. If the Nazis wanted them dead, why bother putting them on a passenger train? It didn't make sense.

The ride to Königsberg was 327 miles and would take around eight hours. The Friedmanns sat together on the train with the other 199 passengers, senior citizens, teenagers, and children, but mostly middle-aged intellectuals like themselves, lawyers and leaders of the *Reichsvereinigung*. But there were also clerks, truck drivers, and simple businessmen: the Cohns, the Rosenthals, the Waldenbergs, the Galinskis, the Strausses and Wolfs, the Simons and their six-year-old son, Marlitt, the Spiegels and their five-year-old daughter, Marianne. Paula Fürst, the head of all Jewish schools in Germany, was on board, as well as Dr. Cora Berliner, a social work pioneer and economics professor. All traveling together to an unknown destiny. They were provided water and food for the journey by the Jewish community and guarded by eighteen members of the *Schupo* (state security police) armed with rifles.

In Königsberg, other Jews who had arrived from other destinations were placed on the train as well. From there, it wound its way over a full day through Korschen and then Prostken in Poland, where more passengers were picked up, then on to Białystok and Wołkowysk.

Here the group, now numbering 770, was transferred onto twenty-six cattle cars by the armed guards. This is when Martha likely began to panic. Albert probably assured her that, at worst, they would be taken to a work camp. It made no sense. Why the long train ride otherwise?

They tried to sleep, but couldn't, with barely room to stand, never mind lie down or even sit. After traveling the whole night, they arrived the next day in Minsk, exhausted but in a state of utter terror. They were ordered off the train car by guards, who pointed MP40 submachine guns at them, while other guards shoved truncheons into their ribs, loading them into waiting vans with about fifty others. The helmeted guards barked that they were being transferred to the camp at Maly Trostenets, a village eight miles outside Minsk. The Nazis had built a concentration camp there on the site of a Soviet kolkhoz, or collective farm, using it mostly as a place to execute Jews from the Minsk ghetto. The sign outside Maly Trostenets announced that all trespassers would be shot without warning.

But as the vans rumbled across the blooming countryside, the Waffen-SS driver sitting up front gripped and then adjusted small levers before pressing the gas pedal down all the way. The sealed passenger compartment of the van filled imperceptibly with carbon monoxide redirected from the exhaust pipe.

While they rode in the windowless vans on the Minsk-Mogilev highway, the birdsong growing louder as they doubled back to the forest, Albert and Martha and their fellow travelers were slowly poisoned to death. They fell asleep and never woke up, their cheeks flushed pink from the poison gas.

Martha's and Albert's bodies were rolled into newly dug pits in the forest, prepared in advance for them and the others who had been on their passenger train from Berlin. When the Red Army invaded at the end of the war, they discovered inside the forest, just a short walk from the highway, thirty-four pits, each fifty-five yards long and thirteen feet deep.

There, with the remains of thousands of others, rested the bones of Jules's beloved in-laws, Albert and Martha Friedmann.

JERRY SIEGEL (STANDING) AND JOE SHUSTER

CHAPTER 22

STARS AND STRIPES

NEW YORK, 1942

JACK DEMPSEY'S BAR IN MANHATTAN'S BRILL BUILDING WAS packed and thick with cigar and cigarette smoke, the floor sticky with spilled drinks. You might not have even known there was a war on except for the darkened marquees and office buildings in the Midtown neighborhood. Dempsey's signature orange neon sign was turned off, but the loud partying continued behind tall curtains pulled shut to hide the lights inside. Harry Donenfeld spent plenty of free time here—and his work time, too—laughing and joking with his hotfoot buddy. Dempsey was often at the Times Square institution, seated at a corner booth smoking a cigar, signing autographs, and posing for photos with fans. Harry also liked to hit nearby Toots Shor's on West Fifty-First Street, with its circular bar and checked tablecloths, where Superman's number one fan, Joe DiMaggio, hung out with his Yankee teammates until he enlisted in 1943. Toots Shor's was once described as a locker room with table service. Wives were not welcome, but other women were.

Sometimes Harry's wartime partying got out of hand, like the night he was arrested by the Miami police for driving the wrong way down a one-way street and not having his identification with him. When he told the cops who he was, the publisher of Superman, they didn't believe him—until a reporter recognized him. An officer called the Versailles hotel, where Harry had been staying, and a friend ran his wallet over to police headquarters. The cops apologized and Harry took down a long list of their kids' names with a promise to send them free copies of the comic book. "If I ever get in jail, I hope it is in Miami," Harry said with a slur. "I've never been shown such hospitality." Hiccup.

There was the time he disappeared for an entire workweek. Lost weekends were for amateurs. Harry was gone for five whole days. No one knew where he was. Not Jack. Not Gussie. Not even Sunny. When Harry finally turned up, he told everyone he had been in Los Angeles, partying with Chef Boyardee. He had, in fact, been on a drinking binge, poolside at the Beverly Hilton hotel with French matinee idol Charles Boyer, shagging everything in sight.

Harry's hundreds of employees were fully aware of his reputation, but they loved him for it. For his fiftieth birthday, the company published a mock newspaper called *The Daily Snooze*, joking about his love of drinking and featuring a comic strip of Harry spanking Superman. Every month, Independent News, Harry and Jack's parent company that published and distributed all their magazines and comics, ran a nationwide newsletter announcing not just sales numbers, but births, marriages, and deaths within the publishing "family." Harry was always a featured character. But top-earning distributors, dealers, and wholesalers were profiled as

well—not just from DC Comics in New York, but from the vast network across America. A Winchell-like column dished the company dirt. There were comics written by Jerry and Joe just about the business—Superman rescuing snowbound copies or fixing the broken presses—and even poems about traveling salesmen and the troops in Europe. At the bottom of the page was the Superman Service Flag, with stars that showed how many sons of the distributors and wholesalers were serving in the war and how many had died.

In February 1942, Clark Kent tried to enlist in the military, but because of his X-ray vision, accidentally reads the eye chart in the next room and fails his exam. The following autumn, the words "Truth, justice, and the American way" were added to Superman's job title as part of the radio show. Superman was no longer an intergalactic citizen but a representative of the good old US of A. And the Nazis were on his hit list.

In syndication, Jerry and Joe gave the troops—and their kid brothers and sisters at home—a Christmas surprise. In a series that ran late November through December 1942, Mussolini, Tojo, and Hitler kidnap Santa Claus from his North Pole workshop to try to convince him to join the Axis powers. "Herr Claus," says Hitler, "I'm told that you are of Teutonic descent—in fact were once known as Kris Kringle. As a true German, preach the doctrine of

HARRY SHOWS
SUPERMAN
WHO'S BOSS

the new order and you can become an important cog in our set-up."
Santa, tied in chains, rebuffs the dastardly trio. "I am not a German,
nor am I French, or American or any other nationality. . . . I live in
the hearts of all good men," says a defiant Santa, who is then sent
off to a concentration camp. Before Christmas can be canceled, and
Santa murdered, Superman flies to Berlin and saves him, then helps
to deliver his gifts.

For Harry's growing staff of comic artists, Hitler became a
staple, gracing more than one hundred covers. There was one featuring Goebbels, and another, much later, with war victims being
led to the ovens. In one strange coincidence, George Reeves—who
would play Superman on television nine years later—starred in the
1943 war film *So Proudly We Hail!* At one point in the movie, a
group of kids is discussing a Superman comic with one of the army
nurses.

Thanks to young GIs' reading habits, and Harry's ability to
export magazines overseas, the sales of comic books doubled from
1941 to 1944. Superman was cheering the troops on, but also reminded them of home and simpler times. By the spring of 1944,
comics made up a third of all magazine sales, surpassing news
magazines, women's magazines, and even movie magazines. Despite wartime paper and gasoline shortages, Harry and Jack put
out twenty-four different publications—everything from *Ha Ha* to
Mutt and Jeff to *Picture Stories from the Bible*. Harry's newest title,
All-Funnies, sold out its first issue nationwide.

Harry and Jack were throwing all sorts of comic book characters
out into the world to see who would fly: Starman, Hourman, Boy
Commandos, and others forgotten by history. But now and then,
one would soar, like Batman and the patriotic Wonder Woman.
Some were created in-house and so belonged outright to Harry and
Jack. Bob Kane, the freelancer who invented Batman, would hold on
to his rights after seeing what had happened to Jerry and Joe. Their

contractual misstep—often called the original sin of comic books—was a lesson for every comic book creator that ever followed.

Though Jerry was making a great living, it still irked him that Superman no longer belonged to him and Joe. One afternoon, while Jerry was in the Grand Central Palace offices, one of the staff members took him into a stairwell and quietly told him that Harry and Jack were making millions through the radio show and merchandising. (Though the comic book cost ten cents, the Daisy Superman Krypto-Ray Gun Projector Pistol cost ten times as much. And Jerry and Joe weren't seeing any of that profit.)

Jerry had a sizable $20,000 nut stashed away in the bank, but he began asking—rightfully so—for more money. In response, DC's editors told him and Joe their work was subpar. In one letter to Jerry, editor Whitney Ellsworth accused him of being "very complacent about the guy you invented." Superman looked like a different character in nearly every picture and became increasingly cruder and cruder, said Ellsworth. Though he complained about Superman's hands and actions, Ellsworth was most upset about the superhero's tight red shorts. "I have written you repeatedly about how the manner in which his jock strap is drawn, and absolutely nothing is ever done about it." Ellsworth also complained to Jerry that he needed to explain to Joe and the other artists how to draw a pretty girl. (Though Jerry was married, Joe would be single for thirty-five years.) Jack complained that Lois Lane was starting to look like a witch, her hair a veritable rat's nest and her clothes dowdy and un-fashionable. Jack "suggests *Vogue*, *Vanity Fair* and *Harper's Bazaar* as likelier spots for dress research," wrote Ellsworth. "The gal ain't being done right." Unless something changed, other arrangements would need to be made. "Altogether," one letter read, "the situation is serious enough to warrant your doing some real worrying."

Though Jerry constantly came up with new characters, Harry and Jack told him to just concentrate on Superman. As early as

1938, Jerry had started pitching Superboy, the adolescent version of Superman, tracing his life growing up in Smallville. But his bosses rejected it. Jerry resubmitted it. But they rejected it again.

Jerry pestered and pestered Jack for more money. And, of course, he and Joe were owed much more than they were receiving, not just for Superman but for all the superheroes they inspired, superheroes that continued to rake in the cash for DC Comics for decades to come: not just Wonder Woman and Batman but the Flash and all the spin-off villains from Superman. In 1942, Superman hit the big screen, starring in ten-minute animated shorts created by Fleischer Studios that would play before the feature film. Harry assured Jerry and Joe that the shorts cost more than they made; they didn't.

Jerry went about asking for money in such an irritating way that Jack and Harry couldn't stop bullying him. For instance, he wrote to Jack and asked him for $500. Jack replied that he had just sent him a check. But Jerry told him he had $19,500 in his account and wanted to make it an even $20,000. Jack reluctantly gave it to him. Jerry's superpower, it seemed, was being super annoying.

Fearing Jack and Harry would give them the complete shaft, Jerry took his frustration out in subtle ways. A Superman story from the winter of 1942, which featured a cover of the superhero holding an American eagle on his forearm, was a master class in passive-aggressive behavior. Jerry's plot involves a young inventor whose rights to his fire-extinguishing powder are stolen by a slick promoter. When the promoter's house catches fire, Superman forces him to give up the rights before agreeing to put out the flames.

A few months later, an unmasked villain in *Superman* exclaims, "Nobody knows me! I wanted to be a celebrity—the creator of a famous comic strip: but no one would buy my strips."

There were rumors that DC Comics had pulled strings to help keep twenty-eight-year-old Jerry out of the army, but after Jerry's barely disguised attacks and constant complaining, some say Harry put in a call and had him drafted. Joe's deteriorating vision kept him out of the military, but Jerry started serving in 1943. On leave two years later for the birth of his son, whom he named after his father who had died of a heart attack in that Cleveland robbery so long ago, Jerry again submitted Superboy for publication. But DC ignored him.

With Jerry stationed in Hawaii writing comedy columns for *Stars and Stripes*, his Superman duties were handed over to DC writers Don Cameron and Bill Finger, Batman's co-creator. Jerry would submit the occasional Superman script to the New York office. But while he was away, Harry and Jack took his old script for Superboy and made Joe illustrate it, without ever telling Jerry or paying him for the rights. Not knowing what to do, a panicked Joe sent a copy of *Superboy* to Jerry in Hawaii. Jerry was understandably furious.

Like Jerry, Harry's son, Irwin, was drafted as well. But with Harry's pull he was sent only as far as Biloxi, Mississippi, to serve as a mechanic in the Army Air Corps. He boxed while in the army because he knew that boxers got weekends off. Irwin, who would go on to work for his father as editorial director, told people years later that he fought a lot of guys in World War II, but they were all Americans. And he was good, too. Maybe not as good as Jack Dempsey, but a good bet to win.

Harry visited him in Biloxi and was treated like royalty, the entire base marching out in formation to greet him. When the commander asked Harry what he wanted for lunch, Harry asked for a pastrami sandwich, much to Irwin's dismay.

"Pop," he whispered, nudging him. "They don't have pastrami in Mississippi."

But somehow, somewhere, the commander found Harry a pastrami sandwich.

DON AND HIS MOTHER, GOLDA

CHAPTER 23

GOLDA'S JOURNEY

POLAND, 1943

JULES AND HIS FAMILY HADN'T HEARD FROM HIS OLDEST SISTER, Golda, since getting a swastika-stamped, Nazi-sanctioned postcard in 1943 mailed from the Kraków ghetto. He had no idea that she and her husband and son had already been sent to Montelupich, one of the worst jails in Poland, where prisoners were severely beaten and starved. Nazis resorted to medieval torture to interrogate and punish inmates, many of whom were professors and other intellectuals from Kraków and members of the underground. Thumb screws and shin screws were used. Nazis killed prisoners by forcing them into freezing-cold baths for hours. Some were simply shot.

Eventually Golda was transferred to Auschwitz with her eighteen-year-old son, Paul. Her husband, Simon, had been taken away on a separate transport to who knows where. It seemed impossible that anything could be worse than Montelupich.

But here it was.

Nazi guards, some with German shepherds, forced Golda and Paul off their truck, pushing them with the butts of their rifles. They were separated into groups of healthy and sick, and then into groups of men and women. In the chaos, Golda did not say good-bye to Paul.

Golda and the rest of the prisoners were forced into large shower rooms and made to wash in cold water. Their heads were shaved to eliminate any lice, but also to make them look inhuman and easier to kill. Then they were tattooed, a line of black numbers inked onto the soft insides of their forearms, to help identify them if they somehow managed to escape. Auschwitz was the only camp that tattooed its prisoners, due to the vast numbers of people coming through its gates. Tattooing began only in 1942 after four prisoners broke into a Nazi storeroom, donned Nazi uniforms, and drove out of the camp to freedom.

For weeks, Golda was jailed in the barracks with the other women, until they were randomly chosen during roll call for death in the gas chambers or sent to another camp, where they would be systematically worked to death. Inside their barracks, the women talked to one another and cried together, remembering home and worrying about their husbands and sons and daughters and parents, but trying to keep up hope that the next stop would be better. Anything would be better than Auschwitz, even death. Some in the camp ran at the fence and committed suicide, either electrocuted by their own hands or shot by the guards.

In the summer of 1944, Golda was sent to the remote Flossenbürg concentration camp in the mountains of Bavaria near the Czechoslovakian border. Though the area surrounding it was beautiful, filled with steep slopes and dense forests, Flossenbürg was a living hell. The back of the village looked down onto the horseshoe-shaped concentration camp, so there was no doubt the German people knew what was going on there: the beatings, the shootings and hangings. The main camp consisted of sixteen large wooden barracks, several guard towers, a kitchen building, a laundry, an infirmary, a brothel, and a building for disinfecting new arrivals, among them Golda.

Around eight thousand prisoners were kept at the main camp to work in the quarry and at nearby factories. To prevent them from escaping, a giant brightly colored X was placed on the back of each striped uniform—clothes that were recycled from the recently murdered. Workers were fed hard pieces of bread and a putrid soup made with sandy carrots and potatoes—not enough to live on, but enough to keep them from dying right away.

But the hell of Flossenbürg would not last. You either died or moved on.

In January of 1945, as a typhus epidemic tore through Flossenbürg, Golda was sent to Gross-Rosen concentration camp near the Polish border because seamstresses were needed there to repair and clean German uniforms. As at Auschwitz and Flossenbürg (and Dachau and Theresienstadt and Sachsenhausen), the camp's yellow arched entryway declared WORK MAKES YOU FREE. But Golda knew now that the real motto of the Nazi overseers—and their industrial companies—was "Extermination through work." Corporations like BMW, Krupp, Volkswagen, Telefunken radio, Hugo Boss, Daimler-Benz, and Siemens all used slave labor, knowingly working and starving their prisoners to death.

The one bright spot in Golda's world was hearing a rumor that Simon had also been sent to Gross-Rosen. He was here. Her husband was here. He was alive.

But there was no sign of Paul.

Upon their arrival at Langenbielau, one of one hundred subcamps at Gross-Rosen, Golda and Simon had gold fillings and gold teeth yanked from their mouths in the infirmary. They were given uniforms with their prison numbers written on them and placed in separate barracks not far from each other—the men located in eight buildings and the women in six.

Though life was still a horror, the twelve-hour work shifts were slightly better here than at Flossenbürg. There was a toilet in the heated clothing factory, and soap, which the women would steal to bring back to the barracks. Once a week, Golda was able to wash out her uniform in cold water, sitting naked and shivering on the straw-filled bunk in her unheated barracks until the dress dried, wondering what she had done in her life—what any of them had done—to deserve such a fate. Was God so cruel? Or maybe—God forbid—God did not exist at all.

On sleepless nights, the women would talk about the past, since their future was so uncertain. Mostly they would discuss what they or their mothers had cooked for the holidays or for Sabbath dinner, the soft golden challah, the baseball-size matzoh balls floating in rich chicken broth, the tender beef brisket braised for hours for Rosh Hashanah, the stuffed cabbage lovingly rolled and tucked side by side, the beet-red borscht made pink with a dollop of sour cream, the light-as-air blintzes folded with sweet cheese, the tzimmes made with fresh carrots and potatoes and apples, gefilte fish made with the carp that their mothers kept live in the bathtub until it was time to cook, the pillowy jelly-filled sufganiyot dusted with sugar, and the perfect triangles of buttery poppy seed hamantaschen. Food was all they could think about, as they slowly starved to death.

Each morning Simon would be woken at three o'clock and forced to walk to an underground factory five miles away. The munitions plants had been placed underground to avoid air raids. In the years before Golda and Simon arrived, prisoners from Gross-Rosen had built tunnels deep into the Owl Mountains, drilling and scraping past dark pine and fir trees, whose scents weren't strong enough to mask the smell of death inside the dank caverns now. Dead bodies were piled up both inside and out.

Like the men who had built the tunnels, Simon worked as a slave laborer, assembling radios, bombs, and weapons to help destroy those he hoped would soon save him. Back at the camp, which they would have to march to at the end of each day, they were housed in wooden barracks, which had originally been constructed as part of a summer sports camp years before for Hitler Youth. They had no heat, running water, or bathrooms, and were now overrun with rats, lice, and fleas. More than forty thousand people had been murdered at Gross-Rosen. Half the camp had died of typhus, spread by lice, but doctors refused to enter the premises because of the rats and growing piles of corpses.

In the winter of 1945, just before the war ended, Golda and the other women were forced to watch from a distance as a large group of men from camp were marched into the nearby woods. Because they were running out of ammunition, the Nazis set the woods ablaze, standing guard with their submachine guns and shooting anyone trying to escape the inferno. Golda and the women wailed throughout the night at the death of their husbands and sons and fathers.

But Simon was not among the men killed that day.

Though Golda didn't know it, he had been transferred in February to a camp called Dora-Mittelbau, to work at another underground factory, Mittelwerk, carved into the Kohnstein mountains of Thuringia. It was here that the rocket scientist Wernher von Braun would watch his V-2 rocket design become a reality thanks to the work of thousands of slaves employed by companies like Siemens. Had Ushi and her colleagues not abandoned their jobs, they could have ended up here as well, transferred by their employer with thousands of other Jews—Jews who would be worked to death, their bodies piled up inside and outside those underground tunnels.

In late January, dozens of V-1 bombs were sent to Mittelwerk for completion; when he arrived weeks later, Simon would become one of the men and women forced to finish their construction in twelve-hour shifts—working, sleeping, not seeing sunlight. The *V* in the bomb's name stood for "vengeance," to exact revenge for the Allied bombings. The remote-controlled bombs were considered "miracle weapons" that the Germans, headed for defeat, hoped would turn the war around.

But prisoners at Mittelwerk ran a resistance organization to sabotage the V-1 bombs and V-2 intercontinental missiles they built day after day, night after night. Some seamstresses were put to work in munitions, their dexterous fingers helping create delicate filaments finer than hair for the V-2 radio tubes. They would often destroy those filaments before placing the final metal pieces on top, guaranteeing the rockets never made it to London, malfunctioning mid-shot and landing instead in the English Channel. Of the ten thousand V-2 rockets fired, more than half exploded while still in flight. But there was a steep price to pay for victory. More than two hundred saboteurs were hung in early 1945 at Mittelwerk, their bodies strung throughout the cave-like tunnels, the other prisoners forced to pass beneath them on their way to work.

A month after his arrival at Mittelwerk, Simon was killed along with twenty-six other workers, just weeks before the Russian and American troops began arriving. It's not clear if Simon and the others were saboteurs or if the Nazis simply wanted to clear out the camp before military defeat. What was left of Simon's body was cremated in the camp's ovens six days later, one of twenty thousand prisoners murdered there over the course of World War II.

Golda and the other prisoners at Langenbielau could glimpse the red glow of firefights and bombs over the mountains that cold spring. The last week of March, the prisoners there somberly celebrated Passover. With more and more guards leaving their posts and running away, a few male prisoners were able to steal some flour, chop up an empty bunk, make a small fire in the barracks, and bake some matzoh inside a makeshift oven. The end of the war was near. The few guards who were left ordered the female prisoners to dig their own graves, but they were so weak that they couldn't finish and were forced back to their barracks. The next day, there was no wake-up call for work; the guards had vanished.

Golda and her fellow camp mates were liberated by the Russians on May 8. The starving prisoners invaded the nearby town, stuffing themselves with food from the shops that were abandoned when the local butchers and grocers fled the invading Russian army. But Golda, less than half her weight from the days before the war, ate just a small amount, fearing that overeating would kill her. She immediately headed back to Kraków to search for her son Paul.

But Paul had been murdered at Auschwitz long ago.

URSULA "USHI" FRIEDMANN

CHAPTER 24

M.I.A.

BERLIN, 1944

THE THUNDEROUS DRONE OF BRITISH PLANES DESCENDING on Berlin at night cut through Ushi's dreams of America and sent her scrambling to the basement of her building to cower with the rest of the Jews and Gentiles living there. Though their religions may have been different, they all prayed to the same God to save them from the bombs about to land, their whistles and then their blasts rocking the once grand boulevards. Ushi placed her small hands on the sides of her head, pressing her curly red hair flat to her ears to buffer the noise.

Of the seven thousand Jews hiding out in Berlin, only fifteen hundred would survive. Some were caught by the Gestapo, some committed suicide under the incredible stress, and some were killed during the Allied bombing of the city. The bombs killed you whether you were a German loyal to the Nazi Party or a persecuted Jew.

Ushi's friend Leja was eventually arrested in the spring of 1944 and taken to the same detention center where Ushi's parents had been taken—to the same school building where Jules had studied as a boy. Ushi could not save her parents. But now that German defeat seemed likely, the Nazis were much less organized. Somehow Leja got a message to Ushi that she had been captured. Ushi boldly went to visit her on Grosse Hamburger Strasse, walking through the doorway where the stone sculpture of boys with their open book gazed down upon her.

Ushi passed beneath the stone boys and brought Leja a bottle of cognac to pack in her one suitcase to use as a bribe for when she was transferred. A few weeks later, Leja was forced onto a third-class passenger train with twenty-nine others. She used the bottle of cognac to convince the German police officer guarding them to let her use a car bathroom rather than the bucket provided them.

"When the train stops you can use the bathroom in the next car," said the policeman. Leja locked the bathroom door, and when the train started up again, opened the window, climbed out, dangled for a few seconds by her hands, and then dropped herself out. She rolled down a slope, then got up, dusted her clothes off, and limped away to freedom. Thanks to Ushi and her bottle of fine cognac.

Most of the other Jews on Leja's transport were transferred to a cattle car, taken to Auschwitz, and were eventually murdered.

The German press spread only lies and propaganda, so it was nearly impossible to know the truth about the progress of the war. But the constant bombings—the Americans by day and the British by night—were a sign that defeat was imminent for Germany. They lit up the streets so brightly at night, you could read by the fire and the antiaircraft searchlights. The bombs gave you hope, even though you might very well die in the process.

As the air attacks increased, it became easier to elude the SS. Chaos had taken hold in Berlin with thousands of bombed-out Germans wandering the streets, looking for shelter. By May 1945, 1.7 million Germans—nearly half the population—fled Berlin. In the very last days of the war, the ground fire grew closer and closer until the Russians finally invaded the city in the Battle of Berlin. Ushi and her fellow submarines hid in bomb shelters and sewers and eventually had to prove to the Russian soldiers they were Jewish by showing the red *J* stamp on their passports. For those who had lost their papers, they were told by Russian Jewish soldiers to sing the Shema Yisrael prayer in Hebrew. Those who could not were often shot. Or raped. Or both. But Ushi knew the prayer well, had been taught it as a child like every other Jew.

Hear, oh Israel, the Lord is our God, the Lord is One
Blessed is his name, whose glorious kingdom is forever and ever.

A few mornings later, on May 8, 1945, Jules and Edith—along with six million other New Yorkers—gathered around their living room radio to hear the president declare an official end to the war in Europe. Less than a month earlier, Roosevelt had died of a stroke, leaving his vice president, now the president, Harry S. Truman, to announce victory. It was Truman's sixty-first birthday.

"The flags of freedom fly all over Europe," said Truman to a listening crowd that broke all records. "United, the peace-loving nations have demonstrated in the West that their arms are stronger by far than the might of dictators or the tyranny of military cliques that once called us soft and weak."

Jules and Edith wept at the news on this Tuesday morning, unaware that Golda had just been liberated that very same day, unaware that she was even still alive. The ships and boats in New York Harbor blew their whistles and horns, mingling with the cars joyfully honking in the streets. Ticker tape flew from the windows down on Wall Street as thousands of civilians, soldiers, and sailors headed to Times Square, blocking traffic, hugging, dancing, and singing songs. People banged pots and pans from windowsills; some knelt in the gutter, praying and crying tears of relief. Mothers who had lost their sons, in whose windows hung a red flag with a gold star, sobbed more bitter tears. By the afternoon, churches and bars were standing room only as rain began to fall gently across the city.

Jules's daughters, Helen and Evy, listened to Truman's radio announcement at school but were let out early. Butcher shops and grocery stores handed out free food, candy stores free candy, and bars free drinks. People drank until they fell down. Harry, of course, was no exception. For the first time in several years, Broadway, Lady Liberty's torch, Harry's Grand Central Palace building, the Waldorf, Jack Dempsey's orange neon, the Piccadilly Hotel, and all of Times Square was fully lit that night—the brownouts, and the war in Europe, finally over.

In Central Park, amid the blooming cherry and magnolia blossoms, a quiet, more serious crowd gathered, offering prayers of thanksgiving, but also asking God to end the war in Japan. Industrial plants in the city, still churning out weapons for the war in the Pacific, were closed for the day, their tens of thousands of workers given the afternoon to rejoice. But they were back at it the next morning. Jules and his sister Mollie wouldn't bother to open their fur stores, but instead gathered together to celebrate as a family in her apartment across town. But for them and for thousands of other Jewish refugees across the world, the war was far from over. Their families were still missing in action.

KAISER WILHELM MEMORIAL CHURCH AFTER THE WAR

CHAPTER 25

RUINS

BERLIN, 1945

FOR HIS 1945 FILM *THE LOST WEEKEND*, BILLY WILDER TRAVeled back to the neighborhood where his mother had once lived in New York City when she was a teenager. He shot on location, one of the spots the tavern P. J. Clarke's, with its beveled stained-glass windows, its gas lamps and dark wood paneling left over from the days of the Gilded Age when Eugenia had called the neighborhood home. The ghost of his young mother haunted those city streets.

Wilder was hired by the army that summer, assigned to the Psychological Warfare Division. Because he spoke the language, he was sent back to Germany, where the end of the war unfolded a bit differently than in New York. Though people were relieved the fighting was over, Berlin and those living there were devastated. Wilder flew over the remnants of the Romanisches Café and the jagged broken spire of the Kaiser Wilhelm Church, the ruins of the zoo and the train station.

Years later, he tried to visit his father's grave, but it had been obliterated. The New Synagogue on Oranienburger Strasse, where Einstein had once played violin, was also in ruins. "I had mixed feelings," Wilder said. "I wanted to see the Nazis destroyed, but to see *the city* destroyed . . ."

Wilder made his way over Berlin's once bustling streets. In the hot summer, the air smelled of rot, German corpses floating in the

Landwehrkanal and lying under collapsed homes. More than six hundred thousand apartments had been destroyed, and nearly half the city's population, just gone. Those who were left were dazed and streaming out into the countryside, their few belongings in wooden carts and baby carriages.

As in dollhouses, rooms sat exposed in bombed-out buildings, the outer walls crumbled away, but tables and chairs still standing, beds lying neatly made. On the once grand Kurfürstendamm, the street where Jules's wedding reception was held, a Panzer tank was stuck in the hot tar, either abandoned or its soldiers dead inside. Airplane parts lay strewn about, propellers and engines left where they had crashed. Saints were toppled onto the ground like corpses outside the Berlin Cathedral. Over the shell-damaged Reichstag, its dome now a skeleton, its walls defaced with bullet holes and obscene graffiti aimed at Hitler from the invading Russian troops, the red Soviet flag sagged in the dead, sweltering air. American GIs handed out chewing gum and chocolate to hungry children begging in the streets, their stunned parents forming long bucket brigade lines to clear the blasted ruins, Ushi and her friend Leja among them.

Wilder met with the Red Cross to try and trace what had happened to his mother and grandmother, but there was nothing. They had likely gone back to Kraków, just like Jules's sister Golda had, and either died in the ghetto or were sent on to a concentration camp.

Wilder's job with the Psywar office, as it was known, was to create documentaries for German consumption, and to pinpoint which German filmmakers were actual Nazis and which, out of fear, had just gone along. During the war, the SS had created a series of propaganda films, including an anti-capitalist account of the *Titanic* sinking, whose director was murdered by the Nazis halfway through production. The ship used in the filming was converted into a prison ship, filled with concentration camp victims, and left as a target for the Royal Air Force, who sunk it at the very end of the war, the death toll triple the actual *Titanic*'s. The Nazis had also made a "documentary" about Theresienstadt, starring actual Jewish prisoners, to convince the world that concentration camps were not so bad. Many of the film's "actors" and "actresses"—forced to participate in a staged soccer game—were later murdered.

Now it was time to show the world the truth. Wilder edited miles of footage shot by the US military, which eventually resulted in a black-and-white film called *Death Mills*. The twenty-minute documentary was made for American-occupied Germany and Austria and was the first of its kind to show what GIs had found when they'd arrived at the Nazi concentration camps.

Maybe Wilder hoped to get a glimpse of his mother or grandmother in that liberation footage, amid reels of gas chambers, crematoriums, and ovens, stacks of infant shoes, boxes of wedding rings and gold fillings, bags of human hair ready for manufacturers, ground-up bone that was sold to local farmers as fertilizer, skeletal camp survivors in striped uniforms, and piles and piles and piles of dead bodies, being bulldozed into giant open graves. There was footage of German citizens being marched to the camps in their towns to face the aftermath of the horrors that they had ignored, to extinguish any hatred or anti-Semitism that might have lingered.

But there was no trace of Wilder's family.

Jules's oldest sister, Golda, was very quiet when she arrived in New York, speaking softly, if at all, her large, tired eyes staring into the void from which she'd barely escaped. Amid the chaos of postwar Europe, Jules was able to locate Golda through a Jewish rescue organization and bring her to Manhattan. He and the family found her a three-bedroom rent-controlled apartment in a gray-brick building on Riverside Drive at Ninety-Fifth Street, not far from

Harry's old place, facing the Hudson River and beautiful Riverside Park, which had been completed long ago. But the beauty of the flowing river and the canopy of trees were not much of a comfort for what Golda had been through, for eyes that had seen all that she had seen.

She rented out the extra bedrooms to boarders to make her $500 rent each month. Golda, a broken woman, was crippled by arthritis from walking in and shoveling snow in the ghettos and concentration camps she had somehow survived. She was the oldest and, it turned out, the strongest of Jules's siblings.

Don, too, made it through the war alive. Golda hadn't seen her son for nearly a decade and barely recognized him, but the joy of hugging him again was a happiness so great that, for a moment, it nearly outweighed her sorrow. Don had been assigned to various posts, including a unit in the Aleutian Islands, handling shipments of planes and ammunition to the Russian front. But because of his ability to speak German, he was given a job with the counterintelligence unit in Staten Island interrogating captured Nazi officers.

When Don got married and had his son, Jeffrey, four years later, they moved into the same seven-story apartment building as Golda, right across the hall. It was the sight of that grandson, her only grandchild, that cured what the view of the Hudson River and Riverside Park could not. Golda began to smile again, taking the boy for walks down to the park and to the river's edge along the promenade. Her legs didn't seem to hurt as much when she pushed his baby carriage all the way to Seventy-Ninth Street and back.

When Jeffrey was old enough, Golda would take him to the movies up at the Riverside and Riviera cinemas on Broadway, laughing again, finally, at the comedies, thrilled by Jewish hero Ben-Hur and his chariot races. Back in her apartment, Golda cooked her grandson all the food she had dreamed of while in the concentration camps: tender beef brisket; delicious gefilte fish made with the freshest carp, kept in the bathtub until she was ready to cook it; and her sweet and savory tzimmes stew, full of fresh apples and potatoes and carrots, so abundant and sand-free now at the local market. But the best times were when Jeffrey came to stay with her every day when he got home from school. Golda would sit quietly with him in her living room in her easy chair, watching the river flow, their third-story view just above the tops of the blooming American elms and black cherry trees below.

She never talked about the camps to Jeffrey, but she hadn't forgotten. Golda applied for reparations from the German government. For Paul's and Simon's murders she was awarded $4,200— each human life worth a mere $2,100.

Since Jules had said goodbye to his youngest sister, Cilly, in Berlin, he had not seen her nor heard much from her. No one had. Many nights, Jules would think of how when they were young, Golda had taken care of them both, helping his own mother to raise them. But Golda had barely managed to survive, herself, during the war.

When Paris was taken by the Nazis, Cilly had stayed, helping arrange illegal transports for some of the Jewish children in the orphanage where she taught. The landlord of the building betrayed her, reporting that she worked for the underground.

All that Jules knew was that Cilly was shot and killed outside 6 Rue Vieille du Temple in the Marais, the center of Paris's Jewish community. No other details were recorded.

Jules would not learn of Cilly's fate for years after the war. But when he finally did, he would sit shiva.

Ushi finally resurfaced, her days as a U-boat drifting aimlessly on the streets of Berlin finally over. With Jules and Edith's help, she was able to make it to America in September 1946, sailing on the

SS *Marine Marlin* from Bremen. She packed what few pieces of clothing she had, along with her once verboten German typewriter, which she had lugged with her everywhere she had hidden.

On her way over on the ship, she met her husband-to-be—a watchmaker also named Jules, who had hid for the entire war like she had, using the German alias Fritz Schlenk. When Ushi arrived, Edith and the family went to meet her at the dock with a bouquet of roses, overjoyed to see her. It was during a September heat wave, but Ushi was wearing a winter suit, probably the only dress clothes she owned. A big black hat covered her curly red hair. She was sweating profusely. At the dock, Ushi put down her suitcase, especially heavy because of the German typewriter inside. She took the flowers from Edith, then slapped her across the face and said, "How dare you leave me behind!" Edith cried and Ushi, lost in an emotional tangle of joy, sadness, and grief, apologized immediately, hugging her sister close.

Ushi lived with Jules and Edith for a year, sleeping in a small bedroom while her hosts slept on their pullout living room sofa. In New York, she landed a job at Alexander's department store in the purchasing department for fancy women's wear and was able to buy several new suits. Even when she wasn't at work, she would accidentally—but happily—answer the phone, "Women's better dresses." When she got married, Edith and Jules threw her a wedding at Zichron Ephraim synagogue on East Sixty-Eighth Street.

Leja and several of Ushi's fellow submarines made it to New York as well, serving as a support group for one another. They all attended each other's weddings—also thrown by Jules—and raised their children together. And eventually their grandchildren. Ushi was as smart and brave as she had been underground in Berlin, and when anyone was in a jam, she was the one they called. One afternoon when an apartment neighbor accidentally locked her door with her infant inside, Ushi wiggled through a hallway window four stories up, climbed over the metal guardrails, and crawled along the ledge and then into the woman's open bedroom window. Just like the superhero she was.

FAIRE SANS DIRE

CHAPTER 26

TO DO WITHOUT SAYING

NEW YORK, 1946

Mr. & Mrs. Sternberg

THE LUXURIOUS JADE ROOM AT THE WALDORF ASTORIA WAS *ungapatchka*—Yiddish for "ornately over the top." When Harry's son, Irwin, got married in July 1946, he invited his old pal Faye and her husband, Murray, to the festivities there. The Jade Room took its name from its jade-green walls, which were decorated with golden carvings and ornamentation. Green marble columns quarried from the Montalto mountains in Tuscany supported an eighteen-foot-high ceiling heavy with gold and crystal chandeliers. For the wedding, each white tablecloth was decorated with three tall white candles amid white freesia and green ferns to match the room. The white menus, held together with golden tasseled silken rope, were embossed with two doves embracing and with each guest's name calligraphed in red Germanic letters. Below the doves were the words *Faire Sans Dire*, French for "To Do Without Saying."

Harry and his son were dressed in black top hats and tails with delicate white stephanotis boutonnieres on their satin lapels. The bride, a willowy blond beauty named Arlene Levy, who was friends with Harry's daughter, Peachy, from the private Fieldston School in the Bronx, carried a long bouquet of matching stephanotis, her gown made of white satin and lace. Faye looked fantastic in a black dress whose chest was embroidered with glittery flowers like a corsage, her upswept hair decorated with a fresh white flower plucked from the round table's centerpiece. Murray even looked dashing in his black tuxedo and bow tie.

Jerry and Joe were there, too. When Joe's sister moved to New York for acting work after the war, he moved back as well, buying a house for the whole family in Forest Hills, Queens. Jerry eventually followed, settling on Long Island. At the wedding, Faye and Murray were seated near Jerry and Joe's table. Faye had never met the creators of Superman and was thrilled to be in the same room with them, though she had no idea about the trouble brewing between Jerry and Harry. Not many people outside DC Comics did.

While in the army, Jerry had met a publicist named Albert Zugsmith—which sounded like a made-up comic book character name—who encouraged him to sue Harry and Jack. Publishing *Superboy* without letting him know or paying him extra had really pushed Jerry too far. And Zugsmith leant a sympathetic ear. Over the last decade, he and Joe had been paid around $400,000 between them, not bad by World War II standards (the equivalent of nearly $6 million in 2022), but a mere pittance compared to what Jack and Harry were hauling in. Soon after Irwin's wedding, with Zugsmith's encouragement, Jerry and Joe would file a lawsuit for $5 million (the equivalent of $71 million today) for money earned from the Superman radio show and merchandising, and for the stolen rights to Superboy. Zugsmith would represent them in court.

Faye, of course, knew none of this. Harry didn't even know what was coming. For now, everyone was having a ball at the wedding, drinking wine and cocktails, singing along to an accordion player and a harmonizing quartet that drifted from table to table. The war was finally over and it was time to celebrate. Superman was as popular as ever, scoring top ratings on his radio show that summer battling the KKK in a sixteen-part episode called "Clan of the Fiery Cross." Now that the Nazis were defeated, he would need to find new enemies. "Anyone who tells you a man can't be a good American because he's a Catholic or a Jew," Superman preached, ". . . you can be pretty sure he's a rotten American himself. Not only a rotten American, but a rotten human being."

When Irwin and Arlene cut the enormous four-tiered wedding cake, decorated with giant bows and baby's breath, Faye was right up front, cheering on the young couple. Before they left for home, Joe drew a picture of Superman in profile—his strong chin jutting out—on the back of Faye's wedding menu. It was an early bar mitzvah present for her son, Neil, the kid who had gone to Harry's office with her to get the affidavit for Jules, who had served as DC Comics' one-boy focus group. Underneath the Superman drawing were signatures of the three men who created the first superhero—Jerry, Joe . . . and Harry.

Harry would attend Neil's bar mitzvah later that year. Neil had the mumps but was a real trooper, his chubby face looking more swollen because of the collar and tie he was forced to wear. Jules was at the party, too, but he would keep his distance from Harry. Keeping his promise, Jules never spoke publicly about Harry's help, even after the war was over. He was probably a little afraid of Harry, with his Mob ties. If Harry didn't want his name mentioned in the escape story, Jules would gladly oblige. The closest he came to mentioning Harry in later years was saying that he knew "the man who had owned Superman." Harry had other reasons for keeping his good deed quiet. Though he didn't seem like a religious man, Harry knew that doing a mitzvah without recognition was more powerful in the eyes of God. *Faire Sans Dire*.

Jules always thanked Faye or her family when he gave a toast or held court at a large gathering—which was quite often. He would get up and tell his story of escape—the story about coming to New York to find a sponsor, pretending to be Clark Gable's agent, about withholding the lollipop and making Helen cry. But he never mentioned Harry.

For those he saved, though, it was Harry who was the true Superman. His good deeds were more than the mitzvah he believed them to be; they were *tikkun olam*—an attempt to repair the world.

Harry created the Donenfeld Foundation, quietly contributing thousands of dollars to dozens of Jewish charities, like the Hebrew Convalescent Home, the Eddie Cantor summer camp for Jewish kids, and the Israel Orphan Asylum. Gussie co-chaired a big fundraiser with the United Jewish Appeal as soon as the war ended to help raise money for Palestine.

But Harry did not do good deeds for everyone.

He and Jack went into full-on attack mode when Jerry and Joe finally filed their lawsuit, using a team of high-powered lawyers to take them down. Despite Harry and Jack's best efforts, Jerry and Joe won their lawsuit against DC Comics for the theft of Superboy, which the judge considered a separate entity from the Superman character. But Judge J. Addison Young ruled in Harry and Jack's favor on the rights to Superman. Jerry and Joe had stupidly signed that dreaded contract back in 1938 and had no claim whatsoever to the superhero. Or its riches.

When the trial was over, Jerry and Joe negotiated out of court with Harry and Jack for the Superboy theft and settled on $94,000, under pressure from Zugsmith, who told them the publishers might win on appeal. (Some said Harry paid Zugsmith off.) It was a hefty sum, but a fraction of what they'd expected. Jerry and Joe were then promptly fired, their creator credits spitefully removed from all future Superman comics and films. It was simply a matter of contract law. The American way.

ACT TWO

NORMA JEANE DOUGHERTY POSING FOR *YANK*,
THE ARMY WEEKLY, AT THE RADIOPLANE FACTORY IN BURBANK

CHAPTER 27

COVER GIRL

HOLLYWOOD, 1945

GIRLS WERE EVERYWHERE. GIRLS IN BATHING SUITS. GIRLS
in shorts. Girls performing various tasks that invariably required
them to bend over. And around these girls were dumb jokes, single-
panel cartoons à la the *New Yorker* that were absolutely nothing like
the single-panel cartoons in the *New Yorker*. They weren't clever
or sophisticated or *wink-wink* droll. They were excruciatingly unfunny. In one issue, a photo of a chimp reading an Italian newspaper carries the caption "Mussolini."

One of Harry's biggest wartime publications, aside from
Superman, was a GI favorite called *Laff*. Harry's smooshes had disappeared and were replaced by more mainstream cheesecake photo
magazines. Times were rough. And any *Laff* was better than no
laugh at all. That was Harry's thinking, anyway. His instructive
magazine title, though misspelled, insisted you try and look on the
bright side of things, even if Germans were shooting at you.

Ads were of the blackhead-removal and ninety-pound-weakling
variety, and "stories" included photo essays, like "How to Dance
the Hula in Seven Easy Lessons." In one feature, titled "Eat Hot
Dogs and Have a Perfect Figure," the author said the secret to the
diet was eating hot dogs for three meals a day, which would give
you "such a bellyache that you can't eat for daze and daze. That's a
sure way to lose weight. The good old American way!" The story

was illustrated with celebrities chomping down on hot dogs, including slugger Joe DiMaggio. "He trains on hot dogs," read the idiotic caption. "We know you thought it was spaghetti."

But the main reason to buy the magazine was for the girls. Some rode atop missiles. Some did karate in their bathing suits. Others were actual circus performers pretzeled into outrageous contortions. One cover featured Harry's favorite pose—a woman, a real woman, not an artist's rendition, with her dress blowing up, her white panties on full display.

And then there was Norma Jeane.

Her full name was Norma Jeane Dougherty. She posed regularly for *Laff*, and with each passing issue, her hair would grow lighter, from brunette to auburn to the blond that would eventually help make her famous. She had soft features, eyes the dark blue color of the Pacific on a cloudy day, and a patina of platinum peach fuzz on her face like you find on a baby, giving her an unusual, ethereal glow. Her smile was bright and perfect, and natural, and had not required years of braces to straighten her teeth. Just a retainer that she slept in for a year. Some of her greatest assets were below the chin, which she knew and used to her advantage. The cheesecake magazine, she would concede later in life, was "a periodical with cover girls who are not flat chested."

Her first national magazine cover was in 1946 for *Family Circle*—distributed by Harry Donenfeld. In the wholesome shot, nineteen-year-old Norma Jeane is dressed like Dorothy from *The Wizard of Oz*, her dark hair tied in a bow and her hemline past her knees as she leans down in a field to pick up a little lamb. She's barefoot and smiling and looks like the teenager she actually is.

Norma Jeane, still a brunette, landed the first of many covers for *Laff* a few months later, dressed in a fairly modest striped bikini, sitting on a rooftop, the California coast curving behind hers. Two months later, shot by Bruno Bernard, a regular *Laff* photographer, she landed the cover again, this time with red hair and a matching orange string-tied bikini. For the January 1947 cover, Bruno shot her with her hand behind her head, her body stretched out in a white bikini in a more cheesecake pose, with the tagline "Beauty Over Brooklyn"—even though she had never left California. And there she was again, the following September, in that string-tied orange bikini in the repurposed Bruno Bernard shots, this time with a cover line Harry could have written: "Can Nite Clubs Cure Insomnia?"

By the end of 1946, Norma Jeane would grace at least thirty-three magazine covers—many of them Harry's. Tying together the strands of her life and his, she would jokingly pose for a candid shot with her body seemingly covered in nothing but those magazines. Maybe she wasn't naked underneath, but she wasn't wearing much—besides those covers. The covers that would make her famous. She was the hardest-working model for the Blue Book Agency, driven and intent on success. When the head of the agency told her she would be even more successful if she dyed her hair blond, Norma Jeane did. And she was.

Even back then, Norma Jeane was no naive waif. She had a superpower of her own and she knew it instinctively—her power of seduction while still appearing vulnerable and innocent. Norma Jeane made those around her want to protect and help her, all the while seducing not just the camera, but the men, or the occasional woman, working behind it. Not to mention those who would eventually look at what was shot. She learned back then in her early modeling days what angles worked best, how natural light was always better, and how to turn on the lights within. It was more than enthusiasm or charisma. It was that magic "It" that cameramen and directors were always going on about. Norma Jeane had It. And then some.

Norma Jeane's aspirations had been instilled in her since birth. Her mother, Gladys, worked as a negative cutter for Consolidated

Film Industries, a menial job splicing film for final cuts. It was an exacting—though not particularly creative—task that involved gluing together pieces of negatives using a hot splicer machine.

Gladys, whose ancestors had come over on the *Mayflower*, had given birth to Norma Jeane out of wedlock. Her husband had left before Norma Jeane was born and was not the baby's biological father. A fan of Jean Harlow, she had partially named her daughter after the Hollywood star.

Unable to both support and take care of the girl at the same time, Gladys paid $5 to various people to board her. But eventually, Gladys got a loan and bought a small house near the Hollywood Bowl, which she shared with young Norma Jeane and an actor couple and their daughter. She bought a secondhand piano that had belonged to the actor Fredric March so that Norma Jeane could learn to play and sing. And on her wall hung a photograph of Norma Jeane's "father" (Glady's former husband), a handsome man with a thin mustache just like Clark Gable's. Norma Jeane had never met her biological father and didn't even know his name. As far as she was concerned, he was Clark Gable. Norma Jeane would stare adoringly at the photo, just like, one day, people would stare at hers.

Gladys would sometimes take young Norma Jeane with her to work in the film-editing studio. The little girl hated the smell of the film, which stuck like the smell of glue in her little nostrils. Eventually, Gladys had a breakdown and was diagnosed a paranoid schizophrenic. Norma Jeane landed in an orphanage at age nine and bounced around with a dozen different foster families. Forced to clean the houses where she lived in poverty, Norma Jeane would often have to take a bath last, in the dirty bathwater everyone in the house had used first. At one of the foster homes, which was also a boardinghouse, she was sexually abused by one of the boarders. But when she told her foster mother, Norma Jeane was slapped and instructed to keep quiet about it.

Sometimes, she would land with a better family, who would give her pocket change to get lost and go to the movies. It was in those darkened theaters, staring up at the giant screen, that she escaped and fell, like Jules, in love with the fantasy that Hollywood created.

Norma Jeane would finally find some happiness in 1938—that remarkable year Harry published Superman and Jules escaped Berlin. At age eleven, Norma Jeane wound up living in West L.A. with Ana Lower, the aunt of one of Gladys's friends. Ana was poor, but kind. Norma Jeane would wait with her in long lines for stale bread during the Depression, but Ana would tell her that one day she would be rich and famous. Ana loved her. And she loved Ana.

But Ana was not healthy. Four years later, a blossoming teenage Norma Jeane was living with another foster family, the Goddards. When the father, Doc, was relocated to Virginia, they left Norma Jeane behind. Some said Doc had tried to molest her. Or maybe his wife, Grace, saw the danger and decided to get him away from Norma Jeane. Either way, the girl was not coming with them.

To avoid having her placed in yet another foster home or orphanage, they asked their next-door neighbor, twenty-one-year-old James Dougherty, if he would marry her. Jimmie took the fifteen-year-old on a few dates, and the following summer of 1942, tied the knot just after Norma Jeane's sixteenth birthday. There's a photo of Norma Jeane and Jimmie looking like kids playing dress-up, standing in front of a fireplace, her dark curly hair covered in a white veil to match the gown Ana made for her; Jimmie in his white tuxedo jacket and black bow tie.

Jimmie would soon enlist in the Merchant Marine and be shipped off to the Pacific. While he was dodging torpedoes, Norma Jeane got a job at the Radioplane munitions factory in Burbank for $20 a week, working ten hours a day spraying and inspecting parachutes. One morning in June 1945, Captain Ronald Reagan sent a camera crew from the army's First Motion Picture Unit over to the factory to shoot some war propaganda of female workers for the weekly magazine *Yank*.

Norma Jeane posed with an RP-5 propeller, blowing away the other girls. The camera crew, impressed by how photogenic she was, asked her where the hell she had been hiding all this time. A few of them asked her on dates (which she refused), but one corporal asked her to model for him in his Sunset Boulevard photo studio. Corporal David Conover, a tall GI with glasses and a wife back home, was all business and seemed like he could be trusted. So she said yes.

Over the next couple of weeks, Conover shot roll after roll of Norma Jeane and encouraged her to continue modeling, sharing his list of contacts with her. By January of 1946, she'd landed her first cover for the Douglas Aircraft in-house corporate magazine. She would work nonstop, modeling for whoever would have her, including Harry's *Laff*.

She was so photogenic and so in demand that she decided she would become an actress, using the name Jean Norman. Acting, she would say years later, was her only escape from the pain of her childhood. It was a way to live in dreams for a few minutes at a time. Jimmie, in pleading letters, was against her plan. That autumn, she filed for divorce.

When he came home on leave, Jimmie tried to convince her to take him back. But Norma Jeane had bigger things in mind. She was a survivor and would show the world that it not only couldn't crush her but that she would succeed beyond anyone's expectations. She started diction lessons and dreamed of working for the studios, like the ones her mother cut film for before she was taken away.

"You don't have to know anything to dream hard," Norma Jeane would say. "I knew nothing about acting. I was ashamed to tell the few people I knew of what I was dreaming." Driving from audition to audition in her used car, she dreamed harder than the thousands of other beautiful girls who traveled to the promised land of Los Angeles, a place that Norma Jeane already called home.

In pursuit of her dreams she would be pawed and propositioned in cafés and on phony and actual audition couches, asked to pull her skirt up a little higher. Higher. Higher. Higher, until the word became a resounding chorus shouted from the rooftops of Manhattan.

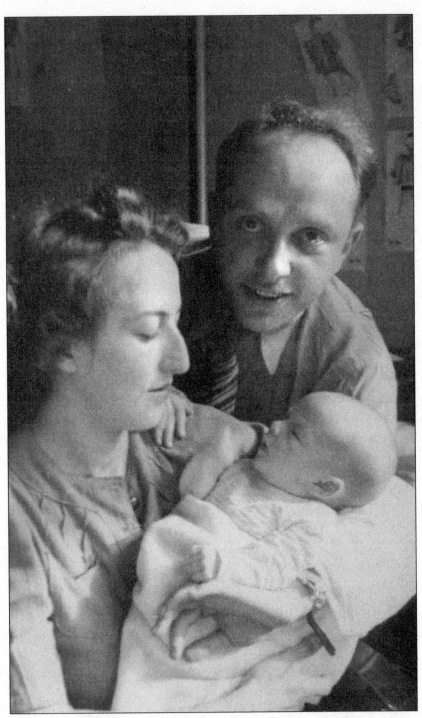

EDITH, JULES, AND THEIR SECOND DAUGHTER, EVELYN

CHAPTER 28

JEWS REEL

NEW YORK, 1947

THE SWISS-MADE 16 MM BOLEX WAS BLACK, WITH STEEL edges and knobs and a handle that had to be cranked every thirty seconds because the camera was powered by a spring-wound clockwork system. It weighed about twelve pounds, with a strap at the top for easy carrying and to hold on to when you were shooting. You had to bring it up to your eye to look through the viewfinder. The Bolex was called the Swiss Army knife of movie cameras, since it was compact and easy to use and had been produced in Switzerland. It had been designed three decades earlier by a Jewish refugee named Jacques Bogopolsky, who lost his Russian family to the Nazis and had taken the last transport from Switzerland to the US in 1939.

Bogopolsky's invention was Jules's new favorite toy. Though it had set them back several hundred dollars, Edith didn't mind the extravagance. The Bolex brought her husband endless hours of happiness and peace.

Armed with his camera, Jules would shoot home movies to help preserve moments in his family's life, lives that would not exist had it not been for Faye and Harry. Most of Jules's Berlin neighbors, childhood schoolmates, and their families had died in concentration camps, their bodies burned in ovens. It was too much for Jules to process, and sometimes he would move through his new life as if in a strange dream or film: a protracted, awful horror film or nightmare that he could not—and would not—wake up from completely, playing constantly in the background of his brain. To try and erase those thoughts, he lived as full a life as he could. And made his own films. Happy films.

When they were old enough, Jules sent his daughters to summer camp in the Berkshires—Camp Kadima for little Jewish boys and girls, where they played sports and rowed boats, a small miracle to Jules, compared with what could have been: saved from an alternate universe where the word "camp" had a very different meaning. When he went to visit his daughters on parents' day, he always brought his movie camera, one of the first fathers to have one. And it wasn't just any camera, but a professional one that actual filmmakers used. An enthusiastic director, Jules would make Helen sing and Evy dance for his home movies. At family gatherings, they were always expected to perform, Mollie's son, Bob, accompanying them on piano. Amid the family crowd that Jules filmed was Golda. And Ushi. But so many others were missing.

One of Jules's favorite film subjects, besides his family, was the formation of Israel. Because his sister Sara and brother Max had settled there, he was always up-to-date on what was happening. For Jules, Israel became not just a symbol of Jewish strength but a fallback if anything as horrific as the Holocaust ever happened again. There was a homeland you could return to if anti-Semitism reached such dire proportions.

Jules filmed the pro-Israel parade down Fifth Avenue and the Jewish State rally at Madison Square Garden, which drew a crowd of one hundred thousand—but also managed to work his loved ones in, out in the audience, cheering. He learned to use title cards to narrate his silent movies, including one that read "Jews Reel"—instead of News Reel—on a round, spinning piece of cardboard, scenes separated by newspaper front pages declaring progress in Palestine. His sister Sara's son, Ishy Lavi, would become a high-ranking officer in the Israeli military, which led Jules to take an even greater interest in what was happening in the Middle East. During the Arab-Israeli War of 1948, he filmed teenage Helen, beautiful and blond, donating blood in New York City. "If you cannot fight for Israel," the intertitles read, "give blood."

But mostly, Jules filmed his family's weddings, bar mitzvahs, confirmations, birthday parties, Passover dinners, and vacations to the Catskills and Miami Beach, which they visited by riding the Silver Meteor overnight train from Penn Station. Unlike Harry, who went to Miami Beach to wine and dine Sunny out in public, or to the dog track and deep-sea fishing with his distributors, Jules spent his time on the beach with his family. With his girls and Edith.

Once, Jules filmed an entire "day in the life" of his two daughters, which he staged and directed. Jules shot Helen and Evy pretending to get up in the morning, eating breakfast, walking to school, their arms filled with books as they made their way up Lexington Avenue past Bloomingdale's (even though it wasn't their regular route to Julia Richman High School). He even filmed each street sign, between shots of the girls, to show that they were heading uptown. They walked slowly, obviously under his direction, and smiled for the camera, barely able to keep from rolling their eyes.

Jules was too frugal to buy a television, so the girls were forced to go to their friends' houses to watch their favorite programs. But he did have a projector and would screen his home movies regularly, celebrating the day-to-day miracle that was their lives. At family events, he would show the films and tell the stories behind them.

His favorite films were the day trips with Edith and the girls in his used 1941 Pontiac Deluxe Six convertible coupe, which he convinced Edith they should buy for out-of-town excursions. Because

Murray and Faye didn't have a car, they would sometimes come along for a ride, crowding with their sons, Neil and Fred, into Jules's Pontiac. But Helen and Evy were always the stars in Jules's films. Helen, who was growing up to be quite lovely, was his perfect model, the winner of a high school beauty contest featured in the *Daily News*. Helen was Jules's very own all-American blond beauty.

Jules filmed their short trips to Coney Island and longer drives to Atlantic City, where his fellow New Yorker Bess Myerson was crowned the first—and only—Jewish Miss America in September 1945. Though the Atlantic City pageant officials had asked her to anglicize her last name, Myerson refused. She also chose a $5,000 college scholarship as her prize rather than a Hollywood movie contract. Myerson's victory, coming so soon after Americans learned of the Holocaust, was an encouraging sign that anti-Semitism here might be near an end. But once she was sent on the usual Miss America national tour, Myerson was turned away with signs proclaiming "No Jews." Some sponsors canceled her appearances altogether. With the Anti-Defamation League's help, she launched a different kind of tour, a series of nationwide speaking engagements titled "You Can't Be Beautiful and Hate."

Myerson's boyfriend rented the apartment beneath Jules on Lexington Avenue, the former Miss America coming and going now and then, the Schulbacks thrilled to see the statuesque beauty in their hallway. But it wasn't just her looks that struck them all. Having just graduated with honors from nearby Hunter College, she was the perfect role model for Helen and Evy—brainy, stunning, and Jewish.

Sometimes, Jules would head out on his own for a drive through the city he loved. He didn't need a destination. The skyscrapers and tenements, fashionable New Yorkers in a rush, the neighborhood girls jumping rope, boys playing stickball and skelly, the corner candy stores and theater marquees and elevated subways all flew past his windshield and never failed to thrill. His Pontiac convertible was no match for the Model A he had left at the dock in Rotterdam. But with its Silver Streak Torpedo style, big chrome grille, and three-speed manual transmission, Jules's car cut quite an impression on the Upper East Side. Jules, always such a careful driver, would run the red lights as he headed down Fifth Avenue along Central Park. Because of the park, there wasn't much cross-street traffic.

And, besides, Jules considered himself a very lucky man.

NORMA JEANE COVERED IN HER COVERS

CHAPTER 29

THE HOTTEST THING

HOLLYWOOD, 1946

IN THE SUMMER OF 1946, BILLIONAIRE AIRPLANE MANUFAC-
turer Howard Hughes took his prototype XF-11 reconnaissance
aircraft on its maiden voyage. After flying for around ninety minutes, Hughes's engine began to fail and, attempting to make an
emergency landing at the Los Angeles Country Club golf course,
he took the roof off a dentist's house in Beverly Hills. He slashed
through a line of poplar trees, then burst into flames as he bar-
reled into the home of Lieutenant Colonel Charles E. Meyer, who
was thankfully serving as an interpreter at a war crimes trial in
Europe—one of the few times an American officer's life was actually saved by the Nazis. The dentist, who was home at the time,
escaped unscathed. Hughes, pulled from the wreckage by a marine
sergeant and a recently discharged GI, wound up with third-degree
burns, a broken nose, several cracked ribs, a crushed collarbone and
chest, a collapsed lung punctured in six places, and a heart shifted
slightly to the right.

But at Good Samaritan Hospital in a full body cast, Hughes's
eyes and mind worked just fine. Suffering in his rigid hospital bed,
he managed to come up with an idea for a new sectional bed that
could lift and lower different parts of the patient's body by turning
various cranks. His engineers designed it and delivered it to Good
Samaritan, where he lay recuperating for several weeks.

The bed was the least of his discoveries that summer. Paging through dozens of magazines during his recovery, he kept seeing, again and again, a wholesome, healthy-looking model. She seemed to be everywhere, but Hughes was especially impressed with a shot on the August cover of *Laff*. The model's cascading red hair matched her orange string-tied bikini. Hughes, who was also head of RKO Pictures, demanded his studio find her and offer her a screen test. His search landed in the column of Hollywood gossip queen Hedda Hopper the first week of August, causing quite the buzz.

"Yes, Howard Hughes is on the mend," wrote Hopper. "Picking up a magazine, he was attracted by the cover girl and promptly instructed his aid to try signing her for pictures. She's Norma Jean Dougherty, a model."

Norma Jeane's agent at Blue Book—credited with planting the item with Hopper—assigned her a film agent, who promptly called 20th Century Fox and told them RKO was about to sign her. Fox studio head Darryl F. Zanuck, never to be outdone by Hughes, arranged for a 5:30 a.m. screen test and stole her away. When Fox offered Norma Jeane a six-month contract, they insisted she change her name. Someone at the studio suggested Marilyn. And so she paired that with her mother's maiden name, Monroe.

Marilyn Monroe. It had a nice ring to it.

On the studio lot, she would spend three hours in drama classes each day and then have lunch in the commissary. That was followed by an hour of dance lessons, an hour of singing lessons, then fencing and horseback riding. Not all the contract players worked that hard, but Marilyn was determined to be ready for when her big break finally came. She may not have finished high school, but she was constantly learning, constantly reading, constantly improving herself, soaking everything up like one of those little sponges the makeup girls used on her baby-down face at the studio. She even learned to do that makeup herself, asking question after question and watching every move they made.

The new Marilyn got a few walk-on parts—as a telephone operator, an extra at a square dance, and rowing a canoe in a comedy called *Scudda Hoo! Scudda Hay!*, a scene that was cut—but Fox eventually dropped her option because Zanuck didn't like her. (Some said it was because she wouldn't sleep with him.) Over at Columbia, she got her first starring role as an innocent burlesque queen in the B movie *Ladies of the Chorus*. When Columbia's studio head, Harry Cohn, invited her onto his yacht, she asked if his wife would be joining them. He threw her out of his office and failed to renew her contract. As one producer once quipped, "Marilyn never slept with a man who could do her any good."

Unsigned, Marilyn finagled an audition and was cast in a small walk-on part in 1949's *Love Happy* with Groucho Marx. But it was quite a walk. For thirty-one seconds, Marilyn worked every bit of screen time, slowly sashaying across the floor in a tight-fitting, shimmering gown, a fur draped over her arm. She was the only reason to see the movie. The producer sent her on the road to promote the film and gave her $75 to buy a new wardrobe. Having never been east, she imagined it would be cold in New York. She bought three wool suits, but when she arrived, she realized it was summer in New York, like in Los Angeles (just as Ushi had arrived in New York wearing her wool suit a few years earlier). The publicist made the best of the situation, giving her two ice cream cones to hold in one hand and a fan in the other, her face shining with sweat. "Marilyn Monroe, the hottest thing in pictures, cooling off," the caption read. "Cooling off" would become a recurring motif.

As part of that tour, she would make a pit stop in Chicago and serve as bat girl at the Movie Star World Series baseball benefit at Wrigley Field. Beside Hopalong Cassidy and Eddie Bracken was a surprise guest—Superman—played by unknown actor Kirk Alyn, who was starring in a new fifteen-part live-action serial showing before matinee feature films in first-run theaters across the country. Alyn would be the first actor to play Superman on-screen, and though he was anonymous, it would launch his career. The baseball benefit would be the only time Marilyn and the Man of Steel would cross paths, Supes rounding the bases and the young starlet coyly smiling for the newsreel cameras.

Despite the publicity tour, and her brush with Superman, Marilyn was still broke when she got back to Los Angeles. She owed $150 on her used red 1948 Ford Super Deluxe convertible. She could barely make the rent and hardly ate, except for the meals her agent/lover, Johnny Hyde, bought her. After three months of missing her car payments, the repo man was knocking at her door, saying for $50 the company would let her have the car back. Marilyn didn't have $50.

Auditioning in Los Angeles without a car was like Superman flying without his cape. It just wasn't possible. For days, Marilyn lay in bed, depressed and crying. She screamed and punched the walls. Until finally she called Tom Kelley, a photographer she had worked with on some Pabst beer ads. Tom had once offered to pay her $50 if she would pose for a nude calendar. She had declined, but now she was having second thoughts. She called Tom and agreed to meet him and his wife, Natalie, at their apartment for a photo shoot. Marilyn was glad she hadn't eaten much lately. She was thin and, of course, looked fabulous. She was a nobody, so it wasn't like anybody would recognize her in the calendar, Natalie assured her.

Marilyn had no hang-ups about sex or nudity. But the rest of America did. A little voice in her head said, "What if you do become famous someday? Those pictures could resurface." The chances of actually making it in the business, though, were slimmer than Marilyn's waistline. Just in case, she used an alias for her photo release, Mona Monroe, then luxuriated on Tom's big red velvet drape on the floor, while he played Benny Goodman's recording of "Begin the Beguine" on the phonograph to get her in the mood. That's what he played for all his nude models, to get them to relax and enjoy the moment. Stretching out, her body partially revealed in diagonal side shots and a more coquettish sitting pose, she was electric. From a ten-foot ladder, Tom shot photo after photo. *Click. Click. Click.*

The next day, she had her red convertible back, and was able to drive to her next rejection.

One night, Marilyn was invited to a big Hollywood A-list party at an agent's house. She wore a cheap dress and even cheaper shoes, but she didn't care. From the hallway, she gazed into the living room, where the beautiful people had gathered. All the stars were there, standing around in evening gowns, chatting casually, not like the superheroes they were, but like regular human beings: Gene Tierney of *Laura* fame. Jennifer Jones. Olivia de Havilland from *Gone with the Wind*. And her costar Clark Gable.

Daddy.

Marilyn couldn't bring herself to say hello. Or to even enter the room.

Clark had no idea Marilyn was there or who she was. Though soon enough he would know her name. Everyone would.

At the end of 1949, Monroe scored her breakout role in John Huston's jewel heist noir, *The Asphalt Jungle*, playing the young mistress of the movie's villain, Louis Calhern. She was so nervous during the audition that she asked Huston if she could lie on the floor to deliver her lines. He agreed. And she got the part. (Huston, a notorious gambler, also happened to owe $18,000 to MGM's talent director, who agreed to wipe out the debt if he auditioned Marilyn.) No matter how she wound up there, Marilyn stole every scene she was in, causing the men in the audience to wolf-whistle in the theater.

That led to *All About Eve*, the Joseph Mankiewicz film for Fox starring Bette Davis that told the story of a hungry young actress who will stop at nothing for success. Marilyn's role was a bit part, the arm candy of actor George Sanders, who was playing a Broadway critic. Sanders's character, like all his characters, was a hilarious snob. (Even when playing a Nazi in *Confessions of a Nazi Spy*, Sanders was a British snob.) Sanders and Marilyn's first scene in *All About Eve* unfolds at a staircase at a fancy cocktail party filled with famous actors and actresses. Art was about to imitate life.

In the film, Sanders sends Marilyn, dressed in a white gown and ermine wrap, into the room to hobnob with a producer. "Why do they always look like unhappy rabbits?" she asks.

Sanders answers, "Go and make him happy." Her character—and, of course, Marilyn—will do what she needs to do to succeed. "I can see your career rising in the east," says Sanders, "like the sun."

GEORGE REEVES AS SUPERMAN WITH SOME MOLE MEN

CHAPTER 30

BACKLASH

NEW YORK, CIRCA 1951

MOLE MEN, SLIGHTLY SHORTER THAN HARRY DONENFELD, emerge from the center of the Earth after a six-mile-deep oil well is drilled. Though they have bald bulbous heads, they are good-natured. After the Mole Men are mercilessly attacked by suspicious humans, Superman comes to their rescue and lecturers the ignorant mob to "stop acting like Nazi storm troopers."

The plot was part of a 1951 B movie called *Superman and the Mole Men*, which tried to convey some sort of a social message: bigotry and racism were unacceptable. The fifty-eight-minute movie, featuring a couple of former munchkins from *The Wizard of Oz* as the Mole Men, wouldn't crack the consciousness of most cinephiles. But it would be the first feature film based on a DC Comics character and serve as the pilot for the *Adventures of Superman* television series. TV was still new and untested, but Harry and Jack knew there was a huge audience of kids out there, kids who were losing interest in comic books because of television. From 1950 to 1951, the number of televisions in American homes jumped from 3 million to 10 million, with Howdy Doody and the Lone Ranger eating into DC's audience base.

The Superman show, starring George Reeves, would bring the superhero to a whole new generation, those too young to remember Superman's comics debut in 1938. Branching out into television was a natural progression for the superhero, and the next step in a long line of successes for Harry and Jack.

But for Superman's creator Jerry Siegel, seeing his beloved character's new incarnation was torture. He and Joe Shuster had been wandering the wilderness since being ousted by DC Comics after their 1947 lawsuit. They had tried to make it in the comics world without Harry and Jack, but things were not going so well. Funnyman, a Jewish comedian/superhero they tried to launch, was painfully unfunny and died a quiet death after only six issues. The $94,000 they'd won in the Superboy fight didn't last very long. In addition to the lawyers' fees and back taxes he owed, Jerry lost more than half of everything he owned when his wife filed for divorce. Bella left him just two months after the settlement, taking the kid, the house, everything in it, and 60 percent of his money.

But Jerry was anxious to get out. A few months earlier, he and Joe had reconnected with their old friend Joanne, the model for Lois Lane. Joe had kept in touch with her over the years and invited her to the Plaza Hotel in Manhattan to the Cartoonists Society ball. Joe even rented her a gown for the event, hoping to reignite their romance. The three old friends had a great time, but Joanne wound up leaving the party with Jerry that night instead of Joe. As soon as Jerry's divorce was final, the two were married. Joanne thought she was marrying a successful writer, but Jerry's worst days were ahead.

He and Joe did some freelance work, Jerry writing stories for the *G.I. Joe* comic book, and Joe dabbling in horror comics. Jerry was hired as the comics editor by another publisher, Ziff-Davis. But their comics division closed after less than a year. Jerry and Joe couldn't catch a break, back to being the hard-luck losers who'd been kicked around at Glenville High School. Except Jerry was now married to Lois Lane.

The new Superman television show was sure to bring in millions in advertising, but Jerry and Joe would see none of it. Bitter and broke, Jerry wrote a letter to the FBI in 1951, telling them to take a close look at Harry and his associates. J. Edgar Hoover, who had been after Harry years earlier for the sex pulps, wrote Jerry back, saying he believed comics caused juvenile delinquency. He was already on the case.

A backlash against the comics industry had been growing for several years. Kidnapping, tying up victims, and sadism were regular staples of comic book stories. (Some parents even complained of Wonder Woman being underdressed.) Back in the 1940s, to quell any complaints, DC had added child psychologists to its editorial board to advise on what was acceptable reading material for children. Graphic violence was to be avoided, as were provocative female characters.

After years of censorship with his girlie pulps, Harry had learned how to play by the rules. But by the 1950s, the fear of juvenile delinquency was growing with the rising population of children from the postwar baby boom. Though crime statistics didn't support their cause, J. Edgar Hoover and politicians stoked the public's fear that radio, television, and, yes, comic books were corrupting their children. Comic book burnings were held by parents, priests, and teachers who claimed their violent content led to juvenile delinquency.

In 1950, a Senate crime investigating committee began looking into whether comics—particularly horror and crime comics—caused actual violence. All the commissioners had to do was look at a back cover of any Superman comic to know that Harry was promoting violence: Full-page ads for BB guns and fireworks had likely helped shoot several eyes out and blow off a finger or two across the country. Leather whips and folding knives were advertised for sale in comics pages. But the content itself?

One of the men leading the charge against the comics was Dr. Fredric Wertham, a German psychiatrist from Nuremberg who had originally come to America in 1922 at the invitation of the Phipps Psychiatric Clinic of Johns Hopkins. Now living and working in New York, Wertham had documented dozens of cases of children acting out in violent ways after reading comic books. With his long, pinched face and his black-rimmed glasses, the humorless Wertham never smiled and insisted there was nothing comical about comic books. His 1948 article in the *Saturday Review of Literature* described a bunch of feral boys tying up a little girl and torturing her after they'd read a comic book. The piece caused quite a stir, catching the eye of several politicians, who questioned whether comic books were inherently good or bad for kids.

"If you want to raise a generation that is half storm trooper and half cannon fodder with a dash of illiteracy," said Wertham in his heavy German accent, "then comic books are good. In fact, they are perfect." Wertham believed all comic books were bad, even the ones featuring Superman. "Comics showing superman types of characters are the worst," he said. "The hero is above all law. He might be a modern Nazi. The villains are small and of dark complexion. Almost any foreigner will do."

To get to the bottom of the problem, the Senate committee sent out a survey to hundreds of probation officers, child welfare workers, juvenile court judges, police, and prison authorities, as well as those in the comics industry. In a 250-page Senate survey released in November 1950, a few outliers called for the banning of comics, citing a boy from Pittsburgh who jumped off a pole thinking he could fly like Superman and a Wisconsin kid picked up for arson who learned his method from a comic book.

But most officials—who had probably read comics in the military and whose own kids grew up on a steady diet of Superman and Batman—believed they were more of a waste of time than an evil influence, and that bad parents were more to blame than superheroes. Henry Palmieri, chief probation officer in Richmond,

Virginia, asked if comic books were really much more violent than the Bible. "Are the comics worse than the stories of David and Goliath, Cain and Abel and some of the fairytales?" Harry and Jack certainly didn't think so. But to nip the hysteria in the bud, they and their fellow comic book publishers established a code similar to the Hollywood production code: Bad guys couldn't win. Cops were always good. Women couldn't be naked or nearly naked.

Ironically, the official Hollywood code was on its way out. In 1952, the Supreme Court unanimously ruled that motion pictures were entitled to First Amendment protection, cracking open the door to more risqué films. And setting the stage for the rise of a certain blond actress from California.

MARILYN MONROE AND JOE DiMAGGIO

CHAPTER 31

FORCE OF NATURE

LOS ANGELES, 1952

THE VILLA NOVA RESTAURANT ON SUNSET BOULEVARD WAS A cozy place with a steeply pitched roof and a mirrored, curved bar lit by hanging lanterns and a skylight. Originally bankrolled by Charlie Chaplin, the Hollywood hideaway was off-limits to reporters: it was where Dean Martin went to meet his agent and where its owner, Vincente Minnelli, had proposed to Judy Garland. If you were going on your first date with the rising new star Marilyn Monroe and wanted some privacy, this was the place to be. So this is where Superman's biggest fan—Joe DiMaggio—took her one night in March 1952.

No longer posing for Harry's girlie magazines, Marilyn was now smiling provocatively from the cover of *Screenland*, a celebrity tell-all that Harry distributed. That same year Marilyn would be voted Miss Cheesecake by *Stars and Stripes*. Though she had hit the big screen, re-signed by Fox the spring of 1951 to a seven-year contract, the GIs already knew her from the covers of magazines like *Laff*. They felt she was their own. DiMaggio, himself a former GI, had seen a recent picture of Marilyn posing at bat with a couple of White Sox players, her white hot pants pressed into the groin of pitcher Joe Dobson. DiMaggio was smitten and asked a mutual friend to introduce them, then arranged for a group date.

That night, Marilyn was late, which was becoming a bad habit.

She really wasn't looking forward to meeting DiMaggio. Marilyn was not a sports fan, had never been to a ball game of any kind, and assumed DiMaggio would be loud and badly dressed. When Marilyn first heard DiMaggio's name, it sounded familiar, but she wasn't sure if he was a baseball player or a football player. He was also a player of a different kind, and was known—after his divorce from his first wife—for his many romances. In fact, a photo spread of DiMaggio with various girlfriends would run in an upcoming issue of *Scope* magazine, whose cover featured Marilyn. But DiMaggio, suffering from the beginning stages of arthritis and several ulcers, seemed to be slowing down. He was thirty-seven and had just retired from baseball, leaving him plenty of time to read his DC comics, flip through Hollywood magazines, and watch lots of television, including *The Adventures of Superman*.

When Marilyn first saw Joe, over the anchovy and pimento appetizers, he looked like a politician or a businessman, not a jock. He was six foot two, slim, and graceful in his gray suit jacket, which matched the bits of gray in his hair, his silver cuff links glinting in the light from the bar. He was wearing a tie with large polka dots, one of which was sitting smack in the center of his tie knot. One of the few things Marilyn said to him at dinner was, "Did it take you long to fix it like that? To get the polka dot right in the center?" Joe just smiled and shook his head. The spaghetti, al dente, with garlic and olive oil arrived.

What she liked best about him wasn't his clothes or the way he looked—he was actually kind of goofy with his big teeth and angular features. What she found most attractive was his quiet and reserve. Marilyn never chattered in public, but usually sat there and took it all in. Just like Joe. What also impressed her was how the other men in and around their red booth—men who would normally be trying to impress her—were now trying to impress *him*. It was a first. She was intrigued.

At one point, just as the veal scallopini arrived, Mickey Rooney came over and fawned over Joe. Marilyn had no idea that Joe had set a record in the summer of 1941 with his fifty-six-game hitting streak. She wasn't sure what that meant exactly, but the men around her were certainly impressed. After espresso, she got up to leave, and he asked to walk her to the door, then to her car, then asked for a ride back to his hotel, the Knickerbocker. She obliged, and he admitted on the drive that he wasn't ready to call it a night after all and asked if she'd mind driving around awhile.

They drove through the City of Angels in Marilyn's convertible for three hours, talking. It was only then that she learned he played center field for the Yankees, that he had grown up in San Francisco, the eighth of nine kids from a big Sicilian family. When Joe was a boy, being Italian was still considered exotic, your last name unpronounceable. You were a joke to some people. A Wop. Dago. Guinea.

Giuseppe Paolo, as his parents had called him, had worn braces on his legs when he was little to correct his knock-knees. But once the braces were removed, he was determined to play ball like two of his brothers, who would also go on to play professionally. His father expected Giuseppe to be a crab fisherman like he and his ancestors had been for generations. It was the safe bet. But Giuseppe hated the smell of fish and used one of his father's broken oars as a bat to play ball in the local lot.

Like Marilyn, he had dropped out of high school sophomore year. He started playing baseball with his brother Vincent's team, the San Francisco Seals. Joe was an incredible hitter and just four years later, in 1936, wound up playing for the Yankees. He would be the first player to make $100,000 a year, enough to buy as many comic books as he liked and open a seafood restaurant on Fisherman's Wharf.

Because his father was Italian-born, he couldn't visit Joe's restaurant—Grotto—during wartime because he was considered an enemy alien, under curfew and prohibited from traveling more than five miles from his home. He also wasn't allowed to fish and had his boat confiscated. Not that he needed it to make a living. Joe bought his parents a big house and was now supporting them. No one had any trouble pronouncing the DiMaggio family name anymore. Despite the government's treatment of his father, Joe enlisted in the army in 1942 and served with the Seventh Air Force in Honolulu. Some say he was bitter about it and felt it ruined his career and first marriage to Universal contract actress Dorothy Arnold. The couple had gotten married back in 1939 and had had a son, Joe Jr., during DiMaggio's big hitting streak. The marriage was brief and rocky, and though they divorced in 1944, the two had stayed friends, even spending Christmas together. Joe and Marilyn bonded over the fact that they were both happily divorced.

Like Marilyn and Harry Donenfeld, Joe was an example of the American dream hard at work. Lack of money and connections could only hold you down so long if you were determined. Not just determined, but with a vendetta or an angry streak. When someone stepped on your neck, or your father's neck, and tried to hold you down, most people submitted and gave up. But there were the strong ones who fought back. Like Marilyn. She had had nothing, and so she had nothing to lose in the fight. She had been disappointed so many times in her short lifetime that the rejection of Hollywood was normal. Pick yourself up, put on some fresh lipstick, and start all over again. Success, after all, was simply persistence and a bit of talent.

When Marilyn finally pulled up to Joe's hotel, he invited her up to his room "to see his trophies." She laughed and told him she really was tired and would take a rain check. He gave her a quick kiss and said good night. The next day, when friends asked her how it went, she told them Joe had struck out.

Joe called her several times, but Marilyn blew him off. It was only when he stopped calling that her interest was piqued.

A couple of weeks later, the studio heads called Marilyn in for a meeting. The nude calendar she had posed for three years earlier had resurfaced and they wanted to know if the skinny strawberry blonde in the photo was, indeed, her. She said yes, of course.

That week, Marilyn was scheduled for an interview with a journalist for United Press named Aline Mosby. Marilyn "confided" in her about the photos, and Mosby sent the story out on the wire. In her exclusive interview, Mosby explained the young star had posed nude out of desperation, describing Marilyn's sad childhood of being bounced around a dozen foster homes. Marilyn explained that she had posed nude to pay her rent. "Oh, the calendar's hanging in garages all over town," said Marilyn. "Why deny it? Besides, I'm not ashamed of it. I've done nothing wrong."

The studio went into crisis mode and considered dropping her, but then the fan mail started pouring in—five thousand letters a week. Because she was so honest and Mosby's piece was such a sob story, the public reaction was swift and sympathetic. Not only did Fox not suspend her but they upped her salary. A month later, because of the nude photo scandal, she landed on the front of *Life* magazine for the first time with the cover line "The Talk of Hollywood." In the story she was described as a "sturdy blonde" who was the "genuine article."

The scandal was the rain for Marilyn's Hollywood deluge. That summer, she would be shot in glorious Technicolor in *Niagara*, scripted by Billy Wilder's writing partner, Charles Brackett. (Wilder, still struggling with the loss of his mother, was busy working on the German POW camp drama *Stalag 17*, even though the studio was convinced no one wanted to think about World War II anymore.) In *Niagara*, Marilyn had top billing for the first time, playing a philandering wife and Joseph Cotten her jealous Korean War veteran husband vacationing in Niagara Falls. Marilyn wore red and, in one scene, a bright pink dress that nearly stole the movie. In an ironic tip of the cap to Joltin' Joe, Cotten's character says in one of his jealous tirades, "She'd like to wear that dress where everybody could see her, right in the middle of the Yankee Stadium."

Reviews of *Niagara* in early 1953 referred to the "grandeur that is Marilyn Monroe." *Variety* described how the camera "lingers on Monroe's sensuous lips, roves over her slip-clad figure and accurately etches the outlines of her derriere." Marilyn was happier with the *Hollywood Reporter*, which called it her "finest acting performance yet." The *New York Times* review headline read: "Niagara Falls Vies with Marilyn Monroe."

She was now an unstoppable force of nature, on her way to becoming the most powerful woman in Hollywood—though the men in charge would never admit it. Though Marilyn had likely never read any Margaret Sanger, she was the poster girl for Sanger's idea that sexual pleasure without procreation was not immoral. In other words, sex was good. She would become the living, walking embodiment of that idea—a proto-feminist of epic proportions who would make it acceptable for women to want sex as much as men, not just on film but in real life. But she would pay a price.

That summer, Marilyn served as grand marshal for the Miss America parade in Atlantic City, posing with each of the contestants for photos in a backless dress with a plunging V in the front reaching down nearly to her navel. Standing in a white Nash convertible sedan, she led a long motorcade down the boardwalk, the crowd calling out to her as she waved. She told an interviewer that day that she usually didn't wear any underwear.

MARILYN ON THE COVER OF *PLAYBOY*'S FIRST ISSUE

CHAPTER 32

CENTERFOLD

CHICAGO, 1953

HUGH HEFNER'S DREAM AFTER GRADUATING THE UNIVER-
sity of Illinois was to be a comics artist. He had developed two comic
strips that had gone nowhere. *Gene Phantos, Psycho-Investigator*,
featuring the adventures of a psychiatrist/private dick, sounded
like something Harry might—but did not—publish in one of his
humor magazines. Hefner's other creation was *Fred Frat*, a funny
look at college life, which apparently wasn't funny enough to be
published—quite a feat, considering how low the bar for humor
was at places like *Laff*.

The failed cartoonist eventually landed a job writing advertising copy for a Chicago department store, then moved to *Esquire*,
where he composed subscription pitch letters. But that didn't last
long. At Publishers Development Corporation, which put out
a magazine called *Modern Man* that included art nudes, Hefner
learned the art of newsstand operations as their circulation manager.

Inspired by *Modern Man* and *Esquire*, his new dream was to
launch his own men's magazine, which he planned to call *Stag Party*
until the publishers of *Stag* magazine sent him a cease and desist
order. Looking for a first-issue gimmick, Hefner briefly considered
a 3D nude centerfold, inspired by Hollywood movies like *It Came
from Outer Space*. He took some 3D test shots and planned on including cardboard glasses with that first issue.

But then he saw it.

An article in a trade paper about Marilyn's nude photos mentioned that Baumgarth, a calendar company in Melrose Park, a suburb of Chicago, owned the rights to the negatives that photographer Tom Kelley had shot years before. Hefner hopped into his used 1941 Chevy coupe, and a few hours later had the negatives—and a bunch of other nude girl shots—for the cool price of $500. Cobbling together a few stories, a men's shopping column, a page of jokes, and the photos, Hefner laid the first issue out in his kitchen. To pay for production, printing, and distribution costs, he borrowed $400 from a neighborhood loan company, took out a $200 bank loan, and raised $3,000 from friends and relatives. In December of 1953, with a new title, *Playboy*, and a still from Marilyn's Atlantic City parade on the cover, Hefner's magazine hit the newsstands.

Its first-ever centerfold: a nude photo of Marilyn from 1949, the one with her in a sitting position, her left arm stretched over her head. Until now, there had been a lot of talk about Marilyn's nude calendar shots—which were hanging on certain garage and barbershop walls. But Hefner delivered Marilyn nude to the general public, to anyone with fifty cents. In a move out of the Harry Donenfeld playbook, Hefner didn't include a date on the cover of the first issue of *Playboy* so that it could sit on newsstands indefinitely. He wasn't sure there would ever be a second issue. The first run was 70,000 and sold 53,000. It launched Hefner's career. And propelled Marilyn's even further. They were both just twenty-seven years old.

Marilyn wasn't paid by Hefner, never met him, and wasn't even given a free copy of *Playboy*. "I never even received a thank you," Marilyn would say. "I even had to buy a copy of the magazine to see myself in it."

Harry, naturally, would become the distributor for *Playboy* magazine. Jack Liebowitz traveled to Chicago to meet with Hefner at his home there. Hefner usually worked after midnight, so Jack showed up late at his place. Binge-drinking Coca-Cola and smoking his signature pipe, Hef welcomed Jack into his study and agreed to a deal. With *Playboy*, Harry and Jack were now raking in an extra $30,000 to $40,000 a month.

Now Fox had plans for Marilyn to star in the film *The Girl in Pink Tights*, which she knew would be another empty-headed-blonde role. She insisted on seeing the script, but Zanuck refused. Around the same time, she discovered that Frank Sinatra, a friend of Joe's and a fellow Sicilian American who had just had a standout supporting role in *From Here to Eternity*, was making $5,000 a week to her $1,500. *Gentlemen Prefer Blondes* had recently earned the studio $5.3 million. And she had been the blonde.

When she refused to accept her *Pink Tights* role, Zanuck suspended her. During her temporary vacation from Fox, Joe proposed to Marilyn on New Year's Eve. She loved Joe but also loved his close-knit Italian family. She admired their warmth and hoped one day to visit Italy with Joe. Marrying him was also a great publicity move. She said yes.

That winter, Joe planned to travel to Japan to help train Japanese players for their upcoming season, and suggested they get hitched and then extend his business trip as their honeymoon. They were married on January 14, 1954, at the San Francisco courthouse, Marilyn in a dark brown suit. The only white she wore was a broad ermine collar and her smile. The judge joked afterward that he had forgotten to kiss the bride. "And I'm sorry," he lamented. Joe wore a suit with a white-diamond-dotted tie with a diamond right in the center of the tie knot.

Joe made up for the judge's loss, kissing Marilyn repeatedly for the cameras, his lips smeared with her red lipstick. Though Joe had wanted a quick and quiet wedding, Marilyn tipped off the papers.

They wound up swamped by five hundred members of the press and onlookers who jammed themselves into the city hall corridor. The mob threw out questions about how many kids they wanted ("Six!" she said) and whether Marilyn slept in the nude (no comment).

Joe and Marilyn planned on spending their free time together in Japan, maybe visiting some small villages and getting away from all the publicity. But before they even got off the luxurious 377 Stratocruiser in Tokyo, a fellow passenger approached the couple. He was a tall, middle-aged Texan with glasses, dressed in uniform. Joe imagined he wanted an autograph or two. But army general Charles Christenberry was a highly decorated officer who had been one of Harry Donenfeld's neighbors on Riverside Drive. He had attended nearby Columbia University and had taught military science at NYU. These days, he was deputy chief of staff in Korea.

He introduced himself and chatted up Joe and Marilyn for a moment and then asked, "Would you like to take a detour on your trip to entertain the troops in Korea?"

"I don't think I'll have time," Joe said.

"I was talking to your wife," General Christenberry said.

"Well, ask her. It's her honeymoon," said Joe, more than a little annoyed.

Marilyn blushed slightly and said, "I would love to."

Joe may have been her first real love, but he was no match for one hundred thousand troops. Before she left for Korea, she told columnist Louella Parsons, "So many GIs have written to me, saying that they'd like to see me, and this is the thing I most want to do. I'll take a guitar player and some pretty clothes and a comedian because I think the boys want laughs as well as glamour." The GIs had been her biggest fans for a decade; singing them a few songs was the least she could do. She toured nearly a dozen bases in Korea's frigid January cold, dressed in a flimsy wine-colored dress, while Joe sat in Japan and stewed. At one of her stops, she had to go on early because the troops were so anxious to see her, they started throwing rocks at the other performers onstage.

"You've never heard applause like that!" she boasted to Joe on her return.

"Yes, I have," Joe snapped back.

Joe didn't get it. Growing up Italian may have been hard. But being an orphan was much harder. The hole in Marilyn's soul couldn't be filled by Joe or any husband. Marilyn would say that she belonged to the public because she had never belonged to anyone.

The more successful she became, the more Joe resented her. Marilyn needed a wife to take care of her, not a jealous husband. The closest she came was her acting coach, Natasha Lytess, a lesbian who was in love with her and despised Joe. Natasha said Joe was "vapid." But the feeling was mutual. When Natasha called the house and asked for Marilyn, Joe told her to call her agent and hung up. Natasha, who had escaped from Berlin under Hitler, spoke with a thick accent and insisted Marilyn overannunciate her syllables. Marilyn hung on Natasha's every acting command, even when it conflicted with the director's instructions, and insisted she be on set whenever she shot a film. Directors only put up with her because it made Marilyn happy.

Sometimes, it seemed Marilyn wanted to spend more time with her acting coach than with her husband. Joe begged her again and again to quit show business and live with him away from the crowds. But Marilyn's life was her career. When Joe complained about Marilyn not wanting to devote her life to him alone, his good friend Norman Brokaw sat him down over drinks at the Polo Lounge and explained it all to him. "I don't know any actress who'd be willing to give up her career when she's on her way to the top," said Norm. He told Joe to think about being with a woman while he was on his hitting streak with the Yankees and having her tell him to stop playing, right when he was about to set the fifty-six-game record. DiMaggio nodded his head and said he'd never thought about it like that before. He would stop asking her to quit. He would try to be a good husband and take care of Marilyn.

But it was too late for that.

Soon after the honeymoon, Marilyn was back under contract with Fox and given a $100,000 bonus and a starring role in Billy Wilder's new film, *The Seven Year Itch*. Wilder would be writing, directing, and producing, with Charles Feldman, a talent agent, putting up the financing for the film. Marilyn was one of Feldman's clients, and was perfect for the lead role. Billy asked for her. And he got her.

By now, Wilder was at the top of his career. His 1950 hit, *Sunset Boulevard*, made over $2 million at the box office and had won him and his writing partner, Charles Brackett, the Academy Award for best screenplay. But it would be their last collaboration. Though he never discussed their breakup in public, Wilder left Brackett—and their heated arguments—behind.

Still a stickler for accuracy and unflinching realism, Wilder had become known in Hollywood for shooting on location—*Sunset Boulevard* in L.A. with his old pal von Stroheim, *A Foreign Affair* amid the rubble of Berlin. So the cast and crew of *The Seven Year Itch* were heading to New York, to the same neighborhood where Wilder's mother had been a girl, full of life and hope and a future. The same neighborhood that a middle-aged furrier from Berlin called home.

THE ORIGINAL POSTER FOR *THE SEVEN YEAR ITCH*

CHAPTER 33

THE GIRL

NEW YORK, 1954

HUMPHREY BOGART, HIS CRAGGY FACE FIXED WITH HIS usual scowl, his homburg hat tilted at a jaunty angle, gets his long-suffering secretary, Miss McCardle, on the car phone. He wants to take his young date, Audrey Hepburn, to the hottest Broadway show in town. "I want two tickets to *The Seven Year Itch*," he barks.

The scene takes place halfway through Billy Wilder's newest film, *Sabrina*. The play *The Seven Year Itch* was all the rage in 1953. When the press dubbed it "The Lust Weekend," Wilder took it as a sign that he had to make the film version. The three-act play, still running on Broadway when Wilder sat down to write the movie script with its playwright, George Axelrod, would go on to be the longest-running non-musical of the 1950s. When Axelrod showed up for his first writing day with Wilder, he brought a copy of the play along with him. Wilder threw it on the floor and said, "We'll use it as a doorstop."

The plot of the play, and the subsequent film, involved a middle-aged New Yorker who is tempted by a pretty young thing living in the apartment upstairs while his wife is away with their son for the summer. Marilyn, naturally, would play the pretty young thing, known only as the Girl. But it was up for debate who would play the lascivious middle-aged creep downstairs. Actor Tom

Ewell was still playing the Creep—named Richard Sherman—in the stage version. Wilder wanted Gary Cooper, William Holden, Jimmy Stewart, or even a young, dynamic new comedian named Walter Matthau for his male lead. But Darryl Zanuck insisted on a proven asset, Ewell.

Ewell, of course, was no match for Marilyn. Wilder knew it before the script was even finished. And Marilyn did, too. She referred to Ewell in her script notes as "Itchy."

When we first see the Girl in *The Seven Year Itch* screenplay, she's carrying a small, newly purchased fan she's bringing up to her steamy second-floor apartment. In another scene, she tells the Creep that she needs to go to her kitchen to change her clothes. "I keep my undies in the icebox," she cheerily announces.

Wilder knew there would be zero chemistry between Marilyn and Ewell. For starters, Ewell had terrible posture, his neck sticking out at a forty-five-degree angle from his body. He wasn't funny. And, not to put too fine a point on it, he was gay. Ewell was probably the only guy on *The Seven Year Itch* shoot who didn't want to get into the Girl's frozen panties. Maybe the only person, period. There was more chemistry between Marilyn and her German drama coach, Natasha.

Ewell's character works for a publisher and, in one scene, shows off the cover of a new psychology text he's editing, whose artwork is right out of a Donenfeld *Spicy Detective* pulp magazine. "Of Sex and Violence," the cover shouts, with a screaming girl in a slinky red dress being attacked on a street corner by a hulking, sinister criminal. When the author balks and asks what the cover has to do with his academic book, the Creep explains, "Gustave Meyerheim, you remember, the mad lover of Leipzig terrorizing one of his victims?" It was a line that Wilder dropped in to make himself laugh. (Meyerheim was a nineteenth-century Polish-German painter of pastoral landscapes. Ha. Ha.)

Sex and violence, the Hollywood version of love and hate. It's what the crowd wanted and what the film industry, and the pulps, gladly served up. Or tried to, anyway. Though the Hollywood code was no longer legal, self-censorship in the industry kicked in. In some places, the rise of sexy stars like Marilyn was causing a conservative backlash. As a result, most of the funny lines from the play were cut. The script became a series of Walter Mitty–like fantasy scenes to avoid the reality that the Creep was committing adultery—a topic that had once been forbidden by the Hollywood code (along with mixed-race couples, gay characters, and corrupt cops). Much to Wilder's horror, a whole scene of Marilyn in the bathtub was scrapped.

All Wilder really needed, he said, was the maid to find a hairpin of Marilyn's in Ewell's bed to get the infidelity message across. But even that was cut. The story was watered down until, as Wilder described, it would "disintegrate into an incomprehensible nothing." The only good thing about the movie was Marilyn.

And the subway grate.

When Sam Shaw, the Fox photographer whose job it was to take publicity shots for the movie, read Wilder's script, the subway grate jumped right out at him. Shaw had taken photos back in the summer of 1941 at Steeplechase Park in Coney Island of a girl holding her red-and-white-striped dress down as a blast of air from a grate forces it up. When the photo ran on the cover of *Friday* magazine, the issue sold out the first day it hit the newsstands. Shaw knew a scene of Marilyn's Girl walking over the subway grate would be the money shot. Before the cast even arrived in New York, Shaw invited every photographer he knew—and some he didn't—to visit the subway grate to drum up publicity for the film.

Shaw had met Marilyn on the set of *Viva Zapata!* before she was a big star. Her lover at the time was the film's director, Elia Kazan, and he had asked her to pick up Shaw and drive him to the studio every morning to take publicity photos, since he was from New York and didn't have a license. By 1954, Shaw and his wife, Anne, were good friends not just with Marilyn but with DiMaggio and would go on double dates to LaStrada restaurant in Hell's Kitchen when the two stars were in Manhattan. DiMaggio even took Sam to Palermo with him once when the two were in Europe, back to his ancestral village.

Unfortunately, DiMaggio was not in Palermo for the shoot of *The Seven Year Itch*.

CHAPTER 34

FLESH IMPACT

NEW YORK, SEPTEMBER 9, 1954

EARLY ON A THURSDAY MORNING, MARILYN LANDED AT Idlewild Airport on the Lockheed Super Constellation, the sleek triple-tailed beauty financed by Howard Hughes—who, of course, had discovered Marilyn years before while propped up in his souped-up hospital bed. At the TWA terminal, she was greeted by press and fans, stopping as always to wave and smile at them all, her long fox stole draped over her shoulders. She traveled to Manhattan in a big black limousine, checking into suite 1105 at the St. Regis Hotel on Fifty-Fifth Street under her usual alias Zelda Schnook, then met with her friends Amy and Milton Greene. Milton, a photographer, had a penthouse studio in the Grand Central Palace, the same thirteen-story building where Harry worked.

Marilyn had met Milton while he was doing a photo shoot for *Look* magazine in Hollywood the year before. She had always admired his work, but was surprised at how young he was. "Why, you're just a boy!" Marilyn said to him the day they met. "And you're just a girl!" Milton replied. When he introduced her to his wife, Amy, the three clicked and became fast friends. What Marilyn liked about them was how they treated her like a regular person and not a starlet.

Whenever Marilyn walked the streets of New York, she took on her secret identity, wearing a dark wig and sunglasses, playing the part of Zelda Schnook. (A schnook in Yiddish is a stupid person, and Marilyn was nobody's schnook.) At the Grand Central Palace, Zelda may well have ridden up in one elevator as Harry was coming down in another. Or maybe they passed each other in the lobby. They were just four floors away from one another, Harry on nine and Zelda on thirteen, the comic book baron and savvy Hollywood starlet passing like taxicabs in the night.

At his studio, Milton shot the famous photos of Marilyn in a ballerina dress. Amy, a former model from Cuba, had bought the taffeta tutu dresses, but they were sample sizes and didn't quite fit

Marilyn. She couldn't zip them up all the way. But it made for an even better shot, the dress hanging open in the back, her feet bare, painted toenails curled like a little girl's. The hairdresser never showed up, so Marilyn's hair was a tousled mess. But it didn't matter.

DiMaggio wasn't planning on coming in for *The Seven Year Itch* film shoot, but his buddy Walter Winchell—smelling the drama of a potential story—convinced him to change his mind. So Joe flew into New York City that Sunday, staying with Zelda Schnook at the St. Regis. It was one of the city's most luxurious hotels, built at the turn of the century by John Jacob Astor, the fur scion behind the Waldorf and those beavers on the wall at the Astor Place subway stop. The St. Regis was most famous for its celebrity watering hole, the King Cole Bar, with a long mural by Maxfield Parrish of Old King Cole. The bar was a favorite of Marlene Dietrich, Ernest Hemingway, and, of course, Joe DiMaggio.

The first scenes of *The Seven Year Itch* were shot the next morning inside and out of a four-story townhouse at 164 East Sixty-First Street, between Lexington and Third Avenues, right around the corner from Jules's apartment. The shoot began at 8:00 a.m., and Marilyn was up early for it. Maybe she had never even gone to sleep. She arrived in her black limousine dressed in costume—a white satin and lace slip covered by a white terrycloth bathrobe—with her mink coat thrown over it.

The black townhouse had a big white arched doorway and white windows and shutters to match her costume. It was a peaceful, tree-lined block, with the occasional Third Avenue elevated subway rattling by in the background, and a quiet neighborhood restaurant, Villa Capri, on the corner. But it wouldn't be peaceful for long. Three policemen blocked off the street to traffic as the fifty technicians and extras went to work. Silver-foiled reflectors, black velvet sunshades, and two thirty-six-inch brute arc spotlights were set up to create the best light for Marilyn.

The scene involved Marilyn leaning out the second-floor window wearing just the slip, blow-drying her hair, messy and curly like in Milton's shoot. Marilyn glowed, as usual. "Flesh impact," Wilder called it. "Flesh which photographs like flesh. You feel you can reach out and touch it." Though most press photographers would be arriving the next night for the subway grate scene, a few members of the press were invited to the day shoot as well. *Life* magazine freelancer Bob Henriques, art photographer Garry Winogrand, and George Barris, who would take the last photos ever of Marilyn, on a Santa Monica beach, were each allowed inside the townhouse. They would shoot her alone at the window in her slip—like johns taking turns in a bordello.

Within minutes, a thousand gawkers clogged the sidewalk across the street, and eventually the street itself, down and up the block, trying to get a good look at Marilyn's flesh. The crowd included Roddy McDowall, a less successful film star, who just happened to live in the neighborhood, and a group of sweaty teenage boys from the nearby Manhattan High School of Aviation Trades. In the avalanche of press that followed, the *Asbury Park Evening Press* erroneously reported that five thousand students from the high school showed up. There weren't even five thousand kids in the whole high school. Marilyn waved to the boys between takes, setting off a flurry of catcalls and whistles.

Jules noticed the commotion that morning when he opened his fur shop around eight o'clock. Excited to have a celebrity on the block, he left Edith in charge, grabbed his Bolex, and positioned himself right in front of the townhouse. The Bolex was loaded with Kodachrome film and was ready to roll—though not exactly for moments like this. Jules was always filming something. He had just shot Edith that weekend at their twentieth wedding anniversary party. The twenty-year itch, he would joke.

Jules usually shot at eighteen frames a second, considered

silent speed. Shooting that slow made the film last longer. Jules usually shot color Kodachrome, which cost almost twice as much as black-and-white and cost more to process as well. He wound the camera up, held it to his eye, and shot Marilyn for several seconds at a time. The mechanical clanging *ting!* ticked second by second, like the meter at a gas station pump, reminding Jules how much time he'd spent on each shot and how close he was to re-cranking. Resting against his face, the twelve-pound camera purred as it wound its way down, its lens wide open and taking in all of glorious Marilyn.

Jules was a fan, not only of the woman but of the furs she had worn both on- and offscreen. Marilyn was a walking advertisement for the fur industry. And he loved her for it. Maybe one day she would even wear one of his. Her furs were designed by the best in the business, Jules's fellow refugees from Europe who had fled pogroms and, later, the rise of Hitler.

The number for Maximilian furs, Jules's competitor on Fifty-Seventh Street and Fifth Avenue, was listed in Marilyn's private phone book. The Maximilian family, who would design for Audrey Hepburn, Helena Rubinstein, and Sophia Loren, had escaped to America in 1939 from Poland and were the ones Marilyn entrusted with her fur storage and repairs, including the upkeep on her giant white fox muff, the first fur she ever personally owned. A foot wide, the muff snapped on to the end of her matching white fox stole and had a small secret pocket where Marilyn could stash her eyeliner or lipstick.

The muff was not just to keep Marilyn's manicured hands warm or her makeup hidden, but to signal that she was now Hollywood royalty. Marilyn was the female manifestation of the American dream, in all its luxury and beauty, a sign that good times had finally arrived. War, and all its horrors, in Europe, Japan, and Korea, was finally over; America was, once again, the promised land. Marilyn was the symbol of what all those GIs had been fighting for: blond, well-fed, and full-figured.

Jules knew that DiMaggio had recently given her a three-quarter-length ranch mink with a wide lapel, bell sleeves, and velvet-lined pockets, the one she had thrown over her robe when arriving on set that morning. There was the white ermine collar she had worn with her brown suit when they'd gotten married. Ermine had been the fur of royalty, used for coronation cloaks for centuries. When she was in New York, Marilyn often wore her black jacket with a wide brown mink collar. She also had a marten fur collar and her white fox cuffs, which could snap together to create a collar as well. There was the white beaver coat and the black fox stole trimmed in silk.

Then there were the studio furs, which Jules had always taken note of. In *Love Happy*, she had draped a light brown mink over her arm, and in *How to Marry a Millionaire* sported a darker brown mink muff and collar. Though, to that film's premiere, she had worn her white fox stole.

In both her scenes in *All About Eve*, she wore film studio furs, first an ermine wrap and then a small skulk of foxes with their sad little heads still attached. In *Gentlemen Prefer Blondes*, she and Jane Russell were responsible for a small massacre of animals, including black minks for cuffs, a silver fox for a wrap, a brown mink for a hooded coat, and a leopard cape and muff.

Jules even remembered the Gold Coast black colobus monkey fur coat that Marilyn wore to the premiere of *The Emperor Waltz* way back in 1948. But nobody really liked to think about that. Monkeys were too close on the evolutionary ladder.

Today there would be no fur. Just bare human flesh. Over three hours, between takes, Marilyn would don her white terry-cloth robe over her slip, since the temperature was only in the sixties, and come downstairs to mug for the crowd from the first-floor window. She would look directly at Jules and wave just at him. She even came out and sat on the stoop. No one paid any attention to her costar, Tom Ewell, who was pacing the sidewalk.

As the shoot was wrapping up, Jules chatted with some of the camera and ground crew. "Where's the next shoot going to be?" Jules asked one of the gaffers.

"Tomorrow night on Lexington outside the Trans-Lux movie theater," the gaffer told him. The theater, which usually showed newsreels and short subjects, was between Fifty-First and Fifty-Second Streets, just four blocks from Harry Donenfeld's office.

"Do you know what time?" Jules asked.

"I think we're starting around midnight," said the gaffer. "It's gonna be a late night." The next afternoon, in preparation, Jules took a nap on one of his fur pillows to rest up.

MARILYN AND THE CROWD ON LEXINGTON AVENUE

CHAPTER 35

IT HAPPENED LAST NIGHT

NEW YORK, SEPTEMBER 15, 1954, MIDNIGHT

INSIDE THE TRANS-LUX THEATER, TENSION WAS HIGH. MAR-
ilyn was always nervous before a big shoot, but tonight was more
nerve-racking than usual. DiMaggio, dressed in a smart dark suit
and the diamond-dotted tie from their wedding, was there with
Walter Winchell, in his typical trench coat and fedora, and the *New
York Post*'s Earl Wilson, whose syndicated column, "It Happened
Last Night," ran six nights a week. Wilson had brought along Italy's latest sex symbol, actress Gina Lollobrigida, to meet Marilyn.
Lollobrigida had told Wilson she was tired of being called the Ital-
ian Marilyn Monroe. And Marilyn seemed annoyed she was there.
But Lollobrigida was not what Marilyn was upset about.

Before the shoot, the studio held a party in the theater's audito-
rium to celebrate the first year of CinemaScope, Hollywood's new
wide-screen technology. A large cake decorated with the Cinema-
Scope logo was brought out, which Marilyn cut with a big knife.
Afterward, she rested in a red velvet movie seat with her strappy
high heels atop the seat in front of her while the crowd gathered
outside, her girl double posing for Wilder to get the lighting just
right.

Though Marilyn was anxious, DiMaggio seemed at ease with
Winchell and the other men, laughing and soaking up the spotlight
that he had given up when he'd retired. Marilyn wished he would

leave already. She wasn't jealous of the attention he was getting. She just didn't want him there when the shoot began. Marilyn knew the scene they were filming and the shot Sam Shaw had in mind to promote the film—her dress blowing up over a subway grate. She wanted to spare Joe the embarrassment. Marilyn had asked him not to come, had begged him, but here he was, refusing to leave. "Joe, you know, you really should go," she said, placing her manicured hands on his chest. "I have to work."

Finally, DiMaggio said he was headed back to the St. Regis, and his nervous wife nodded in agreement. He kissed her good night and said, "I'll see you at the hotel." As he headed for the theater's brass door, Marilyn was able to breathe easier, her smile returning to her glowing, downy face.

Wooden police barricades were set up on Lexington Avenue because of the crowd that was expected, but when DiMaggio walked out of the theater into the chilly night, he was stunned. The crowd had grown to nearly 1,500 people while they were inside, and for now, they erupted in cheers for him. Just him.

Press photographer Weegee was there, as well as Fox's East Coast publicity man, Bill Kobrin; sports photographer Matty Zimmerman; pinup model photographer Tom Caffrey; paparazzo Kas Heppner; Garry Winogrand's mentor, George Zimbel; French-born Elliott Erwitt, whose most famous shot would be a reflection of two young lovers in a car's side mirror; and Hollywood photographer Frank Worth, who would inexplicably hoard thousands of his unpublished celebrity shots and die in poverty.

Glamour shot photographer Bruno Bernard, aka Bruno of Hollywood, was there as well, shooting a story not on the film but on Joe and Marilyn as a couple. He approached Joe, who told him to come by the hotel the next morning. Bruno, who had shot Marilyn early on for those *Laff* covers, had been born in Berlin the same year as Jules and had escaped Hitler as well.

In that night's scene, Marilyn's character, the Girl, goes with Tom Ewell to the air-conditioned movie theater to cool off on a hot summer night. It was the latest—though not the last—in a series of "hot" references throughout Marilyn's career, which had started with the publicity shot of her holding the melting ice cream cones, through the "Heat Wave" dance number in *There's No Business Like Show Business*, and climaxing in a few years with *Some Like It Hot*, also directed by Wilder.

After seeing Hollywood's latest 3D movie, *Creature from the Black Lagoon*, Ewell—dressed in a tan suit, checked bow tie, brown loafers, and a fedora at the back of his head—strolls with Marilyn on the sidewalk, the red and white movie marquee glowing in the background. She is wearing a white pleated halter top dress made of rayon-acetate crepe.

The white dress that would marry her to the whole wide world. To all of mankind.

On her and Joe's wedding day, Marilyn had worn a brown suit. For Jimmie Dougherty, she had worn the white gown and veil that her foster mother Ana had sewn for her, which she later wore for a cover shoot for *Personal Romances* magazine.

This dress was different. This moment would change the way Americans thought about sex from now on.

After leaving the theater, Marilyn and Ewell pass a liquor store, a hat and jewelry store, and then stop in front of Wright's Food market. She stands with her legs apart atop a subway grate. Down below, unseen, a train goes by and creates a breeze. Marilyn purrs, "Isn't it delicious?" In the original script, Marilyn had a line asking Ewell, "Don't you wish you had a skirt? I feel so sorry for you in those hot pants." But that jab was cut by the censors.

Wilder knew the scene would be a big draw for the compromised, now unfunny film, but had no idea what was in store. Sam Shaw was on the street early that night, his Rolleiflex dangling from his neck, making sure the giant fan was positioned just right under the subway grate. Special effects coordinator Paul Wurtzel and a team of electricians were manning the fan. Marilyn was by now notorious for saying she did not wear underwear, so the crowd had arrived, hoping to get a look at her half-naked.

Most were men, except for Natasha, giving step-by-step instructions, much to Wilder's annoyance. Photographer Milton Greene's wife, Amy, was there as well, along with Frieda Hull, a member of the Monroe Six, a bunch of New York teenagers who photographed the starlet whenever they could, outside her hotel or at shoots like this one. Marilyn would befriend the teenagers eventually and invite them to her home, giving them gifts and autographing their photos of her.

Frieda was armed with a still camera, one of the only people shooting Marilyn in full color that night. But not the only one.

A few streets away, Jules was growing closer, taking that ten-block walk from his apartment down Lexington Avenue with his Bolex camera, passing the all-night coffee shops, the closed dry cleaners and silent newsstands, past the synagogue and taxicabs and the lonely cop on the beat. Until there it was, the glow of the klieg lights. Suddenly he was beneath them.

The fifty-seven-degree air was thick with anticipation as Jules, Wilder, and the restless crowd waited for Marilyn to appear. Wurtzel was offered bribes from men who wanted to get under the subway grate. And DiMaggio was still there, stopped on the street by members of the press he knew from his heyday and by fans asking for his autograph. He chatted with adoring cops and movie crew members, reveling in the attention.

Before the actual film shoot began, while Wilder was getting everything set up, the gathered photographers would shoot their still shots of Marilyn. That was the plan. They waited for Marilyn to emerge from the theater. And waited. And waited. For years she was kept waiting, and now she would make everyone else wait. Maybe she was stalling, hoping that Joe would finally leave. But she was always late, and it drove Wilder crazy, though he forgave her after every difficult shoot because she was so truly stunning. "My aunt Minnie would always be punctual and never hold up production," Wilder said. "But who would pay to see my aunt Minnie?"

CHAPTER 36

BIRTH OF VENUS

NEW YORK, SEPTEMBER 15, 1954,
1:00 A.M.

WHEN MARILYN FINALLY STEPPED INTO THE CHILLY NIGHT, holding a red-and-white-striped silk scarf in one hand and a white clutch in the other, wearing the ivory halter top dress designed by William Travilla, the crowd went berserk. They were standing atop cars, on the building rooftops and fire escapes. The applause and shouts soon devolved into catcalls and whistles. Marilyn wore no stockings or slip, but had pulled on two pairs of big white granny underpants, one on top of the other, which the crowd would get to see for hours. As if Superman were using his X-ray vision to stare right through the panties' fabric, Marilyn's dark pubic hair was still visible because of the bright klieg lights. The carpet did not match the drapes, the onlookers joked, elbowing one another and snickering. DiMaggio overheard them, his face growing red.

Flashbulbs popped. Men screamed from the sidelines, "Higher!" as her dress blew clear up over her head. At times her dress would simply puff up, its white pleats forming a scallop shell—her very own Botticelli *Birth of Venus* background slowly drifting down toward Earth.

In New York City, men had been sneaking peaks of women's underwear for decades, starting down at the Flatiron Building on Twenty-Third Street, where the whipping wind provided a free show. But there were no cops giving the old 23 skidoo tonight. Times had changed. The New York City cops simply watched and smiled as Marilyn's dress blew up around her ears. They had forgotten all about DiMaggio, who stood there, his red face now growing pale in the klieg lights.

Tom Ewell looked on and smirked. Sam Shaw shot roll after roll of film, Marilyn looking directly at him and saying, "Hi, Sam Spade." That was her pet name for him. Wilder, dressed in a suit, sweater-vest, dark coat, and his usual fedora, started to get agitated when the crowd's screaming wouldn't end. Maybe they had oversold Marilyn's appearance to the public. How would he possibly shoot this scene with all these people here? DiMaggio paced the sidewalk, fuming, then screamed at Wilder, "What is this circus?" Wilder later described DiMaggio's facial expression as "the look of death." Amy Greene was standing next to DiMaggio and saw him trembling.

The filming started and the screaming continued. The jeers. The whoops. The catcalls and whistles. Higher. Higher. It was the same refrain Marilyn had heard again and again on those casting couches, where the producers had urged her to lift her hem a little bit higher. Higher. Higher.

DiMaggio took hold of Amy's arm and told her he couldn't take anymore. "Tell her I'll see her back at the hotel," he said, walking right into the scene and ruining Wilder's shot. Marilyn looked over toward Joe, her smile gone, as he stormed off. He was headed across town to Toots Shor's for a much-needed drink.

Marilyn took a deep breath and got back to work. She was a professional. Pretending she wasn't freezing her barely covered tuchus off. Beaming. Glowing. Posing. Making love to all mankind on this, her wedding night with the world.

But there was more to it than that, something primitive and sacrificial. Marilyn was the pure sexual life force, the latest Cinema-Scope version in a long line of Aphrodites, female fertility vessels, and Madonnas, on display for all to see. The power of the female figure was greater than anything else. In the battle of Sex vs. Violence, sex would always win. After all, the perpetuation of the species depended on it. Life over death.

For over three hours, she stood there in the cold night pretending she was hot, smiling and offering herself up to the crowd, occasionally pushing Ewell into position, looking off sadly in the distance for her Joe from time to time. Between takes, some in the crowd asked Marilyn for autographs. At one point her strappy high heel got stuck in the subway grate, coming off her foot. But she laughed and bent over and pulled it out. Then put it back on. Some laughed along with her. Most just leered and catcalled.

But not Jules. He was there armed with his Bolex camera, rolling from five feet away, one of the only people on set shooting color film, besides Wilder and teenage Frieda, who was taking color stills. It was dark out, but Jules figured the movie lights would provide enough illumination. And he was right.

A distressed Wilder moved in and out of his shot, annoyed at the screaming crowd. Marilyn shivered and Jules wished he could drape one of his furs over her goose-bumped shoulders. Wilder implored the crowd again and again to keep quiet, but they ignored him. Marilyn smiled and simply put a finger to her lips, and they all fell silent. It held for a moment, a magical silent moment when all the world seemed to stop and hold its breath.

But the silence wouldn't last.

Because of the commotion and shouting, Wilder would shoot fifteen takes and still couldn't get the footage he needed. But as a publicity stunt, the New York shoot was a smashing success. All those photographers. All those photos, disseminated out into the wide world, of just one woman. It became known as the Shot Seen 'Round the World, sent out on the wires early that morning and landing in nearly every newspaper in America. And across the globe.

The crew broke down the set, the sun silently rising on the East River, its celestial glow no match for Marilyn's. Day in and day out, the sun rose over New York City. But Marilyn would be there for less than a week, heading back to her life in Hollywood. As George Sanders had once prophesized on the set of *All About Eve*, "I can see your career rising in the east like the sun."

Bruno Bernard, the photographer from Berlin who was shooting a story on Marilyn and Joe for *Redbook* magazine, got himself some breakfast and then headed over to the St. Regis. He needed a shot of the couple together and Joe had told him to come by. As he was about to knock on the door, he heard screams. The sex part was over and now it was time for the Hollywood violence. Bernard turned and left. Milton Krasner, the cinematographer on the shoot, was staying in the room next door to Joe and Marilyn and heard the screams as well. No one bothered to break it up or call the cops. Wife beaters were an accepted part of American life.

Later that morning, her bruises were covered up by her hairdresser, Gladys Witten. Joe flew back to California. Marilyn was even more of an international sensation than she had been the day before. But her marriage to Joe was over, an offering on the altar of worldwide fame.

That night, pretending everything was normal, Marilyn had dinner with Milton and Amy Greene at a French restaurant and then went dancing with them and some other friends at El Morocco. Milton was not only taking her photos that week but was planning to start a company with her, Marilyn Monroe Productions, to develop better roles for her so she didn't always have to play the dumb blonde. She would be president, Milton vice president.

That night, the Greenes noticed bruises on her back. On her return to Hollywood later that week, Marilyn filed for divorce after just eight months of marriage.

Because of the heckling in the background, Wilder would reshoot the subway grate scene on November 5 on a Hollywood soundstage. This one would be much less risqué, with the edge of the fluttering dress hovering over Marilyn's bare legs. There would be no exposed underwear. No skirt flying up over her ears. Marilyn asked Wilder if he was planning to keep the original footage for his private collection to use at his friends' stag parties. Always the gentleman, Wilder made sure the original location footage was lost. The only evidence of the shoot—one of the most iconic scenes in

Hollywood history—were the stills and a short, grainy black-and-white newsreel announcing the divorce.

And, of course, Jules's lush Kodachrome film, taken from five feet away. The only color-film footage to survive.

Jules developed it, spliced it together with some other home movies, screened it a few times for family, and then placed it with the rest of his growing collection of small domestic masterpieces. The film would stay stashed in his apartment, hiding for half a century.

Eight months after the shoot, to promote *The Seven Year Itch*, the famous shot of Marilyn's dress blowing up was placed in Times Square as a fifty-two-foot-high cutout of the star above the Loew's State marquee, the same theater where Robert Taylor and Maureen O'Sullivan had fallen in love on-screen in April 1938, when Jules had first come to New York. But even the cutout was too risqué and had to be replaced with a more demure version. Staring at the giant version of herself while incognito at a diner across the street, Marilyn told her friend Eli Wallach, "That's all they think of me."

The trailer for the movie would start with a wolf whistle and the shot of Marilyn on the subway grate. Though the original film posters featured her leaning out the window of the townhouse on Sixty-First Street, the PR for the movie—thanks to Shaw—now revolved around the billowing skirt.

The movie premiered on June 1, Marilyn's twenty-ninth birthday. Though they were divorced, DiMaggio went to opening night at the Loew's State with Marilyn, who wore a white cocktail dress with a plunging V neckline and her white fox stole. It wasn't cold enough for the matching muff. Joe, who was still in love with her, told her if he was her he would have divorced himself, too.

The Seven Year Itch would be the highest-grossing film of the year, taking in more than $5 million worldwide. Marilyn, the only good thing about the movie, was still being paid a mere $1,500 a week as per her seven-year contract. After the success of *The Seven Year Itch*, Fox negotiated a new contract, paying out at $100,000 per film.

For the wrap party at Romanoff's Restaurant in Hollywood, cutouts of Marilyn with her skirt blowing up were used as center-pieces on every table, surrounded by roses. It was the party of the year. Marilyn wore a bright red chiffon sweetheart dress and a white ermine wrap. She and Wilder's wife, Audrey, sang, "Let's Do It" for the crowd, which included the Hollywood A-list: Humphrey Bogart and Lauren Bacall, Gary Cooper, Claudette Colbert, agent Swifty Lazar, and producer Darryl Zanuck. And Clark Gable, the star whose name had once been borrowed for Superman's secret identity and whose fame had unwittingly saved the lives of Jules and his family. Like the father of the bride, Clark led Marilyn to the dance floor.

NIGHTS
OF
HORROR

DREAMS FOR
SALE
by
Gar King

ISSUE No. 15

THE COMIC BOOK SERIES THAT UPENDED AN INDUSTRY

CHAPTER 37

NIGHTS OF HORROR

QUEENS, SEPTEMBER 15, 1954

THE BEGINNING OF THE END CAME FOR HARRY DONENFELD on the very same day that Marilyn's dress blew up.

A team of New York City detectives descended on a small print shop across the East River in Richmond Hill, Queens. The quiet tree-lined neighborhood, tucked deep inside the borough, was a world away from Manhattan, unused to crowds or flashy police raids. The respectable Italian-, Irish-, and German-American families living in their modest two-story homes had no idea what had been going on in the Pilgrim Press offset printing operation all summer long. In a basement near the last stop on the elevated A train, twenty-seven-year-old Eugene Maletta had been churning out an edgy comic book called *Nights of Horror*. Maletta, caught in the act, was arrested for selling and distributing obscenity, his metal printing plates confiscated. A group of seventy-five detectives then fanned out across the city, seizing copies of the controversial comic book.

Though Maletta's horror comic had a limited run of a few thousand, all of New York had heard about it that summer. Horror comics had been gaining in popularity in America in the 1950s, providing cheap—seemingly harmless—thrills to teenage boys and adults alike. But screaming headlines that August told of a group of teenagers who were inspired by *Nights of Horror* to launch a crime spree throughout Brooklyn, horsewhipping girls, setting a homeless man on fire, and killing two others. Until Marilyn arrived on the subway grate, those murders were all anyone could talk about.

The accused teenagers were a bunch of Jewish kids from Williamsburg. Many of the poor Jewish immigrants who had settled on the Lower East Side in Harry's day had made the short journey across the Williamsburg Bridge, buying houses and creating a comfortable middle-class enclave. How could such good Jewish boys be led astray? In the months leading up to their trial, parents not just in Brooklyn but all across America were asking themselves, "Could this happen to my kid, too?"

The leader of the Brooklyn Thrill-Kill Gang, as it came to be known, was a tall, skinny eighteen-year-old redhead named Jack Koslow, who said the attacks were part of "a supreme adventure" and an effort to clean up the city streets of bums. His seventeen-year-old buddy Melvin Mittman, a big, beefy guy who played the accordion but spent most of his time at the gym, said he liked to use the bums' bodies as punching bags to see how hard he could hit. Koslow and Mittman were from good Jewish families, but both of them—incredibly—sported sad, teenage Hitler mustaches.

Koslow, the more disturbed of the two, had been trouble since second grade, when he had leapt up in class, pointed to his teacher, and yelled, "Let's get her!" By the time he was twelve, he had taught himself German so he could read and reread *Mein Kampf*.

With one of their accused gang members turning state's evidence, Koslow and Mittman were found guilty of torturing a vagrant by burning the bottoms of his feet, marching him seven blocks to the water's edge, and then drowning him in the East River. Koslow had told a court-appointed psychiatrist—none other than Dr. Fredric Wertham from Nuremberg, the anti–comic book crusader—that he read violent comic books like *Nights of Horror*, a cheap black-and-white booklet on sale in Times Square—and printed in Eugene Maletta's Queens basement.

The things Koslow had done—whipping young women and making his homeless victims kiss his feet—were activities laid out in the illustrated pages of *Nights of Horror*. An S&M fetish comic that made Harry's sex pulps look like fine art, *Nights of Horror* featured women and men dressed in black leather being tortured. Koslow had told Wertham that he had worn his black leather pants on the night of one of his rampages and that the black whip they had used to lash the girls in Williamsburg's McCarren Park was purchased for $2.69 from an ad in a comic book.

Koslow's confession led to the police raiding Eugene Maletta's Queens shop on September 15, eventually leading them to a larger pornography ring that sold magazines and books out of Times Square. Maletta's copublisher, a guy named Clancy who wrote the *Nights of Horror* "story lines," escaped prosecution, tossing his remaining scripts and artwork into Long Island Sound.

"ESTELLE, BY SIGN, INDICATED THAT SHE WISHED
TO HAVE THE MAID CONTINUE."

The terrible twist to the Thrill-Kill story was that a neighbor of Clancy's had drawn the horror comics. That neighbor was Joe Shuster—Jerry Siegel's partner and co-creator of Superman.

To make a living, Joe had done anonymous drawings for all sixteen issues of *Nights of Horror*. His characters looked just like Lois Lane, Clark Kent, Lex Luthor, and Jimmy Olsen, but in leather and brandishing bats, paddles, and whips. The typewritten, crude quality of the comic harkened back to the primitive DIY *Science Fiction* magazine that Joe and Jerry had published in high school back in Cleveland. Except the characters were whipping and torturing one another.

One story was titled "The Bride Wore Leather." Another, called "Slave Camp," starred the devil himself and involved a cruel female Nazi guard with a whip. Characters were named Clark, Jerry, and Joe. It's not clear if Joe was just desperate for cash or if he wanted to mess with Harry and Jack Liebowitz. Here in simple pen-and-ink line drawings were DC Comics' beloved characters, doing things that would make Harry's smoosh characters blush. *Nights of Horror* #17, which Maletta retitled *Hollywood Detective* in the chaos of the Thrill-Kill murders, featured a blond up-and-coming movie star named Nora (Norma!), who looked a lot like Marilyn Monroe, being tortured and stripped nearly naked, then tied up and placed inside an iron maiden.

When Harry first saw the characters in *Nights of Horror*, he no doubt recognized their faces and Joe's telltale style, with its simple, but clean, bold lines. The old pornographer in him probably laughed out loud and shouted, "That son of a bitch!" His and Jack's vengeance on Joe and Jerry had been turned around to bite them right in the ass. Artists both retired and in the current stable at DC Comics likely recognized Joe's style as well, but mum was the word. The connection between Superman and *Nights of Horror* would come to light nearly a half century later when comics expert

Gerard Jones would write about it. (Jones himself would eventually be convicted of possession of child pornography.)

Jack and Harry and the rest of the comics industry went into immediate damage control mode. The day after the Queens raid, they and their fellow comic book publishers held a press conference at the Waldorf, announcing a new-and-improved comics code and appointing their own comics czar, New York judge Charles Murphy, a former adviser to Mayor LaGuardia, to help rid the industry of obscenity and lurid images. They would also create a seal of approval promising that their contents were safe for young minds. Stores, under pressure from parents and priests, wouldn't carry comics without the seal.

When the Thrill-Kill story hit the press, Joe must have been terrified, worried he would be implicated in the case. Thrilled though he may have been that Harry and Jack and the rest of the legit comics industry were squirming, he surely never dreamed his art would cause anyone actual physical harm. Perhaps he encouraged Clancy to throw all the artwork in the Sound.

While the Thrill-Kill trial was still underway in late autumn, Joe ran a heartbreaking ad in the *New York Times* for new work in an attempt to move away from the horror comics:

Artists—Art Services

Comic-Cartoon Productions

For Advertising. Sales Promotion, Education and information, merchandising, Inter-organization relations.

CONTINUITY STRIPS, COMIC CREATIONS, HUMOROUS ILLUSTRATIONS, GAG PANEL CARTOONS.

Art Director: JOE SHUSTER
Artist-Creator of Superman

COMADIC PRODUCTIONS
34 PARK ROW. NEW YORK 38, N Y.
CO 7-3235

The best . . . at piggy bank rates

Season's Greetings to all our
Friends, everywhere

The Thrill-Kill case was tossed like kindling on the fire of the comic book burnings that had been scattered across the country. In February of 1955, the New York State Joint Legislative Committee to Study the Publication of Comics, with Dr. Wertham's help, laid out a point-by-point comparison of *Nights of Horror* and the crimes committed by the Thrill-Kill Gang. "The worst thing about the comic books," said Dr. Wertham, "is that they give complete courses in crime. I'll show you how these Brooklyn boys got their start."

Many publishers and distributors self-censored, folding their horror comics on their own. Bill Gaines, the son of Max, the publisher who had been the link between Harry and Jerry back in the 1930s, helping get Superman off the ground, had reengineered his father's business, and become one of the pioneers of the horror comics. Publishing titles like *Tales from the Crypt*, Gaines had a monthly circulation of 2.6 million before the Thrill-Kill hysteria. He now watched his sales drop off by a third. Due to protests from parents and religious groups, newsstands refused to carry his horror comics. The week of the Queens raid, Gaines announced he would stop publishing all of them—and instead focused on his *MAD* comic book, which he would change to a larger magazine format, partly to avoid the new comics code.

Though he surrendered to censorship, Gaines was nowhere near convinced the horror comics were tied to juvenile delinquency and said his new business strategy would have a whole other group angry at him—his college-age readers. "I don't think anyone was ever harmed by anything they read," said Gaines in the days leading up to the Thrill-Kill trial. "Neuroses are caused by real emotional experiences. Anyone who has studied psychiatry knows horror stories provide a harmless outlet for the hates that are normal to children. They can hate a figure on paper." But, he said, it was "suicidal to buck this kind of censorship." If he didn't appease the parents, they might drive him out of business altogether.

By 1956, Gaines and the rest of the industry had taken a major hit, with 650 comic book titles whittled down to 250 and hundreds of comics artists laid off. The *Nights of Horror* ban was eventually brought before the Supreme Court, which voted 5–4 in 1957 in favor of censorship. FDR's old Jewish friend and appointee Justice Felix Frankfurter, who had refused to believe news of the Nazi death camps, wrote the majority opinion, calling the magazine "dirt for dirt's sake."

Harry's luck was running out.

RADIO SHOW PRODUCER BOB MAXWELL, DISTRIBUTION HEAD
PAUL SAMPLINER, HARRY DONENFELD, JACK LIEBOWITZ, MAX GAINES,
AND EDITOR WHITNEY ELLSWORTH

CHAPTER 38

ALMOST FAMILY

NEW YORK, JUNE 1955

EVERY MORNING, FRED STERNBERG, FAYE'S FIFTEEN-YEAR-old son, would climb out of bed and then out of his family's first-floor apartment window on Tryon Avenue in the Bronx. It was more exciting than using the front door. He would take the subway to the Grand Central Palace, riding the elevator to the DC Comics offices on the ninth floor.

It was the summer of 1955 and Fred, Neil's younger brother, had aged out of summer camp. He was thrilled when Harry offered him a job—at Faye's request, of course—and told all his friends he would be working in Midtown for Superman.

After getting off the elevator, Fred would pass by the artists stable of more than a dozen men bent over their drafting tables creating line drawings, and even a few women inking in those drawings. Women weren't allowed to create comics, since publishers worried they would up and leave to get married at any time. Fred would then make his way past the computer room, which was filled with machines belching out coded cards, and technicians standing around and doing God knows what, figuring out circulation numbers, projecting sales. Fred didn't know and he didn't really care.

It was Fred's job to help ship the new comics out to newsstands, slapping labels on the packages, learning the names of cities all around the country he'd never heard of. But his main job was giving credit to the dealers who had returned the unsold comics, whose covers had been ripped off. DC would either pulp or sell the mangled comics to bargain outlets. Fred would set three or four of the coverless comics aside each day to read on the subway back home every night. He loved his job and was so fired up ripping off those jackets that his four coworkers in the department, all full-timers, got annoyed.

"Slow down, kid," one of them said. "You're making us all look bad."

Occasionally he would be sent into Harry's office on some errand and would be greeted by the nearly life-size picture of the Man of Steel, painted by comic artist H. J. Ward. Harry was usually in a meeting with the other top executives, but greeted Fred warmly, slapping his back and introducing him around as his nephew. As far as Fred knew, Harry was a relative, though he wasn't sure of the exact connection. Harry was part of Fred's *mishpucha*, the Yiddish word for extended or almost family, a rich uncle who came in and out of his life. And Harry was the richest guy Fred had ever met. When he was a teenager, he did the math and calculated that Harry made $1.38 per second.

Some days, Fred would walk into Harry's office and he would be in the middle of a manicure or a haircut. Harry's days of meeting Costello at the Waldorf for a cut and a shave were long over. Harry was much too important—at least for now. Every two weeks, the barber came to *him*, throwing the cutting cape around him in his office chair, the manicurist filing his nails and then painting them in clear polish.

At the end of the summer, Harry slapped Fred on the back once more, smiled, and told him that when he finished college, he had a job waiting for him at DC Comics. But as much as the kid loved it there, he had higher ambitions. "I think I'll probably do something else," Fred told him.

Harry was slightly taken aback when young Fred refused his job offer, but laughed it off and wished the kid good luck. It turned out, by the time Fred was finished with college, Harry would no longer have a job himself.

A month before Fred started his summer job at DC Comics, a Senate investigating committee on juvenile delinquency and pornography convened in New York City, headed by Senator Estes Kefauver of Tennessee. Kefauver had also headed the Senate investigation into organized crime, famously putting Harry's buddy Frank Costello on the stand in 1951. Costello, who was considered the boss of all bosses, had always kept a low profile, so his appearance on the televised hearings was a major event, causing millions of Americans to stop what they were doing and watch him answer the government's questions.

The new 1955 hearings called the publisher of *Nights of Horror*, Eugene Maletta, to testify, as well as a pornographer with ties to the Gambino crime family. The pornographer was not Harry Donenfeld, but a slightly younger, nastier version of Harry—a Jewish New Yorker by the name of Edward Mishkin, known to authorities as the "Sultan of Smut." Harry had given up his girlie magazines long ago. But maybe it was all too close for comfort for Jack.

Because of his friendship with Frank Costello, his past arrests for pornography, and his heavy drinking around town, Harry had become a liability to DC. Hoping to take the company public to eventually increase profits, Jack made himself president and bought Harry out for a million dollars, with a promise to keep Harry's son, Irwin, on the board of directors. Harry was slowly phased out, officially stepping aside finally in 1958 at the age of sixty-five.

His buddy Costello retired that same year, after surviving an assassination attempt in the lobby of his Majestic apartment building in May, his head grazed by a bullet from the gun of a young Vincent "the Chin" Gigante. Word on the street was that his old associate—and now rival—Vito Genovese had put the hit out on him in order to take over the Luciano crime family. The power grab worked; Costello relinquished control to Genovese and now spent most of his time gardening at his Sands Point, Long Island, home.

With a big chunk of the million dollars, Harry bought a fantastic new apartment on Park Avenue, after taking a cruise with Sunny, of course. The apartment was like a mansion in the sky, two full floors with a sunken living room that was about seventy feet long, with multiple couches and sitting areas. Servants greeted guests at the elevator, which opened up into the apartment. Over his fireplace, Harry hung the giant portrait of Superman, the one that had hung in his office, which he took with him when he moved out of the Grand Central Palace. Jack didn't argue. It was part of the divorce settlement.

Harry also bought a house in Sands Point for each of his grown kids, across the street from one another and right near Costello's twelve-room mansion. Costello and his wife never had any kids, and so they had long ago semi-adopted Harry's. Sands Point had been the fictional setting for East Egg in *The Great Gatsby*, whose eponymous character was a bootlegger like Harry once was. Moving his kids to Sands Point, where the Guggenheims and Vanderbilts owned houses, was the final proof that Harry had truly made it. He would have moved there himself, but it was too far from the New York City bars and clubs he loved so much.

Harry still saw Faye and Murray from time to time. When their son Neil got engaged, Harry threw him a big dinner party at his Park Avenue apartment. Neil became a dentist, and Harry his first patient, his chauffer driving him over to his appointments on Eighty-Ninth Street and Second Avenue. Neil's brother, Fred, who had turned down Harry's DC Comics job offer, became a podiatrist. The brothers often joked that they had a hoof-and-mouth group practice.

Though he was no longer working in the Grand Central Palace building, now and then Harry would visit. He would peek in on the stable of comic artists, take his son, Irwin, out to lunch, and maybe even saw Zelda Schnook flitting past in the lobby.

Marilyn Monroe, at the height of her stardom, would abandon Hollywood and move to New York City in the midst of the Thrill-Kill madness of 1954, migrating from apartment to apartment like most new arrivals in their twenties. Marilyn found freedom and new life in the city. She lived at the Gladstone Hotel right around the corner from the subway grate scene, on Fifty-Second Street, then moved into a three-room suite on the twenty-seventh floor of the Waldorf, the hotel where both Sunny and Frank Costello's mistress also lived.

Forming her production company with photographer Milton Greene, Marilyn met regularly with him at the Grand Central Palace to discuss business and to socialize with him and his wife, Amy. They went to dinner at nearby Gino on Lexington Avenue, or she would take her friends out for a big night on the town. One evening they showed up unannounced to see Sinatra at the Copa—which was partially owned by Frank Costello—and were seated ringside at a special table as the audience and Sinatra just watched, silently, mouths agape. She also spent time in the Greene's Connecticut country home, surrendering to domesticity, cooking and cleaning.

Marilyn took classes at the Actors Studio on Forty-Sixth Street and eventually settled into a beautiful eighth-floor apartment in Sutton Place, one of Manhattan's most exclusive enclaves. The building had a doorman and its own taxi lantern to attract cabs when the well-off tenants needed a ride. The lobby was luxurious, with a black-and-white-checkered floor and a fireplace and plush furniture. Across the street was a small pocket park with a view of the East River and the 59th Street Bridge, where Marilyn would sit on a bench sometimes with her little white Maltese terrier, a gift from Sinatra, which she named Maf (short for Mafia Honey). Her living room also had a view of the river and of Queens. With binoculars, she could have seen Eugene Maletta's print shop.

Marilyn's apartment was lined with shelves full of books that she had indeed read. Free of Hollywood and its sexist limits, Marilyn was happy in New York. At least for a while. She had her new production company and a new contract with Fox, starring in *Bus Stop*, where she played—surprise!—a burlesque singer, this time with an Ozarks drawl. In her first film production, she would play opposite Laurence Olivier, the showgirl to his prince. Though she was still playing showgirls, these scripts were smart and well written, a step up from *The Girl in Pink Tights*. Marilyn was not the dumb blonde they all thought she was or wanted her to be. She was uneducated, but she was always one step ahead.

Not so accidentally, she bumped into Brooklyn boy Arthur Miller at the Broadway premiere of *A View from the Bridge* in September 1955. They had met four years earlier on the Hollywood film set of the forgotten *As Young as You Feel* and had occasionally written to one another. But now Marilyn was a star. And living in New York City, Miller's hometown. She knew that America's favorite playwright could create a role for her that did not involve stripping. The prettiest girl in class was renouncing the jock for the brainy kid. This is not to say Marilyn wasn't attracted to Miller or felt no love for him. But Marilyn, in an era when women were not allowed to have any real desires besides home and family, was looking out for her own interests. The photographers, the film directors, the studio heads, the press, the publicists, the magazine editors and publishers—all the men who would claim they had helped her get to where she was going—had all been working for her. Her talent, her brilliance really, was making them think that they were doing her a big favor. And she did it all disguised as a dumb blonde.

Miller, forty, was already married with two children when he fell in love with Marilyn. He was a nerd with glasses, but a tall, charming nerd who was at the height of his fame. He was also the voice of the common man, which likely appealed to Marilyn. And though he could be arrogant and sometimes too intellectual for his own good, he was the champion of the underdog. Marilyn was so famous, and so beautiful, that even Miller's wife of sixteen years, Mary Slattery, couldn't argue when he fell in love with her. According to Miller, his marriage to Mary had already been floundering. They parted amicably, and Marilyn became friendly with Miller's children, Bobby and Jane.

Before marrying Miller, Marilyn converted to Judaism, meeting with a reformed rabbi and explaining her affinity not for just one Jewish man, but for the whole Jewish race. "Everybody's always out to get them, no matter what they do, like me," she explained. She would study from a Jewish prayer book from Miller's Avenue N synagogue in Brooklyn and even place a mezuzah on her doorframe.

Before the wedding, Marilyn visited Miller's parents in Midwood, Brooklyn, and, still searching for a family of her own, hit it off with them immediately. Outside the redbrick and white-clapboard house, the neighborhood kids climbed on each other's shoulders to get a look at the starlet through the Millers' windows. Miller's mother—whose name was Gussie—threw open a window and yelled, "Get out! Go on home!"

Gussie taught Marilyn to make gefilte fish, borscht, tzimmes, and matzoh balls. After eating several bowls of matzoh ball soup, Marilyn cracked, "Isn't there any other part of the matzoh you can eat?" Her mother-in-law also taught her some key Yiddish phrases like *bubbaleh*, *oy vey*, and *tuches*, prompting Marilyn to joke about her nude *Playboy* photo: "There I am with my bare *tuches* out."

As a conversion present, Gussie gave Marilyn a big brass-plated menorah. In its base was a mechanism that, when wound up, played the Israeli national anthem, "Hatikvah." The anthem's lyrics, about searching for a homeland, struck a chord with Marilyn, who had never really had a proper home. "Our hope is not yet lost," the song went. "The hope of two thousand years." America's favorite shiksa was now officially a member of the tribe.

The couple eventually settled around the corner from Marilyn's Manhattan place, in an all-white apartment on East Fifty-Seventh Street with a fireplace, a view overlooking the river, and a piano, the very same one that Gladys had bought Norma Jeane years before when she was a girl. Marilyn hoped she had finally found a family and was determined to have her own child with Miller. When she became pregnant, Marilyn happily filled her closet with maternity dresses, weights sewn into the hems so that they wouldn't blow up in the wind.

CLARK AND MARILYN ON THE SET OF *THE MISFITS*, 1960

CHAPTER 39

THE FALL

AMERICA, THE 1960S

EACH OF MARILYN'S THREE PREGNANCIES WOULD END IN A miscarriage, and her marriage to Miller would end in divorce, though she would stay close to his parents, taking his father as her chaperone to President Kennedy's birthday party at Madison Square Garden.

In their Manhattan apartment and in their Connecticut country home, Miller had penned Marilyn's last film, *The Misfits*. A Western about a group of horse wranglers who befriend a pretty divorcée, *The Misfits* was directed in 1960 by John Huston, who had given Marilyn her breakout role a decade earlier in *The Asphalt Jungle*. Her costars in *The Misfits* included her Actors Studio pal Eli Wallach, Montgomery Clift, and Clark Gable, whose character tells her, "When you smile, it's like the sun coming up."

The day after filming ended in the hot Nevada desert, Gable, fifty-nine, suffered a heart attack. His widow blamed Marilyn, saying her no-shows and late arrivals, making Clark wait in the brutal sun day after day after day, had caused him stress. Marilyn cried for two days when he died that November. The guilt added another layer to Marilyn's growing depression and anxiety. It wouldn't only be Clark's last film, but hers as well. Her last days were also the last days of the studio star system, an outmoded, financially unsound, sexist institution.

Wilder, who stayed friends with Marilyn, partially blamed Miller for her sadness and her downfall. Miller "was a little too resentful of his wife. I was not married to her. I didn't have to be patient and loving. But he was her husband and I thought he could have been more understanding." Her marriages didn't work, he quipped, "because Joe DiMaggio found out she was Marilyn Monroe and Arthur Miller found out she wasn't Marilyn Monroe."

To keep himself out of trouble, Harry traveled with Sunny and stepped up his philanthropy, donating money to build a youth center in Florida and helping create the Albert Einstein College of Medicine in the Bronx. His trips to Cuba, now a Communist stronghold, had come to an end. Harry made a 180-degree turn politically, joining the national council of the right-wing organization Common Cause. The CIA-backed, New York–based group was formed in 1947 to combat Communism and included such high-profile members as Hearst, Douglas Fairbanks Jr., and Samuel Goldwyn of MGM. Maybe Harry joined to cover up his Socialist past. But he made an about-face, and Superman went along with him.

Superman was no longer the Socialist champion of the masses he'd been in the thirties, but was now battling Communists and cheering on capitalism. He would eventually settle down, surrounded by Krypto, his superdog, and his long-lost cousin, Kara Zor-El, aka Supergirl. Unknown survivors of Krypton, Supergirl and her relatives would show up like illegal immigrants at Superman's door, wanting a part of the American dream. By the 1960s, Marvel's ironic, quirky superheroes more attuned to the counterculture made the overly patriotic Superman look uncool and corny. But Superman fought on, as he always did.

Harry, of course, partied on. Because of his *Playboy* distribution deal, Harry and his son, Irwin, were designated VIP key holders of the Playboy Club when it opened in Chicago in 1960, their key numbers, lucky 7 and *11*. When Harry or any VIP guest signed in, their nameplate would appear on a directory at the front of the club, so that when you entered, you knew exactly what other big-wigs were inside. The waitresses, famously dressed as bunnies in their satin, skintight outfits, matching ears, and white cotton tails, served cigarettes, cocktails, and red meat to the mostly male guests, who constantly pawed and groped them. From certain VIPs, some bunnies would accept room keys for extra money to continue the partying in private. It was as if Harry had died and gone to heaven.

While Harry was living the high life, Jerry Siegel was struggling to pay the rent on a one-bedroom apartment in Great Neck, Long Island, which he shared with his second wife, Joanne (aka Lois Lane) and their young daughter, Laura. Over the years, Jerry tried all kinds of strategies to shine a light on DC Comics' mistreatment of him and Joe. He went on a hunger strike. He picketed outside Harry's home. Finally, Joanne wrote Jack Liebowitz a letter in 1959. She asked him if he wanted to see a headline: "Creator of Superman Starves to Death." So Jack rehired Jerry to write scripts, but without any creative control or even a byline. DC Comics lowered his rate from $50 to $10 a page—right back to where he and Joe had started in 1938. It was humiliating for Jerry, but he was desperate. And, of course, still angry. A few years later, with the rights to Superman about to expire, Jerry filed for renewal of the copyright. But so did DC. They won. And Jerry was banished, this time forever.

In 1966, he and Joanne moved with their daughter to California. Joanne was unwell and they thought the climate would help. And maybe Jerry could land some writing work. But all he could find was a job as a clerk typist for the state's Public Utilities Commission.

Somehow, Joe Shuster was doing even worse. He had left the

horror comics behind, but anonymously drew for pornographic magazines. But even that petered out. By the 1960s, he was nearly blind, living with his mother on Long Island and working as a storeroom clerk and deliveryman. Legend has it that at one point, he delivered a package to the DC Comics offices, causing Jack to toss him a few bucks to buy a new coat, telling him to never return to the building again. Some say Harry stepped up and paid for Joe's eye surgery. But Harry never talked about it. There was the story about Joe being picked up by a cop while freezing without a coat on a bench in Central Park. The cop took pity on him and bought him a bowl of soup. When some kids went by holding Superman comics, Joe drew his famous character for them on a paper napkin. They looked at him like he was crazy.

In 1961, Gussie suffered a fatal heart attack while staying at the Fontainebleau in Miami Beach. And though it freed up Harry to be with Sunny full-time, something important was lost for Harry. Gussie had been with him since he was a nobody and knew him better than anybody. Now there was no one to give him a hard time when he drank too much or didn't come home at night, or for weeks at a time.

The following year, Harry booked a cruise with Sunny and had planned on marrying her during their trip. A week before they sailed, Harry really tied one on while clicking through the channels on his gigantic color TV console, more a piece of furniture than a screen. Replacing Superman in the ratings were the Beverly Hillbillies and the Jetsons, one family poking fun of the nouveau riche and another blasting into cartoon space. The landscape, not just of television but of the world, was changing right before Harry's tired eyes. Pushing himself up in his armchair to get more ice and a small refill, Harry fell and hit his head. When he opened his eyes, he realized he'd been out for quite a while. There was some dried blood on his head, but he was still pretty drunk, so he simply crawled into bed and was found the next morning by the housekeeper.

Another version of the story had him falling in the shower with Sunny at the Waldorf. His kids would joke that Gussie had come down from heaven and kicked him.

However the fall happened, Harry wound up in a three-week coma. After surgery, he woke up with a hell of a headache and no memory, no recollection of Irwin or his daughter, Peachy, or of Jack or Superman. He couldn't remember his childhood on the Lower East Side, the gangs, the mobsters, the Prohibition booze and girlie pulps. Not a flicker of those Marilyn magazine covers or of World War II, Cuba, or his Socialist days in the East Village. All of it, nearly every last memory, erased. Now and then he would look around for Gussie and ask her to bring him a Heineken. He also talked incessantly of the 1923 New York Giants, who had lost the World Series that year to the Yankees.

The December after Harry's fall, a Playboy Club finally opened in New York, less than two miles from his apartment, and though Harry was still a VIP key holder, he would never go. He had no idea what *Playboy* even was. Crippled by paralysis, he would sit in his luxury apartment and receive visitors he couldn't recognize. Frank Costello would drop in from time to time. But Harry had no idea who he was. He didn't even recognize Sunny. And it broke her heart. Sunny loved Harry, but not enough to hang around and take care of him for the rest of his life. Still in her early fifties, she married another admirer that year, a fifty-nine-year-old widower with a grown daughter and several grandchildren. Sunny refused to be called Grandma.

A few months after Harry's fall, Marilyn would also be found in bed by her housekeeper. But unlike Harry, Marilyn wouldn't hang on. She would die of a drug overdose in her new Brentwood home, her back tan, her blond hair tousled like on that Milton Greene ballet dress shoot, one hand on the telephone receiver. In the weeks before her death, she had been in the process of decorating her new house, still searching for the home she'd never had. The small end table—one of the only pieces of furniture in the bedroom—was cluttered with prescription pill bottles. The brass, musical menorah Gussie Miller had given her was sitting silently on the mantelpiece in her living room.

DiMaggio claimed the body and arranged her funeral, placing a half dozen roses on her grave twice a week for the next twenty years.

Harry died three years later at the age of seventy-one; Sunny, naturally, went to the funeral. In his will, Harry not only left her a small fortune but called her "my beloved." It made Sunny cry.

After Harry's death, DC Comics was acquired by the parking lot giant Kinney, a Jewish-owned company that had moved into mergers and acquisitions. Kinney delivered a $60 million payday for Jack, but the sale forced Harry's son, Irwin, out of the picture. Kinney, with the rights to DC's characters, then swallowed up Warner Bros., which would pioneer the superhero film genre with 1978's *Superman* starring Christopher Reeve. The DC and Marvel films would make untold fortunes, and eventually devour the Hollywood movie industry whole. A-list stars and directors—the Marilyns and Wilders of a new generation—would bow down to the superhero blockbuster film gods.

In 1975, while the first blockbuster Superman movie was still in production, Jerry Siegel put out a press release placing a curse on the film. "I hope it super bombs!" he wrote. He called Jack Liebowitz out for leaving him and Joe destitute while Jack and Warner Bros. were about to reap millions. "You hear a great deal about The American Dream," Jerry said. "But Superman, who in the comics and films fights for 'truth, justice and the American way,' has for Joe and me become An American Nightmare."

Because the film was so high-profile, newspapers and television talk shows ate up the story, shaming Warner Bros. into taking action. Jerry and Joe, who had been whitewashed from DC's history for nearly thirty years, would finally win one battle against Goliath: an annual stipend of $30,000 and their names restored as creators in the movie's opening credits—and in the many Superman films and comics that followed.

American justice was delayed. But had finally arrived.

JULES AND EDITH

CHAPTER 40

A LEGEND MOST

NEW YORK, 1969

IN THE SUMMER OF 1969, THE ADOPTED COUNTRY THAT Jules loved was nearly unrecognizable to him, young people protesting a new unwinnable war, Charles Manson and his followers murdering Hollywood's elite, Muhammad Ali convicted of dodging the draft, and the gay community fighting the cops down at the Stonewall Inn—a former speakeasy during Prohibition. But that summer, both young and old were gathered together to celebrate decades of mitzvahs that Jules had performed, little actions that had made life easier for his fellow men and women on the Upper East Side. Jules was feted by a neighborhood group and given an award for his work in the community. The whole family, many of whom had escaped Nazi Germany or were the offspring of those survivors, were seated in the hotel ballroom on a Sunday afternoon at round banquet tables, crystal chandeliers dangling overhead, a band playing.

Despite—or maybe because of—his sadness over the deaths of his sister Cilly and Edith's parents, Jules went at life full-force. He was unfailingly cheerful in public, always helping new arrivals find jobs in New York City, throwing weddings at the local synagogue and receptions in his apartment for refugees, then driving them home all the way to Brooklyn in his big convertible when the festivities were over. "When there is room in the heart, there is room in the house," he would say. He loved meeting new people, partly because it guaranteed a new rapt audience for the stories that his family had heard dozens of times. He told of his life in Berlin and his escape. He talked of his love of New York and its politics. And of Israel and his siblings living there. And of the night he shot the footage of Marilyn Monroe, though by now the film was lost somewhere amid dozens of family films.

Though he had been forced out of Germany, he still considered himself a proud Berliner. Jules loved spending time in Central Park, especially when the German soccer teams practiced there. He would chat them up in his native tongue and bounce their ball off his balding head. When he was out to dinner with his grandchildren, he would always scold them for being too noisy and say, "German children are so much better behaved than you." But Jules would never return to Germany for fear of what he would find, preferring to remember what it was like before the war.

Despite his love of Germany, Jules was also a staunch Zionist. He helped found the Jewish Friends Society, raising money for Israel, visiting the sick and lonely in New York, and helping raise money for the needy both in the States and overseas. Not out of guilt or for glory. But because he knew he was lucky to be alive. He was here for a reason. Like that lone survivor from Krypton.

Jules would become president of both the Fifth Avenue Synagogue and his Lexington Avenue/Sixty-First Street block association, flying from one small disaster to another on his bicycle, calling ambulances for people, getting prescriptions filled in the middle of the night, assisting an old woman who had fallen off a stepladder, or simply coming by to talk to those who were lonely. Instead of 911, neighbors called Jules. He was a member of the precinct neighborhood watch and so had strong connections to the NYPD. When someone was in trouble, Jules came to the rescue.

He and Edith planted trees on the block, invited young couples new to the city over for Sabbath dinner, and delivered prayer books to those who needed them. And Jules continued to be the most entertaining guy in the room, pretending to play Edith like an upright bass at every party and family gathering, including this one. By this time, the entire family had gotten in on the routine, each one pretending to play their favorite imaginary instrument, with Mollie—who had the best voice—singing lead.

Jules was thrilled to be the official center of attention and would greet every guest at the door as they checked the white-tableclothed table for their assigned-seating cards. There were hugs for those he hadn't seen lately. And kisses for those he had.

With a long list of his rescues and good deeds, Jules was welcomed to the stage. He thanked the emcee and then recounted the story, once again, of his escape from Berlin, of his coming to New York in search of a sponsor. Like all those who had escaped the Nazis, his survival had been a combination of intuition, intelligence, and luck. If it wasn't for all those who had died, the series of incredible events would make you think that maybe there was a God after all. Jules certainly still believed there was.

In his speech, he would thank God and remember those who never made it over to safety. He would tell the crowd to always keep their loved ones alive in their stories. Because it was only there that they survived. Whole villages had been murdered in the Holocaust, with no one left to even remember their names.

Stories, he would say, are what bind us together not just as Jews, but as humans. Not just stories like the ones from the Torah, though they had been written to give us a shared connection, shared ancestors. But Hollywood stories and comic book stories and the stories you told one-on-one or to a crowd like this today. They brought us together as listeners, but also bound us in more direct ways. They connected us. If you dug down deep enough, your story was intertwined with every other person's story. It wasn't just a matter of coincidence. We were all part of a vast network of interconnected narratives, so shouldn't we try and help each other to make the narrative a happy one?

You had to keep your eyes and ears sharp to know when that window opened or that door was flung wide. Harry had connected with Faye, who had connected with Jules, and that connection had saved his life. Marilyn had connected with Harry's magazines and they had been seen by Howard Hughes in that adjustable hospital bed and that had led to her fame. Clark Gable had served as Jules's cover to get back into Nazi Germany to save his family, but had also been undone by the force of nature that was Marilyn. Jules had connected with Marilyn on that cold summer night in September 1954 and so she, too, had become part of his story. The story of his life. Once you were gone, all that was left were the stories. At the end of the day, they were all we had.

So Jules once again told the story of his return to Berlin to fetch Edith and young Helen, nodding at Edith in the crowd, who sat smiling at their guest-of-honor banquet table, the chair next to hers empty. Edith had heard this story before, of course, and could recite it herself word for word in her head. But she always smiled when he told about lying his way past the Nazi guards with his fib about being Clark Gable's agent. He was now rounding his way home, to the part of standing on that long visa line with Edith, pinching young Helen's bottom to make her scream, when an actual scream went up from the audience.

Edith had slumped over at their table. Jules jumped from the podium and in a flash was at his wife's side. She had a pulse, but was unconscious. A mumbling wave of chatter and then panic rippled through the crowd as a doctor, the husband of a concert pianist in the audience, ran over. Dr. Herman examined Edith, and with Jules's help moved her body to the ballroom floor. "Call an ambulance," someone yelled. "I already did," someone yelled back.

"She's had a stroke," Dr. Herman said to Jules, kneeling beside him. Jules felt dizzy and nearly fell to the floor.

As the crowd murmured, most not knowing whether they should stay or leave, some joining in a circle around them, Dr. Herman saw that Edith was no longer breathing. But her heart was still beating. He called to one of the banquet waitresses and carefully told her, "I need you to bring me a sharp steak knife and a plastic straw." She looked dazed. "Now," he said. "Hurry." He turned to Jules and explained. "I need to perform an emergency tracheotomy."

When the waitress returned seconds later, Dr. Herman made a small slit in the hollow of Edith's throat, blood trickling out, and gently shoved the straw inside, pushing it in about two inches. He bent over and breathed twice into the straw and, suddenly, Edith started breathing again.

A few moments later, Edith was taken away in an ambulance, Jules by her side, holding her hand the whole way, trying to stay calm. He had to be strong for Edith. "Don't leave me, my love," he would gently whisper to her in German. "We've survived so much. Don't leave me now." Jules would pray to God in the ambulance and ask him to please save his wife. From the God that had taken so much from him, this man who had done so much for so many would ask this very small favor. Edith's life.

At the hospital, Edith was given only weeks to live. Half her body was paralyzed and she couldn't speak. Doctors wanted to do experimental surgery, but Jules wouldn't allow them, afraid she would die on the operating table. Edith was more than just his wife; she was his fellow escapee, the person who had survived beside him, the only person on the planet who had lost as much as he had. She not only knew his story but had witnessed it with him. If not for her and Helen, he may not have ever even left Berlin. They had been his future, his reason for living.

Edith spent nine weeks in Lenox Hill Hospital and five weeks in a convalescent home. So that Jules didn't have to carry Edith up and down three flights of stairs, a neighbor rented him a ground-floor apartment in a townhouse around the corner, charging him $560, the exact amount of Jules's reparations check each month from Germany. The new place was across the street from the brownstone where that first scene with Marilyn had been shot for *The Seven Year Itch*.

When Jules saw the backyard of the new apartment, he had a flashback to his and Edith's Berlin place, with its cobblestones and ivy-covered wall, the same courtyard where Helen had taken her first baby steps. They had been so happy there as a family. So long ago. Could it be three decades had passed since they'd fled Nazi Germany? Now his Edith was dying. How could it be?

Though the doctors wanted to keep Edith hospitalized, Jules insisted she spend her last days at home with him. She was only fifty-four years old. The rest of his life without her stretched like a seemingly endless void before him in his imagination.

But Jules's prayers were answered. Weeks turned into months, months into years. Years stretched into decades.

Jules renovated the sunny backyard, which he called the Garden of Edith, planting white-edged hosta, flowering rhododendrons, and English ivy. He made it look just like the courtyard in Berlin where they had been newlyweds. Now they were growing old, but would grow old together.

The couple spent countless hours in the garden, an old and ailing Adam and Eve, their grandchildren running around on the slate and white pebbles amid the mimosa and spruce trees. Dustin Hoffman lived in an apartment in the building behind the garden and they would sometimes see the actor come and go. But more often his cat would come and visit, curling in Edith's lap or playing with the grandchildren, who called Jules *Opi* and Edith *Omi*—German terms of endearment for Grandpa and Grandma.

Jules always put out cut-up strawberries, vanilla ice cream, and red pistachios, which would turn his grandchildren's fingers pink. He would tell them about when he came to New York back in 1938 for the first time, searching for a sponsor. The film of his life should be called *The Signature*, he told his grandchildren, since so much had depended on that sponsor.

Dr. Herman and his wife became dear friends and would come for dinner in the garden from time to time, Jules thanking him over and over for saving Edith's life. He would tell them about Marilyn, too, but they didn't believe it, without Edith to back him up. The stroke had left her unable to speak.

Jules closed his fur shop, but kept a pelt room in the second bedroom of his new apartment. It was in this pelt room where his films were kept. He had all kinds of fur scraps and would occasionally put the leftover pelts to good use—making tall black Russian hats for the cast at his granddaughter's grammar school production of *Fiddler on the Roof*, giving a fancy fur collar like the one Marilyn sported in New York to his niece as a present, or making matching white lambswool coats and muffs to keep his grandchildren warm, just as he had for his own girls. They were blond, beautiful, and all-American.

The December after the stroke, Jules was feted yet again for his service to the community. His sister Golda died that year at the age of seventy-one, her body worn out by the hard labor she'd been forced to perform at the camps. Edith was in her wheelchair and stayed at home with their daughter, Evy. This time the Jewish Friends Society celebrated Jules's good deeds at a luncheon at the Piccadilly Hotel, where he had stayed back in 1938 when he'd first come to New York and where he and Edith would come to ballroom dance. It was December 7, Pearl Harbor Day, and the fourth day of Hanukkah.

After Jules's nine-year-old granddaughter, Rayna, lit the Shabbas candles on the long table of honor, he stepped up to the podium and gave his speech, telling his tale of escape once more and praising Edith for her courage and help in serving the community all these years. He paid tribute to those in the family who had not survived and to Golda, who had survived so much.

As the guests ate dinner, an Israeli folk musician, Miriam Bernett, sang songs in Yiddish and Hebrew: the Israeli national anthem, "Fryer Foigol" (Free Bird), "Saeinu" (Sun of the Desert), and the haunting ballad "Laila" (Night). "Night" told the tragic story of three knights coming to the rescue in the dark. One is killed by a beast. A second is killed by the sword. And the third, the singer tells the listener, does not remember your name.

Night, night—the wind blows stronger
Night, night—the trees whisper
Night, night—only you still wait
Go to sleep, the road is empty.

Though Edith never regained her speech or her ability to walk, she was fully cognizant, her gray, sad eyes very much alive. Jules dressed her fashionably every day and lovingly combed her dark hair each night. They couldn't ballroom dance anymore, but Jules was more devoted to his wife than ever.

He took Edith to see films at the neighborhood theater, which always made room for her wheelchair. He cooked and cleaned and lovingly decorated the apartment with hip Fiorucci posters from the nearby Italian designer store, one featuring a model in a leopard skin outfit, as well as several celebrity Blackglama fur ads that read "What Becomes a Legend Most?" Sophia Loren, Liza Minnelli, and Pavarotti in black-and-white, swathed in fur, stared into the room, greeting the relatives and friends who would visit.

Edith would outlive most of their relatives, surviving another twenty-six years. Thanks to Jules. Like a superhero couple, Jules and Edith, even in her wheelchair, continued to visit the sick and comfort the lonely. They volunteered at Hunter College, demonstrating to faculty and students in the physical therapy program how to care for a wheelchair-bound loved one. Rain, snow, or shine, Jules would push Edith eight blocks over to the campus. Jules also volunteered at Lenox Hill, making calls to discharged patients to make sure they carried through on their follow-up appointments, arranging transportation and whatever help they needed. He rode his bicycle with the basket on the front all over town because it was good exercise and gave him the ability to weave in and out of the ever-growing Manhattan traffic. Without a cape, the bicycle was the best mode of transportation in the metropolis. He sometimes brought Edith along to Lenox Hill to visit those who were sick, to give them hope and inspire them to keep fighting.

For their fiftieth anniversary a friend sent a tribute: "The history of the human spirit does not rest on great wars and great nations. Life on this earth is not perpetually affirmed by the great feats of mankind. . . . For the past half century your sharing and giving to each other teaches us about life and love at its very best."

The true superhero tales were all around us, not in comic books and blockbuster films, but in those like Jules who survived and helped those around him survive. Day after day after day after day. Night after night after night.

Jules remembered your name and he was coming.

FAYE AND MURRAY STERNBERG

CHAPTER 41

THE FINAL FIGHT

NEW YORK, 1980S AND LOS ANGELES, 1990S

WHEN MURRAY STERNBERG DIED IN 1981, JULES SENT A LET-
ter of condolence telling Faye that he would say Kaddish for a year,
thanking them for their help in getting him and Edith and Helen
out of Nazi Germany by asking that once-in-a-lifetime favor of
Harry. "Although on every occasion we paid tribute for saving our
lives, it cannot be uttered often enough," he wrote, "as it was written 'he who saves a life' is as if he has saved the whole world."

The following year, the Piccadilly Hotel was knocked down,
its ballroom reduced to rubble.

One of Jules's final missions was battling a huge development
that was going up in the early 1980s a few doors down from him.
The thirty-six-story building, a planned mix of retail and luxury co-
ops costing up to a million dollars each on the corner of Sixty-First
Street and Third Avenue, was completely out of scale with the rest
of the neighborhood—the brownstones, the doll hospital, and the
townhouse right across the street, where Marilyn had filmed that
first scene for *The Seven Year Itch*. Jules led the charge against the
megadevelopment with his neighbors at community and planning-
board meetings. But the young developer of the building had the
money and the muscle behind him to win the fight.

The $125 million building was completed in 1984, built by
workers controlled by Fat Tony Salerno, head of the Genovese

crime family, who was later indicted by the US Attorney for the Southern District of New York—Rudy Giuliani. Salerno was convicted of bid-rigging on the project.

The co-op was so high it blocked out the sun in the Garden of Edith. But that was the least of the neighborhood's problems. During construction, a stone derrick rigger from Staten Island working on the project fell thirty-three floors, bouncing off the building, his body parts landing in the backyards of Jules's neighbors. A group of co-op owners eventually sued the developer for over $10 million for shoddy workmanship and building materials after cement from its curved, cracked balconies also fell into the neighborhood. They also asked the judge to force the developer to take his name off the building.

The young developer's name was Donald Trump.

Clear across the country, Billy Wilder was fighting his own battles. Wilder didn't speak of his mother in public, but his failure to get her out of Europe became a private obsession. He assumed she was sent to Auschwitz, but never learned the details of her death. Around 1992, seeking some closure, the eighty-five-year-old legendary director visited fellow director Steven Spielberg in an effort to purchase the rights he held to a novel by Australian writer Thomas Keneally. But Spielberg was about to travel to Poland to start filming. He apologized to his idol but said he had come knocking a little too late. The book was called *Schindler's Ark*.

Though Wilder never knew it, Eugenia's half brother, Michael, submitted testimony to the Yad Vashem Holocaust memorial in the 1950s about Eugenia's fate. She had indeed been moved to the Kraków ghetto, whose first death transports began in 1941. But like Golda, she was able to stay in the ghetto for an extended period. Because her husband, Bernard, supplied bottle stoppers to the German military, they were left alone in their small one-bedroom apartment with the bathroom in the hall. But two years later, in 1943, the ghetto was liquidated.

Eugenia was moved not to Auschwitz, but to the notorious Kraków-Płaszów concentration camp, which had been built atop two Jewish cemeteries. Those who were too old for forced labor were shot on-site. The camp was run by Amon Goth, an especially sadistic Nazi who was known to release his two Great Danes on prisoners and would not have breakfast each morning until he shot at least one person himself from his balcony. Some prisoners from Płaszów were sent to Czechoslovakia to work at an enamel factory, where conditions were good. The factory, which also produced ammunition to guarantee it remained open during the war, was owned by a man named Oskar Schindler. But Wilder's mother never made it to Schindler's factory. She was sixty-one years old and unwell, with gallbladder problems and nerve damage in her right hand. She was immediately shot or was quickly worked to death at Płaszów, one of about eight thousand prisoners murdered there.

One of the main characters of Spielberg's *Schindler's List* was Amon Goth, played by Ralph Fiennes, and the camp in the film was the same one where Eugenia was murdered. It was a terrible coincidence.

After the film's release, Wilder wrote an essay for a German magazine lamenting the fact that younger generations were growing more and more ignorant of the Holocaust. Some were even doubting that it had happened at all. "If the concentration camps and the gas chambers were all in my imagination, then please tell me, where is my mother?" he asked.

Billy Wilder died at the turn of the new century without knowing exactly what had happened to Eugenia.

The secret location of the original footage from *The Seven Year Itch* also died with Wilder. He was buried in the same cemetery as his friend Marilyn Monroe. His tombstone, partially quoting the last line of *Some Like It Hot,* reads:

I'M A WRITER

BUT THEN

NOBODY'S PERFECT

When Hugh Hefner passed away, he was buried in the same cemetery, in a crypt right next to Marilyn's, which he had bought for $75,000, even though he had never even met her. Hefner's comics were never published.

In 1992, right around the time that Joe Shuster died, DC Comics killed off Superman, a publicity stunt to draw attention to the superhero amid declining comic book sales. Of course, once sales shot back up that year with six million sold, Superman would be resurrected in 1993. Jerry Siegel died four years later, still bitter about his treatment at the hands of Harry and Jack. Jerry's daughter, Laura, would continue the legal battle against Warner Bros., once again claiming ownership of the copyright. "Just like the Gestapo," she dramatically wrote to DC, "your company wants to strip us naked of our legal rights." Harry, meanwhile, would remain conspicuously absent from the official history of DC Comics and Superman, his name not even a whisper on its website.

His name was not even mentioned by those he had saved from the Holocaust, sworn to secrecy by Harry himself. But those original seven—Jules, Edith, Helen, Mollie, David, and their sons, Bob and Fred—and their two generations of children and grandchildren—twenty-one people in all—owed him their lives.

JULES AT THE TURN OF A NEW CENTURY

CHAPTER 42

LOST AND FOUND

NEW YORK CITY, 2004

IN HIS FINAL YEARS, JULES WAS A DEAD RINGER FOR FELLOW Berliner Albert Einstein, with his unkempt white hair and big droopy white mustache. He was mistaken for him while riding his bicycle near Columbus Circle one afternoon by a crew from Italian *Vogue*, who asked if he would pose with the tall, leggy models in a layout called "Beauty and the Brain." He obliged, of course. Jules cut quite a figure, dressed in his seersucker suit, suspenders, bow tie, and cap. He was still as sharp as ever.

After Edith's death in 1993, Jules spent another decade in their apartment until he was evicted by the Andrew W. Mellon Foundation, which had bought the townhouse and wanted to reconfigure the property. Jules and his family fought the eviction as hard as he had fought Trump, holding out as long as possible. The Mellon Foundation jackhammered around him, turning his home into a construction zone, closing the main entryway and making ninety-two-year-old Jules shuffle, bent with age, through a tunnel to the delivery entrance each day. Still, Jules refused to move. This was a man who had survived the Nazis. He was not about to let anyone take his home from him ever again.

He loved the Garden of Edith, even if the monstrous Trump building now blocked most of his light. His life was here in these four rooms, his papers, his photos, his keepsakes, his fur pelts and old home movies. At a neighborhood meeting, Mellon representatives came to try to win over the community. But Jules's neighbors, many of whom he had saved with an ambulance call or a kind gesture, were livid, shouting down the intruders.

Because of his age, his living conditions, and the protracted yearlong battle that he was too old to fight, Jules began to deteriorate. All that was left of his memory was the greatest hits reel—his escape from Germany, taking care of Edith, the night he shot the footage of Marilyn, and resentment at President Kennedy for his "*Ich bin ein Berliner*" speech. Being an actual Berliner, Jules had been annoyed by it and still was—four decades later—as if JFK had said it yesterday.

After fighting for six months, the family finally reached an agreement with Mellon: Jules would move into a new garden apartment across from Central Park on the West Side in 2004, with Mellon agreeing to pay the $5,000 difference in rent each month for the rest of his life. His daughter Evy would move with him and be his caretaker. Six months after the move, Jules died in his sleep. After surviving Hitler, a near-death escape not once but twice, Jules was done in by the cruel world of New York City real estate. Evy was killed six months later, hit by the sideview mirror of a passing car while riding her bike without a helmet on the Central Park transverse road.

While packing up her grandfather for that fatal move across town, Jules's granddaughter Bonnie came across a giant stash of film in the pelt room. No one ever really liked to go back there because it was such a mess. Some of the film was in metal canisters, but most was not even on reels. It was in big tangled balls, as if there had been a major projector mishap decades ago, some film loose and some shoved inside shopping bags. Bonnie's husband was a filmmaker and, like Bonnie, had always been fascinated by one of her grandfather's more outlandish tales, one that surely couldn't be true. It was the tale of the night he had shot footage of Marilyn Monroe.

Bonnie had heard the story dozens of times. But if it was true, she thought, how come she had never seen it?

Bonnie and Jeff gathered the hundreds of unlabeled reels and took them home to their apartment downtown on West Sixteenth Street. That night, Jeff carefully wound the loose film, some of it brittle and in danger of breaking. After a few repairs with splicing tape, they started looking at the reels, one by one, using a light box, spooling the film by hand from reel to reel. Jeff counted about seventy-five rolls of 8 millimeter and fifty rolls of 16 millimeter. There were the family outings to Atlantic City and Evy's graduation, Helen's wedding and the pro-Israel rallies. Ushi and Golda, smiling for the camera, happy to be safe in America. Reel after reel after reel. But then, off its reel in a plastic D'Agostino's grocery bag, Jeff found another film. When he held it up to the light to look at it, he could see it: The white dress. The blond hair and supple skin. He yelled to Bonnie, who was in the next room, "I found it! It's really here!"

Bonnie knew right away that he meant Marilyn. So they sat down and watched it together, a half century after it was shot. When Bonnie called her grandfather, she excitedly said, "We found the Marilyn footage!"

"Of course you did," said Jules nonchalantly.

The three-minute-and-seventeen-second film starts with a short series of black-and-white stock filler that Jules must have bought in a film store, which proclaims WORLD PREMIERE in bold white letters. Behind the title is the drawing of a baby's head, with baby clothes and a row of baby bottles, followed by silhouettes of kids pulling a wagon that reads KIDDIE KAPERS. Scratched onto two frames are the words *20 Year Itsch*—which is so small and fleeting that it can't be seen unless you completely stop the film. It was a private little joke for Jules, who had celebrated twenty years with Edith in September 1954. Or maybe it was his way of secretly marking his rare footage, in case it was stolen. Because what he shot was a treasure.

Suddenly, in crisp, colorful 16 millimeter, there is Marilyn. The first minute is Marilyn on Sixty-First Street, standing on the stoop of that black townhouse in her white bathrobe, as she waves to the adoring aviation high school students and to neighbor and actor Roddy McDowall and whoever else showed up that Monday morning bright and early. She waves straight at Jules's camera. Sam Shaw flits past. Tom Ewell makes his way up the street as Marilyn blow-dries her hair in the second-floor window.

White dots intrude into the frame, which means that the roll has ended. But instead of the subway grate scene, we see a Shriners parade. The Shriners, a fraternity affiliated with the Masons, visited New York for their national convention in the summer of 1953. Their colorful parade marched past Jules's apartment and so, naturally, he had filmed it. He spliced it in here as a joke, to make us wait for the main event, Marilyn. At thirty-two seconds, the Shriners parade is excruciatingly long.

A Shriner string band from Cincinnati dressed in bright orange outfits makes its way down Sixty-Second Street on a float, as fellow Shriners watch from behind a blue police barricade at the curb. A collection of clowns, one dressed as a baby and being pushed in a stroller, glides by. A Shriners contingent from Atlanta passes with Confederate flags flying and the head of their temple held aloft in a sedan chair by eight of his fellow Shriners. A man dressed as the devil with horns and a pitchfork walks past, right off the cover of one of Harry's *Hot Tales* magazines, as well as a man dressed in prison stripes bound in fake chains. A cop clown, a hobo clown. Men in old-fashioned bathing suits ride on a tiny Ferris wheel atop another float, followed by Shriners from Kentucky dressed like hillbillies with long fake rifles. A clown smoking a cigar rides a giant tricycle. Trick cars pop wheelies down the street. Life's rich pageant in all its absurd glory.

Another intertitle finally announces OUR BABY, with the baby head from the film's first frame floating inside a big heart.

And suddenly, there she is again, Marilyn, her full body in view from five feet away. It's the shot we've all been waiting for. The shot seen around the world, not in still, but in moving, living, luxuriously saturated Kodachrome. The lost footage of one of the most iconic moments in American film history.

For a minute and a half, Marilyn moves and breathes and is alive again, not on television or up on a wide screen, but in a home movie that hardly anyone has ever seen. The American dream in flesh and blood. She holds a red-and-white-striped scarf in one hand and a white clutch in the other and tries to hold down the famous white pleated dress. It billows up like a paratrooper's parachute, like those parachutes she sprayed and inspected so long ago at the Radioplane factory just before she started modeling. Back when World War II was still raging, the concentration camps about to be discovered by the American and Russian GIs.

Marilyn yawns. Marilyn smiles. Marilyn glows. Her skin is just like Billy Wilder described it decades ago, flesh that photographs like flesh. You feel you can reach out and touch it. Hold it. Squeeze it.

For a moment, the film crew crowds in and Jules shoots through a gap between their bodies. He captures only Marilyn's face, which looks off to the left, serious and unsmiling. DiMaggio is there in the crowd, though you can't see him. But Marilyn can. And she watches him walk away.

Tom Ewell comes into the shot and Marilyn pushes him into place. Wilder, dressed in his winter coat and fedora, moves in and out of the shot. Marilyn's dress flutters as she holds it down and chats with Ewell. But it flutters up again and she laughs, throwing her head back. The dress flies clear up over her head, revealing the two pairs of white silky underpants and the dark patch that they have failed to camouflage. The skirt hovers behind her like angel's wings. And for a second, it looks like she may just fly up, up, and away, over the metropolis rooftops and the screaming, leering crowd that we cannot see or hear.

Then, as suddenly as she appeared, Marilyn is gone. The dream is over. Three seconds of black is followed by a single frame from a home movie: a middle-aged Schulback relative strolls on green grass, a teenage boy behind her, both on a typical, miraculous family outing. A family that, had it not been for Harry or Faye or America, would simply not exist.

FROM THE BOOK *SECRET IDENTITY: THE FETISH ART OF
SUPERMAN'S CO-CREATOR JOE SHUSTER* BY CRAIG YOE,
FROM THE ORIGINAL ART IN THE AUTHOR'S COLLECTION.

ACKNOWLEDGMENTS

First and foremost, enormous thanks to the immediate and extended family for sharing precious memories, letters, documents, testimony, and pictures: Helen and Stephen Siegler, Rayna Dineen, Nomi Joy Parker, Jeff Retig and his family, Fred and Rosalie Sternberg, Grace, Edwin, and Howard Freedman, Fran Schaeffler-Siegel, Rafi Lemberger, Fred Payne, David Payne, Clarissa Uvegi, Ruth Ansel, Marcia Erdberg, and especially Elizabeth Sternberg Goldreich and Audrey Cohen for going above and beyond the call. Neil Sternberg and Anita Payne, no longer with us, shared their memories before this book was even a concept.

Thank you to the Donenfeld grandkids, Amy, Harry, and Luke, for opening up their homes and hearts to us and sharing photos and reminiscences. We owe an immeasurable debt to Jude Richter at the United States Holocaust Memorial Museum for his deep dives into the archives and careful fact-checking. To Rebecca Erbelding and Ronald Coleman for helping us understand the process of emigration from Europe in the thirties and with tracking down documentation. To Elizabeth Edelstein, Joana Arruda, Jacqueline Smith, Alexandria Jason, and Treva Walsh at the Museum of Jewish Heritage for their education, guidance, and access to survivors as well as recorded testimony. To Elizabeth Burnes at the National Archives in Kansas City for Jules's immigration records. To Dr. Aaron Eckstaedt, head of the Moses Mendelssohn School in Berlin, for opening his doors and giving us a tour. To Katja Baumeister-Frenzel for meeting us in Berlin and sharing her love of the Romanisches. To Ulrike Ludlam for her invaluable translating skills, on call day and night for two years. To Christoph Neimann and Lisa Zeitz for warmly welcoming us to Berlin. To Erik Spiekermann for generously sharing German typefaces. To Dr. Ewald Blocher at Siemens Historical Institute for opening up the company's dark history. To World War I scholar Sam R. Williamson for his time deciphering the Austrian military photo. To Tobias Kniebe for providing the Wilder article. To Michael Jackson for giving us such incisive notes. And to Ancestry.com for being the best rabbit hole in the world.

To Ken Quattro, comics detective extraordinaire, thanks for responding to a cold email and being our guide through a world we knew very little about. To those comics researchers who paved the way, especially Larry Tye, whose Superman archive at Columbia was a game changer, and to Karen L. Green for helping us "access" it virtually during the pandemic. To Brad Ricca for graciously answering our emails. To Nicky Wheeler-Nicholson for sharing information on her grandfather. To Gail Sitomer for her photos and memories of Sunny. To Steven Lomazov, David Saunders, John Gunnison, and Douglas Ellis for their pulp expertise and collections.

To Rebecca Federman and Iris Weinshall at the New York Public Library for help in mailing all those books during the pandemic. To Michael Feldman for copies of the in-house Independent newsletters. To Esther Katz for information on Margaret Sanger's sponsorship of refugees. To Chris Napolitano for sharing his knowledge of *Playboy* and Hugh Hefner. To Meta Shaw Stevens and Edith Shaw Marcus for helping us through the Shaw Family Archives. To Andrew Zimbel for patiently looking through his father's negatives for us. To Scott Fortner for his Marilyn wisdom. To Craig Yoe for his scholarship and finding those copies of *Nights of Horror*. To Alison Russell and Lea Iselin for their memories of the Upper East Side.

Last but not least, thanks to Lisa DiMona for introducing us to each other and to Bill Ferguson for running the original story in the *New York Times*. To agents Larry Weissman and Sascha Alper for believing in the project and shepherding us through the process.

To our editor, Megan Hogan, for her enthusiasm, thoughtful edits, and trust that we would pull all the threads together. To Rob Sternitzky for his close read. To Steve Walkowiak for making all the images perfect. To Paula and Will Christen for their horticultural knowledge. To Irene Stapinski for her memories of Times Square and life during wartime. To Stan Stapinski for his Marilyn documentary news flashes. To Wendell Jamieson for his edits, World War II knowledge, and unwavering love and emotional support. To Dean and Paulina Jamieson for suffering through—this time in such close quarters—the writing of yet another book and offering their feedback and the picture of Marilyn. You inspire me every day. To Seth Godin, who was the first to encourage me to share this story. To Anne Kreamer for being our enthusiastic first reader. To Penny Shane and Judy Goldberg for being an invaluable support system. To Jeff Scher for absolutely everything. To Buster and Oscar Scher, you know what you did. Love you both like crazy. And lastly, to Opi, who upon meeting Buster, insisted we have another.

CITY EDITION

DAILY NEWS

NEW YORK'S PICTURE NEWSPAPER ®

4¢

Vol. 36. No. 87   Copr. 1954 News Syndicate Co. Inc.   New York 17, N.Y., Tuesday, October 5, 1954*   4¢ IN CITY LIMITS | 5¢ OUTSIDE CITY LIMITS

MARILYN SPLITS WITH JOE OVER SEXY PICTURES

Story on Page 3

Joe approved of this recent night club picture—but not of cheesecake!—Story page 3.

BIBLIOGRAPHY

BOOKS

Adin, Mariah. *The Brooklyn Thrill-Kill Gang and the Great Comic Book Scare of the 1950s*. Santa Barbara, CA: Praeger, 2014.

Allen, Maury. *Where Have You Gone, Joe DiMaggio?: The Story of America's Last Hero*. New York: Dutton, 1975.

Anonymous. *A Woman in Berlin: Eight Weeks in the Conquered City: A Diary*. Translated by Philip Boehm. New York: Henry Holt, 2005.

Banner, Lois. *Marilyn: The Passion and the Paradox*. New York: Bloomsbury, 2012.

Barreaux, Adolphe. *Sally the Sleuth*. Winnipeg, Canada: Bedside Press, 2018.

Barris, George. *Marilyn: Her Life in Her Own Words*. New York: Birch Lane Press, 1995.

Berenbaum, Michael. *Witness to the Holocaust*. New York: HarperCollins, 1997.

Boschwitz, Ulrich Alexander. *The Passenger*. New York: Metropolitan Books, 2021.

Caro, Robert A. *The Power Broker: Robert Moses and the Fall of New York*. New York: Alfred A. Knopf, 1974.

Chabon, Michael. *The Amazing Adventures of Kavalier & Clay*. New York: Random House, 2000.

Chandler, Charlotte. *Nobody's Perfect: Billy Wilder: A Personal Biography*. New York: Simon & Schuster, 2002.

Chase, W. Parker. *New York, the Wonder City*. New York: Wonder City, 1932.

Collins, Max Allan. *A Killing in Comics*. New York: Berkley Publishing Group, 2007.

Cramer, Richard Ben. *Joe DiMaggio: The Hero's Life*. New York: Simon & Schuster, 2000.

Crowe, Cameron. *Conversations with Wilder*. New York: Alfred A. Knopf, 1999.

Daniels, Madison, ed. *Marilyn Monroe unCovers*, compiled by Clark Kidder. Edmonton, Canada: Quon, 1994.

Dauber, Jeremy. *American Comics: A History*. New York: W. W. Norton, 2021.

DeHaven, Tom. *Our Hero: Superman on Earth*. New Haven: Yale University Press, 2010.

DeStefano, Anthony. *Top Hoodlum: Frank Costello, Prime Minister of the Mafia*. New York: Citadel, 2018.

Diehl, Lorraine B. *Over Here!: New York City During World War II*. New York: HarperCollins, 2010.

Duin, Steve, and Mike Richardson. *Comics: Between the Panels*. Milwaukie, OR: Dark Horse Comics, 1998.

Ellis, Douglas. *The Art of the Pulps: An Illustrated History*. San Diego: IDW Publishing, 2017.

———. *Uncovered: The Hidden Art of the Girlie Pulps*. Silver Spring, MD: Adventure House, 2003.

Erbelding, Rebecca. *Rescue Board: The Untold Story of America's Efforts to Save the Jews of Europe*. New York: Doubleday, 2018.

Feiffer, Jules. *The Great Comic Book Heroes*. Seattle: Fantagraphics, 2003.

Feldenkirchen, Wilfried. *Siemens 1918–1945*. Columbus: Ohio State University Press, 1999.

Friedländer, Saul. *Nazi Germany and the Jews, Volume I: The Years of Persecution, 1933–1939*. New York: HarperCollins, 1997.

Friedrich, Otto. *Before the Deluge: A Portrait of Berlin in the 1920s*. New York: Harper & Row, 1972.

Gabler, Neal. *Winchell: Gossip, Power and the Culture of Celebrity*. New York: Alfred A. Knopf, 1994.

Gay, Nick. *Berlin Then and Now*. San Diego: Thunder Bay Press, 2005.

Goldhagen, Daniel Jonah. *Hitler's Willing Executioners: Ordinary Germans and the Holocaust*. New York: Alfred A. Knopf, 1996.

Gross, Leonard. *The Last Jews in Berlin*. New York: Carroll & Graf, 1992.

Guiles, Fred Lawrence. *Norma Jean: The Life of Marilyn Monroe*. New York: McGraw Hill, 1969.

Hannah, Kristin. *The Nightingale*. New York: St. Martin's Press, 2015.

Harris, Marlys B. *The Zanucks of Hollywood: The Dark Legacy of an American Dynasty*. New York: Crown, 1989.

Herr, Michael. *Walter Winchell*. New York: Alfred A. Knopf, 1990.

Hirschfeld, Al, and Gordon Kahn. *The Speakeasies of 1932*. Milwaukee, WI: Glenn Young Books, 2003.

Hitler, Adolf. *Mein Kampf*. Boston: Houghton Mifflin, 1969.

Hull, David Stewart. *Film in the Third Reich: A Study of the German Cinema, 1933–1945*. Berkeley: University of California Press, 1969.

Ioanid, Radu. *The Holocaust in Romania: The Destruction of Jews and Gypsies Under the Antonescu Regime, 1940–1944*. Chicago: Ivan R. Dee, 2000.

Isenberg, Noah, ed. *Billy Wilder on Assignment: Dispatches from Weimar Berlin and Interwar Vienna*. Translated by Shelley Frisch. Princeton, NJ: Princeton University Press, 2021.

Isherwood, Christopher. *The Berlin Stories*. New York: New Directions, 1963.

Jalowicz Simon, Marie. *Underground in Berlin: A Young Woman's Extraordinary Tale of Survival in the Heart of Nazi Germany*. New York: Back Bay Books, 2014.

James, M. E. Clifton. *The Counterfeit General Montgomery*. New York: Avon Books, 1954.

Jones, Gerard. *Men of Tomorrow: Geeks, Gangsters, and the Birth of the Comic Book*. New York: Basic Books, 2004.

Kahn, Roger. *Joe and Marilyn: A Memory of Love*. New York: William Morrow, 1986.

Klurfeld, Herman. *Winchell: His Life and Times*. New York: Praeger, 1976.

Koszarski, Richard. *The Man You Loved to Hate: Erich von Stroheim and Hollywood*. New York: Oxford University Press, 1983.

Lambert, Angela. *The Lost Life of Eva Braun*. New York: St. Martin's Press, 2006.

Levi, Primo. *Survival in Auschwitz*. New York: Touchstone, 1958.

Levitz, Paul. *75 Years of DC Comics: The Art of Modern Mythmaking*. Los Angeles: Taschen America, 2010.

Lutes, Jason. *Berlin*. Montreal: Drawn and Quarterly, 2018.

Madsen, Axel. *Billy Wilder*. Bloomington: Indiana University Press, 1969.

Maeder, Jay. *Big Town, Big Time: A New York Epic: 1898–1998*. New York: New York Daily News, 1999.

Malaparte, Curzio. *Kaputt*. New York: New York Review Books, 2005.

Matetsky, Harry. *The Adventures of Superman Collecting*. West Plains, MO: Russ Cochran, 1988.

Maxtone-Graham, John. *The Only Way to Cross*. New York: Macmillan, 1972.

McBride, Joseph. *Billy Wilder: Dancing on the Edge*. New York: Columbia University Press, 2021.

Megargee, Geoffrey P., ed. *USHMM Encyclopedia of Camps and Ghettos: 1933–1945*, vol. 1–3. Washington, DC, 1999–.

Mendelsohn, John. *The Holocaust: Selected Documents in Eighteen Volumes*. New York: Garland, 1982.

Miller, Arthur. *Timebends: A Life*. New York: Grove Press, 1987.

Miracle, Berniece Baker, and Mona Rae Miracle. *My Sister Marilyn: A Memoir of Marilyn Monroe*. Bloomington, IN: iUniverse, 2012.

Monroe, Marilyn. *Fragments: Poems, Intimate Notes, Letters*. New York: Farrar, Straus and Giroux, 2010.

Monroe, Marilyn, with Ben Hecht. *My Story*. New York: Cooper Square Press, 2000.

Morris, Heather. *The Tattooist of Auschwitz*. New York: HarperCollins, 2018.

Niven, Bill. *Hitler and Film: The Führer's Hidden Passion*. New Haven: Yale University Press, 2018.

Ozick, Cynthia. "The Shawl." *New Yorker*, May 26, 1980.

Phillips, Gene D. *Some Like It Wilder: The Life and Controversial Films of Billy Wilder*. Lexington: University Press of Kentucky, 2010.

Preston, Jennifer. *Queen Bess: The Unauthorized Biography of Bess Myerson*. Chicago: Contemporary Books, 1990.

Quattro, Ken. *Invisible Men: The Trailblazing Black Artists of Comic Books*. San Diego: Yoe Books, 2020.

Rhoades, Shirrel. *A Complete History of American Comic Books*. New York: Peter Lang, 2008.

Ricca, Brad. *Super Boys: The Amazing Adventures of Jerry Siegel and Joe Shuster—The Creators of Superman*. New York: St. Martin's Press, 2013.

Rosenbaum, Ron. *Explaining Hitler: The Search for the Origins of His Evil*. New York: Harper Perennial, 1999.

Sanger, Margaret. *The Autobiography of Margaret Sanger*. Mineola, NY: Dover, 2004.

———. *Woman and the New Race*. Middletown, DE: Odin's Library Classics, 2020.

Shirer, William L. *Berlin Diary: The Journal of a Foreign Correspondent, 1934–1941*. New York: Alfred A. Knopf, 1941.

Sikov, Ed. *On Sunset Boulevard: The Life and Times of Billy Wilder*. New York: Hyperion, 1998.

Spiegelman, Art. *Maus: A Survivor's Tale*. New York: Pantheon Books, 1986.

———. *Maus II: A Survivor's Tale: And Here My Troubles Began*. New York: Pantheon Books, 1991.

Spoto, Donald. *Marilyn Monroe: The Biography*. New York: Cooper Square Press, 1993.

Steranko, James. *The Steranko History of the Comics*, vol. 1. New York: Crown, 1970.

———. *The Steranko History of the Comics*, vol. 2. New York: Crown, 1972.

Talese, Gay. *The Silent Season of a Hero*. London: Walker & Co., 2010.

Taraborrelli, J. Randy. *The Secret Life of Marilyn Monroe*. New York: Grand Central Publishing, 2010.

Trimborn, Jürgen. *Leni Riefenstahl: A Life*. Translated by Edna McCown. New York: Farrar, Straus and Giroux, 2007.

Tye, Larry. *Superman: The High-Flying History of America's Most Enduring Hero*. New York: Random House, 2012.

Urwand, Ben. *The Collaboration: Hollywood's Pact with Hitler*. Cambridge, MA: Belknap Press, 2013.

Vaz, Mark Cotta. *Empire of the Superheroes: America's Comic Book Creators and the Making of a Billion-Dollar Industry*. Austin: University of Texas Press, 2021.

Voloj, Julian, and Thomas Campi. *The Joe Shuster Story: The Artist Behind Superman*. New York: Super Genius, 2018.

Waldman, Louis. *Labor Lawyer*. New York: Dutton, 1944.

Walker, Stanley. *The Night Club Era*. Baltimore: Johns Hopkins University Press, 1933.

Watson, Robert P. *The Nazi Titanic: The Incredible Untold Story of a Doomed Ship in World War II*. Boston: Da Capo Press, 2016.

Wayne, Jane Ellen. *Marilyn's Men: The Private Life of Marilyn Monroe*. New York: St. Martin's Press, 1992.

Wertham, Fredric. *Seduction of the Innocent*. New York: Rinehart & Company, 1954.

Weyr, Thomas. *Reaching for Paradise: The* Playboy *Vision of America*. New York: Times Books, 1978.

Wheeler-Nicholson, Nicky. *DC Comics Before Superman: Major Malcolm Wheeler-Nicholson's Pulp Comics*. Neshannock, PA: Hermes Press, 2018.

Wiesel, Elie. *Night*. New York: Hill and Wang, 1958.

Winder, Elizabeth. *Marilyn in Manhattan: Her Year of Joy*. New York: Flatiron Books, 2017.

Wood, Tom. *The Bright Side of Billy Wilder, Primarily*. New York: Doubleday, 1970.

Yoe, Craig. *Secret Identity: The Fetish Art of Superman's Co-Creator Joe Shuster*. San Diego: Yoe Books, 2009.

Zivier, Georg. *Das Romanische Café: Berlinische Reminiszenzen 9*. Berlin: Haude & Spencer, 1965.

Zolotow, Maurice. *Billy Wilder in Hollywood*. New York: G. P. Putnam, 1977.

———. *Marilyn Monroe*. New York: Harcourt Brace, 1960.

FILMS

Annakin, Ken, Andrew Marton, and Bernhard Wicki, dirs. *The Longest Day*. Hollywood: 20th Century Fox, 1962.

Bloch, Yossi, and Daniel Sivan, dirs. *The Devil Next Door*. Netflix documentary, 2019.

Bolsey, Alyssa, dir. *Beyond the Bolex*. Portland, OR: Collective Eye Films, 2018.

Chaplin, Charlie, dir. *The Great Dictator*. Hollywood: United Artists, 1940.

Greenspan, Bud, dir. *Jesse Owens Returns to Berlin*. Toronto: Sports Network Inc., 1968.

Hathaway, Henry, dir. *Niagara*. Hollywood: 20th Century Fox, 1953.

Hirschbiegel, Oliver, dir. *Downfall*. Munich: Constantin Film, 2004.

Kramer, Stanley, dir. *Judgement at Nuremberg*. Hollywood: MGM, 1961.

Levin, Gail, dir. *Marilyn Monroe: Still Life*. PBS, "American Masters," first aired July 19, 2006.

Pierson, Frank, dir. *Conspiracy*. New York: HBO Films, 2001.

Polanski, Roman, dir. *The Pianist*. Berlin: Babelsberg Film Studio, 2002.

Resnais, Alain, dir. *Night and Fog*. Paris: Argos Films, 1955.

Riefenstahl, Leni, dir. *Olympia*. Berlin: Olympia-Film, 1938.

_____. *Triumph of the Will*. Berlin: Reichsparteitag-Film, 1935.

Ruttmann, Walter, dir. *Berlin: Symphony of a Metropolis*. Fort Lee, NJ: Fox Film Corporation, 1927.

Schirk, Heinz, dir. *Hitler's Final Solution: The Wannsee Conference*. Munich: Infafilm GmbH Manfred Korytowski, 1984.

Sholem, Lee, dir. *Superman and the Mole Men*. Hollywood: Lippert Pictures, 1951.

Shoychet, Matthew, dir. *The Accountant of Auschwitz*. Toronto: Good Soup Productions/TLNT Productions, 2018.

Siodmak, Robert, and Edgar G. Ulmar, dirs. *People on Sunday*. Screenplay by Billy Wilder. Berlin: Babelsberg Film Studio, 1930.

Spielberg, Steven, dir. *Schindler's List*. Hollywood: Universal Pictures, 1994.

Tourneur, Jacques, dir. *Berlin Express*. Los Angeles: RKO Pictures, 1948.

Wilder, Billy, dir. *Death Mills*. Washington, DC: United States Department of War, 1945.

_____. *Five Graves to Cairo*. Hollywood: Paramount, 1943.

_____. *A Foreign Affair*. Hollywood: Paramount, 1948.

_____. *Sabrina*. Hollywood: Paramount, 1954.

_____. *The Seven Year Itch*. Hollywood: Fox, 1955.

VIDEOS AND RECORDINGS

"Berlin in July 1945." Berlin Channel. YouTube, uploaded April 28, 2015. https://www .youtube.com/watch?v=R5i9k7s9X_A.

"Hitler Back in Berlin from Vienna (1938)." British Pathé. YouTube. https://www .youtube.com/watch?v=hkt9iagqkk8.

"Hollywood Stars Appear at the 1949 Benefit for City of Hope at Wrigley Field in Chicago." Grinberg, Paramount, Pathé Newsreels. Getty Images. https://www .gettyimages.co.uk/detail/video/infield-of-wrigley-field-eddie-bracken-sonny -tufts-signs-news-footage/506426228.

"Jergens Journal with Walter Winchell—December 7, 1941." SoundCloud recording uploaded 2015 by Sammy Jones. https://soundcloud.com/sammyjones-1/jergens -journal-with-walter.

Jones, Gerard. Interview with Harry Donenfeld at the 2016 San Diego Comic Fest. Michael D Hamersky. YouTube, uploaded February 19, 2016. https://www .youtube.com/watch?v=ZNOWPb9QaRU.

Friedkin, William. Interview with Fritz Lang on February 21 and 24, 1975. Mario Mangione. YouTube, uploaded November 22, 2014. https://www.youtube.com /watch?v=or0j1mY_rug.

"New York in the Mid 1930's in Color!" Rick88888888. YouTube, uploaded August 3, 2019. https://www.youtube.com/watch?v=ZpXnEvW0XD0.

"Superman Day New York World's Fair 1940." Scotty V. YouTube. https://www .youtube.com/watch?v=A27ii9cIPGw.

Truman, Harry. May 8, 1945, victory speech. America's National Churchill Museum. YouTube, uploaded May 8, 2020. https://www.youtube.com/watch?v=Pix7G2SKXlY.

Wilder, Billy. "Billy Wilder Receiving the Irving G. Thalberg Award," 1988. Oscars. YouTube, uploaded July 1, 2009. https://www.youtube.com/watch?v=kebqj_grGC0.

EDITH, MARTHA, USHI, ALBERT, AND JULES, 1933

NOTES

CHAPTER 1 : IN THE METROPOLIS

Family photos, interviews, and a personal visit to Berlin to Wannsee, Münz-strasse, the New Synagogue, and the Babylon theater—where *Metropolis* was once again playing—provided much of the information for this chapter.

Further information on Wannsee is from the United States Holocaust Memorial Museum's online Holocaust Encyclopedia; from the films *The Wannsee Conference* and *Conspiracy*. A translated copy of the Wannsee Protocol can be found in Mendelsohn, *The Holocaust, Vol. 11: The Wannsee Protocol* and a 1944 Report on Auschwitz by the Office of Strategic Services.

Other Berlin background can be found in Friedrich's *Before the Deluge* and Shirer's *Berlin Diary*.

Go to the Jewish Galicia and Bukovina website for information on Kolomyia.

Hitler's cinematic tastes are from Niven's *Hitler and Film*.

CHAPTER 2 : SMOOSHES AND BOOZE

Three of the Donenfeld grandchildren, Amy, Luke, and Harry, generously shared family stories and photographs.

US Census records and Ancestry.com provided dates on immigration, residences, and family background.

Ken Quattro himself and his well-researched *Comics Detective* blog provided countless leads and steered us to Waldman's *Labor Lawyer*, which tells firsthand of Harry's Socialist background.

Jones's *Men of Tomorrow* gives a great account of Harry's early years. His interview with Harry's grandson Harry at the 2016 San Diego Comic Fest can be found on YouTube.

The comics fanzine *Alter Ego*, no. 26 (July 2003), features an interview with Irwin Donenfeld, Harry's son, by Mark Evanier, Robert Beerbohm, and Julius Schwartz.

Harry's FBI file, including information on his arrests, his adulterous activity, and his business dealings, can be found online from Mitchell Kotler's MuckRock FOIA request from 2013.

Gussie filing for divorce can be found in the New York *Sun*, February 17, 1925.

The foundation for Harry's pulp background and the beginnings of DC Comics was laid out in Will Murray, "DC's Tangled Roots," *Comic Book Marketplace*, no. 53, November 1997, page 26.

For Harry's pulp history, we interviewed David Saunders, author of the website Pulp Artists. Also providing background were Douglas Ellis's *Uncovered* and *The Art of the Pulps*; Terence Towles Canote's *A Shroud of Thoughts* blog from August 29, 2007; Jay Deitcher, "With Great Chutzpah Comes Great Responsibility: DC Comics's Socialist," Unleash the Fanboy, June 21, 2013; and Todd Klein, "Schnapp, Donenfeld and the Pulps," parts 1 and 2, *Todd's Blog*, July 30 and 31, 2012.

Magazine collector Steven Lomazow and the New York Public Library shared their extensive pulp collections with us.

Information on distribution and magazine dumps came from John Gunnison, who runs Adventure House, which sells and reprints original pulp fiction.

Information on Prohibition can be found in Walker's *The Night Club Era* and Hirschfeld's *The Speakeasies of 1932*.

Jack Leibowitz's oral history from 1993, taped by Linda Stillman, is available at Columbia University in the comics archive of Larry Tye's exhaustive research collection for his book *Superman: The High-Flying History of America's Most Enduring Hero*— which served as our Superman bible.

More information on Margaret Sanger can be found in her autobiography, as well as in *Woman and the New Race*.

The "boy meets girl" quote has been repeated countless times but seems to have originally been uttered by novelist Jack Woodford.

CHAPTER 3 : DAREDEVIL REPORTER

Katja Baumeister-Frenzel, an expert on the Romanisches Café and bohemian life in 1920s Berlin, provided photographs, background, and other essential materials and documents, including Georg Zivier's book *Das Romanische Café*.

Isenberg's *Billy Wilder on Assignment*, a collection of Wilder's articles from the 1920s and '30s, gives firsthand accounts of his time in Berlin.

Quotes from Wilder come from Crowe's *Conversations with Wilder*.

Sikov's *On Sunset Boulevard* was also a major source, as was Chandler's *Nobody's Perfect*, and Phillips's *Some Like It Wilder*.

Lutes's graphic novel *Berlin* was a source, as was Isherwood's *The Berlin Stories*.

Wilder's *People on Sunday* and the film *Berlin: Symphony of a Metropolis* also provided visual tours of the city in the late 1920s.

CHAPTER 4 : STONE BOYS AND BEASTS

Family letters, photographs, and a visit to the Schulback and Friedmann homes and businesses in Berlin provided much of the information and color for this chapter. The staff at the Moses Mendelssohn school gave us a tour and historical background not only on the boys' school but on the neighborhood and the cemetery as well.

Don Retig's 1992 survivor testimony for the Fortunoff Video Archive for Holocaust Testimonies at Yale University and Jackie Retig, Don's granddaughter, provided the story of his days as a student in Nazi Germany.

Personal interviews with Jeff Retig, Olga's grandson, were a primary source.

Exhibits at the Museum of Jewish Heritage in New York City provided information on the April 1933 boycott.

Friedrich's *Before the Deluge* gave us more background on the Nazis' rise in Berlin.

Fritz Lang's personal account of leaving Berlin can be found on YouTube.

CHAPTER 5 : PULP NONFICTION

Chase's *New York, The Wonder City* was an excellent guide to the buildings and people of the era.

Harry's Grand Central neighborhood and building are described, respectively, in Christopher Gray, "Covering Its Tracks Paid Off Handsomely," *New York Times*, August 19, 2010; and David Dunlap, "When Trade Shows Were Both Grand and Central," *City Room* blog, *New York Times*, December 18, 2012.

DeStefano's *Top Hoodlum: Frank Costello, Prime Minister of the Mafia* was a source on Costello's New York story.

Harry's FBI file, the *Pulp Artists* blog, and Jones's *Men of Tomorrow* provided essential information.

CHAPTER 6 : DIRECT TRANSMISSIONS

Crowe's *Conversations with Wilder*, Sikov's *On Sunset Boulevard*, Zolotow's *Billy Wilder in Hollywood*, and Chandler's *Nobody's Perfect* were all sources for this chapter.

Information on *What Women Dream* came from McBride's *Billy Wilder*.

Excerpts from Hitler's *Mein Kampf* and Rosenbaum's *Explaining Hitler* provided background.

Shirer's *Berlin Diary* and Isherwood's *The Berlin Stories* describe events leading up to the war.

Billy Wilder's personal account of his immigration through Mexico can be found in his 1986 acceptance speech for the Irving G. Thalberg award at the Oscars on YouTube.

Information on *Bluebeard's Eighth Wife* came from Niven's *Hitler and Film*.

CHAPTER 7 : ALWAYS SUNNY

The *New York Times*, the *Daily News*, the *Tablet of Brooklyn*, and the *New York Age* all covered the magazine raid story and hearings. The *Daily News* story from March 9, 1934, gives a detailed account of the raid. The *Tablet* from March 24, 1934, the hearing. The *New York Times*, March 3 and 8, 1934.

Harry's FBI file also includes information on the arrests.

The *Spicy* hybrids are discussed in S. J. Perelman, "Somewhere a Roscoe . . . ," the *New Yorker*, October 7, 1938.

For more on Sally the Sleuth and her creator, Adolphe Barreaux, see the 2018 Bedside Press collection *Sally the Sleuth: 1934–1953*, Hope Nicholson, ed., Winnipeg, as well as Quattro's *Invisible Men*.

Lomazov provided copies of his *Spicy* magazines for research.

Crime rate information came from Barry Latzer, "Do Hard Times Spark More Crime?" *Los Angeles Times*, January 24, 2014.

The US Census, NYC Municipal Archives, and Ancestry.com provided both Harry's and Sunny's backgrounds, travel, and address information.

Interviews with Sunny's niece, Gale Sitomer, provided information for this chapter.

Development near the West Side Highway can be found in Caro's *The Power Broker*. Also see Lucie Levine, "Looking Back at the Depression-Era Shanty Towns in New York City Parks," *6sqft*, February 26, 2020.

Harry's granddaughter, Amy, provided us with his fiftieth birthday party tribute, which included information on his love of singing and his favorite songs.

For more on Cherry Street, see "Gotham Court and the Lost Neighborhood of Cherry Street," *Bowery Boys: New York City History* blog, May 28, 2015.

Information on the Hotel Nacional de Cuba can be found on its website.

CHAPTER 8 : IN THE GARDEN

Most of the information in this chapter comes from Jules's wedding photos, letters of tribute from Jules and Edith's fiftieth wedding anniversary, family interviews, and our visit to Berlin.

The United States Holocaust Memorial Museum's Holocaust Encyclopedia provided background on the Nazi campaign against the Jews in the 1930s, as did the Museum of Jewish Heritage in New York City.

For more on the 1936 Berlin Olympics, see the television documentary *Jesse Owens Returns to Berlin*, as well as Riefenstahl's film *Olympia*. Riefenstahl's *Triumph of the Will* also provided background on 1930s Germany.

Jesse Owens quote from the Jesse Owens Museum website.

Owens's reception in Manhattan is documented in "Olympic Stars Get Welcome of City," page 21 of the *New York Times*, September 4, 1936, and his White House snub in "Snub from Roosevelt," page 25, *St. Joseph News-Press*, Oct. 16, 1936.

CHAPTER 9 : THE TEN-BLOCK WALK, TAKE 2

Jerry Siegel's unpublished autobiography, a copy of which sits at Columbia University in the Tye archive, is the basis for this chapter.

Voloj and Campi's *The Joe Shuster Story* gives Joe's version of events. As does a November 23, 1975, letter from Joe to Jay Emmett at Warner Bros., also in the Tye archive at Columbia.

Nemo: The Classic Comics Library, no. 2, contains an interview with Jerry and Joe, with a reprint of *The Reign of the Super-Man* and a pencil sketch of the original version of the Superman.

Jules Feiffer's "The Minsk Theory of Krypton," *New York Times*, December 29, 1996.

Biographical information as provided by John Kobler, "Up, Up and A-a-Way: The Rise of Superman, Inc.," *Saturday Evening Post*, June 21, 1941.

"Superman a Money Maker," *Kansas City Star*, May 22, 1941, reveals that Harry's Superman enterprises was grossing $5 million.

Comics fanzine *Alter Ego*, no. 56, from February 2006 features an interview with Jerry from 1975, among other treasures.

Ricca's *Super Boys* is a major source, as is Jones's *Men of Tomorrow*, Tye's *Superman*, and DeHaven's *Our Hero*.

Feiffer's *The Great Comic Book Heroes* also provided information on the comics industry, as did Levitz's *75 Years of DC Comics*.

CHAPTER 10 : THE MAJOR AND THE MINORS

The Major's granddaughter, Nicky Wheeler-Nicholson, gave us an interview, and her *DC Comics Before Superman* was a major source for this chapter, as was Jerry's unpublished autobiography, which provided a step-by-step explanation of Superman's birth, as well as this chapter's last, crushing line.

Ken Quattro's August 19, 2019, *Comics Detective* piece "The Ballad of Herbie Siegel"; Tye's *Superman*; and Jones's *Men of Tomorrow* all provided information. As did Rhoades's *A Complete History of American Comic Books* and Steranko's *The Steranko History of Comics*, vols. 1 and 2.

Quattro's "DC vs. Victor Fox" led us to the *DC vs. Bruns* court case transcript of Harry's testimony on his whereabouts in the winter of 1938. See Ken Quattro, "DC vs. Victor Fox: The Testimony of Will Eisner." *Comics Detective*, July 1, 2010.

Alter Ego, no. 56, includes an interview with DC artist Jack Adler.

Baron Bifford's online archive at Scribd includes Jerry's and Joe's letters and contracts with Harry and Jack.

Information also from "Jack Liebowitz, Comics Publisher, Dies at 100," by Eric P. Nash, *New York Times*, December 13, 2000, Section B, page 10.

CHAPTER 11 : THE WAIT

Dr. Rebecca Erbelding, author of *Rescue Board*, and Ronald Coleman of the United States Holocaust Memorial Museum offered guidance on what documents would be necessary to emigrate from Germany to America. Dr. Erbelding also explained how the sponsor system worked for refugees, sharing government letters from the late 1930s.

Jules's nephew, Don Retig, spoke of his emigration from Germany in his 1992 survivor interview for the Fortunoff Video Archive, shedding light on Jules's experience.

Interviews with Faye's son Fred Sternberg and her daughter-in-law Rosalie provided us with biographical information on Faye. Fran Scheffler-Siegel, Faye's niece, also provided background on the family, as did David Payne and Clarissa Uvegi.

Jules's own stories, notes, letters, and photos, and the recollections of his daughter Helen Siegler and her husband, Stephen, provided information for his escape narrative.

For more information on the *Queen Mary*, see Maxtone-Graham's *The Only Way to Cross*.

The *New York Times*, March 17, 1938, describes Hitler's return to Berlin in the page 2 story "1,500,000 Acclaim Hitler in Berlin." Video of his parade can also be seen on YouTube.

Background also from "U.S. Asks Powers to Help Refugees Flee from Nazis," *New York Times*, March 25, 1938.

Shirer's *Berlin Diary* and newspaper accounts from the week of March 17 in the *New York Times* provided information on the Anschluss.

The *New York Times* theater and entertainment listings for March 1938 provided the movies, concerts, and plays, and its real estate listings show how much apartments in Yorkville cost at the time.

The New York Architecture website describes the Piccadilly Hotel and includes a collection of old postcards and photos.

"New York in the Mid 1930's in Color!" on YouTube provides almost forty-two minutes of incredible footage.

CHAPTER 12 : THE SIGNATURE

Neil Sternberg told the author of the day he went with his mother to visit Harry's office for the affidavit. Anita Payne, Mollie's daughter-in-law, spoke of the day as well. Fred Sternberg and his sister-in-law, Rosalie, were also interviewed.

The Jewish Museum Berlin displays a copy of an affidavit from 1939.

The United States Holocaust Memorial Museum's "Americans and the Holocaust" website page details the process to come over from Germany to America.

CHAPTER 13 : THE WAY BACK

Jules's personal recollections and the memories of his daughter Helen are the basis for this chapter. Jules's nephew Jeff Retig was also interviewed about his grandmother Golda and provided sponsor letters.

The United States Holocaust Memorial Museum in Washington, DC, provided background on life for Jews in Berlin in the spring, summer, and fall of 1938.

Boschwitz's *The Passenger* describes what it was like to be a Jew in November 1938 in Berlin.

CHAPTER 14 : BROKEN GLASS

For information on Kristallnacht, we read Berenbaum's *Witness to the Holocaust*, volume 3 of Mendelsohn's *The Holocaust*, the testimony of Gerald Liebenau given to the United States Holocaust Memorial Museum, Wyatt's "The Girl Who Witnessed Kristallnacht," as well as Yad Vashem's online "The November Pogrom" interviews and photos.

Information on Sachsenhausen and the New Synagogue damage was found on-site in Berlin.

Jeff Retig and Helen Siegler provided information about Golda and Jules.

Information on the S.S. *Veendam* came from "1922 Veendam (II)" by Albert J. Shoonderbeek, *Captain Albert's Blog: Stories from the Sea, Past and Present*, February 2008.

Story of the *Veendam* suicide is from "Refugee Gone from Ship: Woman, 65, from Vienna Vanished on the *Veendam*," *New York Times*, October 26, 1938.

Story about the Upper West Side fur shops is from Dennis Hevesi, "Upper Broadway Loses Last of Its Fur Salons," *New York Times*, July 25, 1990.

CHAPTER 15 : A JOB FOR SUPERMAN

Maury Allen, in *Where Have You Gone, Joe DiMaggio?*, tells the story of Lefty Gomez buying Superman comics for DiMaggio.

Circulation numbers and syndication information come from the *DC v. Bruns* case transcript.

The reader survey information is taken from Jack Liebowitz's oral history.

The letter from Jack to Jerry is quoted in the *Siegel v. Warner Bros.* case from 2009.

Information on Bob Maxwell, the radio show, and Jerry's and Joe's new-and-improved lives are taken from John Kobler, "Up, Up and A-a-Way: The Rise of Superman, Inc.," *Saturday Evening Post*, June 21, 1941.

Jerry's corrections come from Jones's *Men of Tomorrow*.

The list of Superman merchandising objects comes from a Smithsonian Museum letter to Larry Tye, from his Columbia University archive.

Film footage from Superman Day at the World's Fair can be found on YouTube. Personal family photos show Neil at the festivities.

Superman profit from *DC v. Bruns* transcript.

Information on the pulps folding comes from Ellis's *Uncovered*.

Beresford background comes from the StreetEasy website. Information on Costello's apartment from DeStefano's biography.

H. J. Ward's painting background comes from James Barron, "The Mystery of the Missing Man of Steel," *New York Times*, April 18, 2010.

Palm tree story from "Radio Comment, Programs" by Marion Stevens, the *Miami Herald*, December 4, 1940, Section B, page 3.

"Superman in the Slums" is from the online DC Comics Database.

"How Superman Would End the War" is from *Look* magazine, February 27, 1940.

CHAPTER 16 : TAKING SIDES

Detailed descriptions of the Jassy massacre can be found in Malaparte's *Kaputt*; the United States Holocaust Memorial Museum, "The Massacre of the Jews of Jassy" report from the Central Zionist Archives, 1941, translated from the French original; and Ioanid's *The Holocaust in Romania*.

Interviews with the Siegler, Payne, and Retig families provided information about Golda.

Goldhagen's *Hitler's Willing Executioners* provided information on German collusion.

Washington Post story on Harry, October 22, 1940, declares "Superman to Sweep World for Democracy, His Boss Says."

Randall Bytwerk, a professor at Calvin University, found and translated the Nazi response to the *Look* magazine story in 1998.

The Margaret Sanger Papers Project at NYU provided information on her sponsorship of Jewish refugees to America.

Information from "Edward G. Robinson, 79, Dies," from *New York Times* obituary, January 27, 1973, by Alden Whitman, page 1.

For Carl Laemmle sponsoring Jewish refugees, see Jackie Mansky, "This Hollywood Titan Foresaw the Horrors of Nazi Germany," *Smithsonian* magazine, January 17, 2017.

The Anti-Nazi League boycott is told about in "Hollywood Ad Hits at Leni Riefenstahl: Anti-Nazi League Bids Industry Close Doors to Hitler Agent," *New York Times*, November 30, 1938.

Information on Charlie Chaplin's inspiration is from Trimborn's *Leni Riefenstahl*. Also, the Associated Press story on Chaplin's Jewish ties, "British Spies Stumped by Charlie Chaplin Mystery" by Jill Lawless, *Norfolk Daily News*, February 17, 2012.

Film quotes from *The Great Dictator.*

CHAPTER 17 : COLLATERAL DAMAGE

Descriptions of New York City from December 7, 1941, from newspaper accounts of that day in the New York *Daily News* and the *New York Times*; from Wendell Jamieson, "Enemy Planes Off City" from *Big Town, Big Time*, New York *Daily News*, 1999; and from Diehl's *Over Here!*

Walter Winchell's broadcast can be heard on SoundCloud, courtesy of Sammy Jones.

The Museum of the City of New York provided information on the city's black-and brownouts during the war.

Information on the S.S. *Veendam*'s fate again came from *Captain Albert's Blog*.

Miami Herald, December 15, 1943, reports on Harry's Versailles Hotel wartime activities: "Donenfeld to Give Farewell Party," Section 2, page 6.

Independent's in-house newsletters from March, April, and May 1944, courtesy of Michael Feldman, also provided information on Harry's activities during the war.

For Nabokov information see Andrei Babikov, "Superman Returns," *Times Literary Supplement*, March 5, 2021, and Alison Flood, "Vladimir Nabokov's Superman Poem Published for the First Time," *The Guardian*, March 4, 2021.

Information on Superman's popularity in the military comes from Tye's *Superman*.

The Donenfeld grandchildren provided information on Harry's relationship with FDR.

Yorkville information from Diehl's *Over Here!*

Author's recollections and interviews with Jules's daughter, Helen, and granddaughter, Rayna Dineen; Ushi's daughters, Audrey Cohen and Marcia Erdberg; photos and visits to his old apartments provided details and color.

CHAPTER 18 : BLEEDING LETTERS

Letters were provided by Helen Siegler, as well as Audrey Cohen and Marcia Erdberg.

The United States Holocaust Memorial Museum's (USHMM) exhibits in Washington, DC, and their online encyclopedia provided historical background on Nazi Germany in the 1940s and on America's reluctance to let refugees in. See their encyclopedia page on Breckinridge Long, assistant secretary in the US State Department.

Information on Felix Frankfurter's inaction can be found online at the David S. Wyman Institute for Holocaust Studies website.

The Breckinridge Long Memo from June 26, 1940, lays out the government's policy on postponing immigration.

Information on Wannsee is from the USHMM's online Holocaust Encyclopedia; from the films *The Wannsee Conference* and *Conspiracy*. A translated copy of the Wannsee Protocol can be found in Mendelsohn, *The Holocaust, Vol. 11: The Wannsee Protocol* and a 1944 report on Auschwitz by the Office of Strategic Services.

Details on Golda's life in the Jewish ghetto in Kraków were provided by the one and only Jude Richter at the USHMM's National Institute for Holocaust Documentation; a Kraków ghetto resident questionnaire from November 11, 1940, for Golda and Simon; a deferment on deportation from the ghetto from November 22, 1940; a June 25, 1940, letter from the Security Police commander asking the city for a deferment for certain tailors and cobblers; a document extending Golda's ghetto residence permit from March 3, 1941; certification that an ID card was issued for the ghetto from March 8, 1941.

Additional background on the Kraków ghetto from the USHMM online encyclopedia.

CHAPTER 19 : FAKE NAZIS

Information on the making of *Five Graves to Cairo* came from Sikov's *On Sunset Boulevard* and Zolotow's *Billy Wilder in Hollywood*, from watching the film itself, and from the excellent audio commentary by film historian Joseph McBride (Kino Lorber Studio Classics).

The David Freeman profile on Wilder, "Sunset Boulevard Revisited" in the *New Yorker*, June 13, 1993, provided information on his relationship with Charles Brackett, as did Sikov's *On Sunset Boulevard* and Chandler's *Nobody's Perfect*.

Urwand's *The Collaboration* provided information on the moguls' investment in the German film industry.

For more on Erich von Stroheim, see Wilder's newspaper stories in Isenberg's *Billy Wilder on Assignment*, as well as Koszarski's *The Man You Loved to Hate*.

For more on Operation Copperhead see James's *The Counterfeit General Montgomery*.

Stories in the *New York Times* from the fall of 1942 and the winter of '43 provided historical background on Rommel in North Africa.

CHAPTER 20 : STOLEN BREAD

Interviews with Ursula "Ushi" Friedmann's daughters, Audrey Cohen and Marcia Erdberg, and the 1996 recorded testimony of Leja Steinhauer from the USC Shoah Foundation provided the bulk of the information in this chapter.

Jude Richter, at the United States Holocaust Memorial Museum's National Institute for Holocaust Documentation, provided documentation of Ushi's employment at Siemens from May 14, 1940, through February 1943; a registered list of Jews who had been hiding in Berlin from August 1945; another list from the British and French sector of Berlin from October 6, 1945; a passenger list from the SS *Marlin* to the US from September 6, 1946; Ushi's Tracing Documentation File from 1963.

Ushi's story was filled in with archival information from Ewald Blocher at Siemens Historical Institute, as well as from Feldenkirchen's *Siemens 1918–1945*. The 1979 testimony of Siemens worker Esther Cymbalista provided by the Museum of Jewish Heritage helped with details as well.

The contents of the Friedmann apartment are listed in Ushi's and Edith's letters from the 1940s to the 1970s to the German government requesting reparations for what was taken from them. Letters provided by Landesarchiv Berlin.

More background on living underground in Berlin can be found in Jalowicz Simon's excellent memoir *Underground in Berlin*.

The story about Ushi hiding with Hildegard was found in a May 20, 1961, article in an unidentified German newspaper, "Two Years of Fear" by Winfried Maass, provided by Ushi's daughters, Audrey and Marcia.

Information on the bombing of the Charlottenburg neighborhood came from Katja Baumeister-Frenzel in Berlin and from photographs taken at the end of the war by Robert Capa.

CHAPTER 21 : GROSSE HAMBURGER STRASSE

Jude Richter, at the United States Holocaust Memorial Museum's National Institute for Holocaust Documentation, provided Nazi deportation and transport records for the Friedmanns from June 26, 1942. Additional information on Transport 16 from Berlin came from Yad Vashem. Their Untold Stories database also provided information on the gas vans used by the Nazis.

The USHMM Encyclopedia of Camps and Ghettos: 1933–1945 and the Jewish Virtual Library also provided historical background, as did Goldhagen's *Hitler's Willing Executioners*.

CHAPTER 22 : STARS AND STRIPES

Information on Dempsey's Bar was found in the New York *Daily News*, "Then and Now Jack Dempsey's Bar" by Anthony Connors, May 16, 1999, page 15 of the weekend Showtime section, and in "Dempsey in the Window" in the *New York Times* by Robert Lipsythe from June 25, 1970, page 65.

NOTES

Harry's grandsons Luke and Harry Donenfeld provided some background on Harry's drinking habits and shenanigans, as did Independent's in-house newsletters.

The story of Harry being arrested in Florida is from the *Miami Herald*, November 29, 1943, "Superman Would Do It Differently," page 1.

In his syndicated newspaper comic strip the week of February 15, 1942, Superman tried to join the military.

In newspaper syndication from November 23 to December 19, Santa is kidnapped.

Information on the list of publications and GI reading habits from the Independent newsletter, as well as Tye's *Superman*.

Original sin concept is raised in Dauber's *American Comics*.

Jerry's unpublished autobiography and his 1975 press release regarding the Superman movie address in detail their being cheated out of money and about his creation of Superboy.

Whitney Ellsworth's February 21, 1942, letter to Jerry is from the Letters of Note website, January 20, 2010, in the Tye archives, Columbia University.

Ricca's *Super Boys* references Jerry asking for $500 more, being drafted, and DC stealing his Superboy story.

"The Invention Thief," Jerry's passive-aggressive plotline, can be found in *Superman* #14 from February 1942. The unmasked villain appears in the December 1942 issue, *Superman* #19. Synopses can be found at the DC Database online.

"Superman's Creator Now Pvt. Siegal [*sic*]," *Washington Post*, August 14, 1943, provided information on Jerry in the army.

Information on Irwin's time in the military comes from interviews with the Donenfeld grandchildren, the pastrami sandwich story from Luke Donenfeld.

CHAPTER 23 : GOLDA'S JOURNEY

Golda and Simon's story was stitched together from family interviews, her son Don's testimony, and information from Jude Richter at the United States Holocaust Memorial Museum's (USHMM) National Institute for Holocaust Documentation, including Golda's Tracing and Documentation file from 1955; wartime prison records from January 18, 1945, indicating she was moved from Flossenburg to Gross Rosen; the Langenbielau Jewish Committee list of liberated prisoners from May 8, 1945; a list of former prisoners from May 23, 1945; a list from the Central Committee of Polish Jews from August 1945; a survivor information card from the Records and Statistical Division of the Central Committee on Polish Jews from January 1946, as well as a committee list of survivors from January 1947; a February 11, 1945, list of prisoners at Mittelbau; a March 6, 1945, "strength report" from Mittelbau, which references Simon's death; a March 11, 1945, list of prisoners cremated at Mittelbau, including Simon; an August 1967 list of prisoners compiled by former Polish prisoner Roman Olszyna mentions Simon being transferred from Gross Rosen to Mittelbau.

Background came from the *Encyclopedia of Camps and Ghettos* and the Jewish Virtual Library. Yad Vashem also has a web page describing Montelupich prison.

A personal interview conducted with survivor Alice Ginsburg provided details on life at Auschwitz and Langenbielau. A *Jewish Journal* story from January 21, 2015, includes an account from Erika Jacoby on life at Langenbielau.

With the help of the USHMM and the Museum of Jewish Heritage, we listened to many survivor testimonies from Langenbielau, Flossenburg, and Dora-Mittelbau, including Eleanor Weile Erlich, Betti Frank, Ann Cyncynatus, Katalin Tyler, Fanny Federman, Elizabeth Klein, Wanda Wos Lorenc, Judith Szpiro, Mila Bachner, and Henry Oertelt, as well as GIs who liberated the camps, William Johnson and Lon Redmon. Mordechai (Motke) Wiesel's testimony courtesy of Yad Vashem.

Information was also found on both the Auschwitz and Flossenburg camp websites.

The books *Survival at Auschwitz* by Primo Levi, *Night* by Elie Wiesel, and *Maus* and *Maus II* by Art Spiegelman, and the short story "The Shawl" by Cynthia Ozick, provided context, as did the films *The Pianist* by Roman Polanski, *Schindler's List* by Steven Spielberg, Alain Resnais's *Night and Fog*, Stanley Kramer's *Judgement at Nuremberg*, Matthew Shoychet's *The Accountant of Auschwitz*, and the Netflix documentary *The Devil Next Door*.

CHAPTER 24 : M.I.A.

Leja Steinhauer's testimony and family interviews provided much of the information for the first half of this chapter. Jude Richter provided her camp deportation documents, a list compiled by the allies of Jews living illegally in Berlin, as well as a passenger list of her trip to the United States aboard the SS *Marine Flasher* on June 8, 1946.

Berlin's last days of the war are described in detail in the anonymous memoir *A Woman in Berlin*.

Press accounts of May 8, 1945, from the *New York Times* and the *Daily News* provided color for VE Day in New York. Irene Stapinski and Helen Siegler also shared their childhood memories.

The films *Downfall* and *The Longest Day* provided background as well.

President Harry Truman's speech and footage from May 8 can be found online from America's National Churchill Museum, uploaded to YouTube May 8, 2020.

CHAPTER 25 : RUINS

Wilder's *Death Mills*, as well as Sikov's *On Sunset Boulevard* and Zolotow's *Billy Wilder in Hollywood* provided the building blocks on Wilder's stint with the Psywar office.

For more on the Nazi *Titanic* see Watson's book of the same name.

Accounts in the *New York Times* from the spring and summer of 1945 provided background on the state of postwar Berlin.

Tourneur's *Berlin Express* and Wilder's *A Foreign Affair* provided footage of postwar Berlin, as did the Berlin Channel's color footage *Berlin in July 1945* from Kronos Media, which can be seen on YouTube.

Also providing color was "VE Day: The Fall of Nazi Berlin in Pictures," BBC News, May 8, 2020.

Information on Golda comes from Jeff Retig and Don's testimony. Information on Ushi from her daughters, Audrey and Marcia, and from Helen Siegler.

CHAPTER 26 : TO DO WITHOUT SAYING

Amy Donenfeld shared her father's wedding album with us, as well as her family memories and information on the Harry Donenfeld Foundation, Inc.

Other background on the Jade Room was found at the Waldorf Astoria Archive. The menu was provided by Faye's granddaughter, Elizabeth Sternberg.

Information about Neil comes from Fred and Rosalie Sternberg, family photos, and the author's recollections.

Lawsuit information and decision are from New York Supreme Court documents, 1947, *Jerome Siegel and Joseph Shuster v. National Comics Publications Inc.*

Ricca's *Super Boys* and Tye's *Superman* provided background as well.

CHAPTER 27 : COVER GIRL

Steven Lomazow provided us with copies of *Laff* magazine as well as Marilyn Monroe's other early magazine covers. Other information was culled from Kidder and Daniels's *Marilyn Monroe unCovers*.

For information on Marilyn Monroe's job at the Radioplane factory, see Michael Bechloss, "Marilyn Monroe's World War II Drone Program, *New York Times*, June 3, 2014.

Biographical information came from Marilyn's autobiography, *My Story*, as well as Barris's *Marilyn: Her Life in Her Own Words*.

Zolotow's *Marilyn Monroe*; Taraborrelli's *The Secret Life of Marilyn Monroe*; Spoto's *Marilyn Monroe*; and Guiles's *Norma Jean* also provided information.

For information on Marilyn Monroe's ancestral roots see "Inside Marilyn Monroe's Family Tree" from Biography.com by genealogist Juliana Szucs, May 31, 2016.

CHAPTER 28 : JEWS REEL

The Siegler family provided Jules's films.

Information on the Bolex came from Jeff Scher and from Bolsey's *Beyond the Bolex*.

For more on Bess Myerson see Preston's *Queen Bess*.

The story about Jules's driving through New York comes from an interview with Jules's grand-nephew Edwin Freedman.

CHAPTER 29 : THE HOTTEST THING

"Howard Hughes Near Death After Plane Hits Four Houses" from page 1 of the *Los Angeles Times*, July 8, 1946, described Howard Hughes's crash in detail.

Hedda Hopper's column "Looking at Hollywood" published in the *Harrisburg Telegraph*, August 1, 1946, page 28, mentions Hughes's sickbed discovery.

Michelle Morgan and Astrid Franse, "How Married and Bored Norma Jeane Became Sex Bomb Marilyn Monroe," *New York Post*, November 21, 2015, also recounted the Howard Hughes story.

Baseball game footage from 1949 from Getty Images.

We watched every Marilyn Monroe film ever made.

Information also from Marilyn's autobiographies, and from Taraborrelli's *The Secret Life of Marilyn Monroe*, Zolotow's *Marilyn Monroe*, and Spoto's *Marilyn Monroe*.

CHAPTER 30: BACKLASH

The film *Superman and the Mole Men* provided information for this chapter.

Libby Coleman's "America's Very Own Book Burnings" from September 30, 2015, on Ozy.com was a resource, as were Tye's *Superman*, Jones's *Men of Tomorrow*, and Ricca's *Super Boys*.

Wertham's article appears in the *Saturday Review of Literature*, May 29, 1948.

Newspapers across America, including the *Richmond Times-Dispatch* and the *Clarion-Ledger* of Jackson, Mississippi, carried the story of the Senate survey results on November 12, 1950.

Joseph Burstyn, Inc. v. Wilson, Supreme Court decision, 1952, decided on Hollywood's First Amendment rights.

CHAPTER 31 : FORCE OF NATURE

The story "How to Dine Out in Los Angeles Like Marilyn Monroe" by Crystal Coser in Eater Los Angeles, from January 28, 2015, and Alison Martino's Vintage Los Angeles post from February 18, 2011, provided information and photos of the Villa Nova restaurant.

Background on DiMaggio is from Talese's *The Silent Season of a Hero* and Cramer's *Joe DiMaggio*.

Aline Mosby's UPI story appeared on March 13, 1952, in papers across America.

Life magazine, April 7, 1952, features Marilyn on the cover.

The film *Niagara* provided background.

Reviews are from *Variety*, December 31, 1952; the *Hollywood Reporter*, January 20, 1953, " 'Niagara' Gripping Meller Full of Sex and Suspense"; and the *New York Times*, January 22, 1953, "Niagara Falls Vies with Marilyn Monroe," page 20.

Marilyn in Atlantic City from "Life Hereabouts" by Jack Weiner, *Camden Courier-Post*, September 3, 1952, page 2.

Also information from Spoto's *Marilyn Monroe*, Taraborrelli's *The Secret Life of Marilyn Monroe*, Zolotow's *Marilyn Monroe*, and Monroe's *My Story*.

CHAPTER 32 : CENTERFOLD

For more on Hugh Hefner, see Weyr's *Reaching for Paradise*.

Harry and Jack's involvement in *Playboy* is documented in Leibowitz's oral history from 1993.

Stories from January 15 and 16, 1954, in the *Camden Courier-Post*, the *Wisconsin State Journal*, the *News* of Paterson, NJ, and newspapers nationwide on the Monroe-DiMaggio wedding.

For more on Monroe and DiMaggio's Japan and Korea adventures, see Monroe's *My Story*, Taraborrelli's *The Secret Life of Marilyn Monroe*, as well as Liesl Bradner's piece "When Marilyn Monroe Interrupted Her Honeymoon to Go to Korea" in *Military History Quarterly*, December 3, 2019.

See Taraborrelli's *The Secret Life of Marilyn Monroe* for the Brokaw quote.

CHAPTER 33 : THE GIRL

Sabrina and *The Seven Year Itch* provided details.

See Zolotow's *Billy Wilder in Hollywood* and *Marilyn Monroe* and Sikov's *On Sunset Boulevard* for the making of *The Seven Year Itch*.

Annotated script at Fine Books & Collections auction, July 2, 2021.

Sam Shaw information from personal interviews with his daughters, Meta Shaw Stevens and Edith Shaw Marcus, who also provided photos from the Shaw Family Archives.

Friday magazine cover from July 25, 1941, shows a woman with her dress blowing up in Coney Island. Photo by Sam Shaw.

CHAPTER 34 : FLESH IMPACT

Photos and stories on Marilyn landing at Idlewild ran in dozens of newspapers on September 10, 1954, including "Marilyn Monroe Causes Near-Riot on N.Y. Visit" in the *Philadelphia Inquirer*.

Coverage on the first day of shooting from the *Daily News* and other papers (including the *Asbury Park Evening Press*) on September 14, 1954.

PBS's *Marilyn Monroe: Still Life* provided interviews with photographers who were at both the September 13 and 15 shoots.

Information also from Spoto's *Marilyn Monroe*, Taraborrelli's *The Secret Life of Marilyn Monroe*, Zolotow's *Marilyn Monroe*, and a personal interview with Lois Banner, author of *Marilyn: The Passion and the Paradox*.

Information on Jules's film is from the Siegler family, Jeff Scher, and Rayna Dineen.

Fur information is from the Marilyn Monroe Collection website and from a personal interview with its founder, collector Scott Fortner.

Obituary of Anna M. Potok of the Maximilian fur family, from the *New York Times*, April 23, 1987, provided information on their escape from Poland.

Scott Feinberg's taped interview with Amanda Greene from April 12, 2020, includes her firsthand account of Marilyn's time in NYC.

CHAPTER 35 : IT HAPPENED LAST NIGHT
AND CHAPTER 36 : BIRTH OF VENUS

Earl Wilson's syndicated column appeared in dozens of newspapers, including the *Pittsburgh Post-Gazette*, on September 16, 1954.

Coverage of that night is from the *Daily News*, Long Island *Newsday*, the *Hartford Courant*, and other papers, September 16, 1954.

Feinberg's taped interview with Amanda Greene includes information on the night of the shoot.

The French website Canalblog includes an exhaustive collection of photos from the night of the shoot on its "Divine Marilyn" page.

Billy Wilder information is from Chandler's *Nobody's Perfect*, Sikov's *On Sunset Boulevard*, Zolotow's *Billy Wilder in Hollywood*, and Crowe's *Conversations with Wilder*.

Information and photos are from the Shaw Family Archives.

Spoto's *Marilyn Monroe*, Zolotow's *Marilyn Monroe*, Banner's *Marilyn: The Passion and the Paradox*, and Taraborrelli's *The Secret Life of Marilyn Monroe* provided information on Marilyn as well.

CHAPTER 37 : NIGHTS OF HORROR

Newspaper coverage on the arrest and trial of the Thrill-Kill Gang from August through December 1954, from the *World-Telegram and Sun*, the *Daily News*, *Newsday*, the *Brooklyn Daily Eagle*, and the *Asbury Park Press*, as well as nationwide coverage including a story in the *Charlotte Observer*, October 18, 1954, and *Time* magazine on December 27, 1954, provided the factual information for this chapter.

Information on the raid can be found in the *World-Telegram and Sun*, September 15, 1954.

Gaines quoted in newspapers nationwide on October 17, 1954, including the *San Bernardino County Sun* and the *Fort Worth Star-Telegram*.

Wertham's post-trial campaign against the comics industry can be found in newspaper stories in the winter of 1955 in the *Daily News*, the *Record* of Hackensack, the *Morning Call* of Allentown, as well as the *Evening Standard* of London and the Los Angeles *Mirror and Daily News*.

Wertham's *Seduction of the Innocent* lays out his evidence and philosophy.

Jones's *Men of Tomorrow* was the first to report Joe Shuster's involvement with *Nights of Horror*.

For more on *Nights of Horror*, see Yoe's *Secret Identity*.

For more on the Thrill-Kill murders, see Adin's *The Brooklyn Thrill-Kill Gang and the Great Comic Book Scare of the 1950s*.

Joe's ad can be found in the *New York Times* classifieds on December 20, 1954.

On-the-ground reporting in Richmond Hill, Queens, provided color.

Supreme Court decision on *Kingsley Books Inc. v. Brown* can be found in the case decision online at FindLaw. Newspaper stories on the decision can be found nationwide on June 24, 1957, including "Supreme Court Backs Ban on Obscenity" on page 1 of the *Baltimore Evening Sun*.

NOTES

CHAPTER 38 : ALMOST FAMILY

Interviews with Fred and Rosalie Sternberg provided much of the information for this chapter.

Stories on the Kefauver-led hearings can be found in the *Spokane Chronicle*, as well as other newspapers across the country in February 1955.

The Donenfeld grandchildren, Ricca's *Super Boys*, and Jones's *Men of Tomorrow* provided information on Harry's retirement.

For more on Marilyn's time in New York City, see Winder's *Marilyn in Manhattan*; Pat Ryan, "Marilyn in Manhattan, Both Public and Private," *New York Times*, January 6, 2011; and Scott Feinberg's taped interview with Amanda Greene from YouTube, April 12, 2020.

Monroe's *My Story*, Spoto's *Marilyn Monroe*, and Taraborrelli's *The Secret Life of Marilyn Monroe* provided information on Marilyn's time in New York and her conversion to Judaism.

The August 6, 2021, story "9 Stunning Jewish Facts About Marilyn Monroe" by Arielle Kaplan in *Kveller* and "The Jewish Marilyn Monroe—Gone but Not Forgotten" by Bob Bahr in the *Atlanta Jewish Times* from August 28, 2019, provided more information on her conversion.

A *Washington Post* story by Isaac Stanley-Becker, "Jewish Prayer Book Annotated by Marilyn Monroe, Who Converted in 1956, Could Fetch Thousands in Auction," from October 16, 2018, provided information on Marilyn's prayer book, and "You Can Own Marilyn Monroe's Menorah—That's Lit!" in the *Forward* from November 1, 2019, by P. J. Grisar described her menorah.

On-the-ground reporting on Sutton Place and in Brooklyn provided color on Marilyn's apartments with and without Arthur Miller and on Miller's family home in Midwood. A personal interview with Miller's sister, Joan Copeland, provided information about Marilyn's visit to Brooklyn.

A real estate story, "Marilyn Monroe's Former Sutton Place Penthouse Is on the Market for $6.75M" in *6sqft* by Michelle Cohen from June 16, 2016, described Miller and Monroe's apartment as well.

The maternity dress information comes from Miracle's *My Sister Marilyn*.

CHAPTER 39 : THE FALL

Newspapers nationwide carried stories on Clark Gable's heart attack and subsequent death from November 7–18, 1960.

See Taraborrelli's *The Secret Life of Marilyn Monroe* for Marilyn's marriage to Miller.

Information on Harry's philanthropy is from Amy Donenfeld.

Common Cause information from Ken Quattro's *Comics Detective* 2019 piece, "Harry Donenfeld the Young Socialist." Superman's right-wing turn is from DeHaven's *Our Hero*.

Information on the Playboy Club and Harry's final days are from grandsons Luke and Harry Donenfeld interviews and Sunny's niece, Gale Sitomer. Information on Harry's fall is from an *Alter Ego* interview in 2003.

Information on Harry's obituary in the *Daily News*, February 28, 1965.

Information on Marilyn's death from newspapers nationwide, August 6, 1962, including the *Los Angeles Times* and the *Daily News*.

Information on Jerry's and Joe's later years are from *New York Times* stories by Mary Breasted, "Superman's Creators Nearly Destitute, Invoke His Spirit," page 31, November 22, 1975, and "Superman's Creators Get Lifetime Pay" by David Vidal, page 25, December 24, 1975. Also the *Los Angeles Times* stories by Erik Knutzen, "Man of Steel Splinters an American Dream" from February 25, 1979, and John L. Mitchell, "Superman's Originators Warm Up After Long Freeze-Out" from June 18, 1981.

Jerry's curse is from his 1975 press release, which can be read in its entirety on the *20th Century Danny Boy* blog.

The Wilder quote on Marilyn's marriages is from Chandler's *Nobody's Perfect*.

The story on Hefner's grave, "For Sale: Eternity with Marilyn Monroe," is by Jeff Gottlieb, *Los Angeles Times*, August 14, 2009.

CHAPTER 40 : A LEGEND MOST

This chapter is taken from family interviews and photographs, letters, and programs from tributes to Jules.

CHAPTER 41 : THE FINAL FIGHT

The Trump Plaza building accident was reported in "Falls 33 Floors to Death" on page 4 of the *Daily News* on May 3, 1983, by Peter McLaughlin and Mary Ann Giordano. The building's poor workmanship was reported in the *Record* of Hackensack, February 15, 1990, "Trump High-rise Built Poorly, Suit Says," page A22.

Trump's ties to Salerno is from David Cay Johnston, "Just What Were Donald Trump's Ties to the Mob?," *Politico*, May 22, 2016.

Wilder's interest in *Schindler's List* is from a conversation with Steven Spielberg and from an essay, "You Saw Only Handkerchiefs Everywhere," by Wilder in *Süeddeutsche Zeitung Magazin* in Germany, February 18, 1994.

Information on Eugenia is from Jude Richter, including her identification card and registry in the Kraków ghetto from 1940 to 1941, her questionnaire, her resident extension in 1942, and her brother Michael's Page of Testimony with Yad Vashem from 1953.

Laura Siegel's letter is from Ricca and also on the *Danny Boy* blog.

CHAPTER 42 : LOST AND FOUND

From Jules's film collection and family interviews.

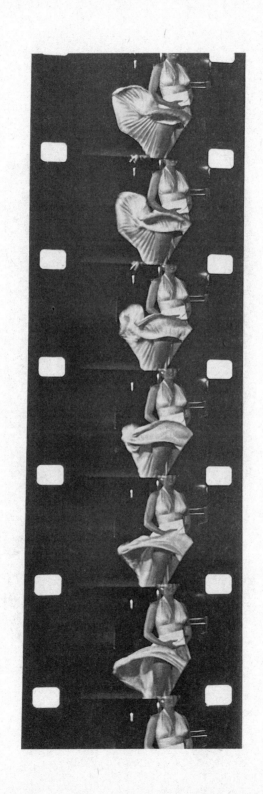

JULES'S LEICA, ACTUAL SIZE

PHOTO CREDITS

ILLUSTRATION BY JOE SHUSTER

ABOUT THE AUTHORS

HELENE STAPINSKI is the nationally bestselling author of three memoirs: *Five-Finger Discount*, *Murder in Matera*, and *Baby Plays Around*. Having run out of her own family stories, she's been adopted by her friend Bonnie to help tell her family saga. Though raised Roman Catholic, Helene has some Jewish ancestors on her father's Polish side and is sure she's somehow related to Bonnie. Helene writes regularly for the *New York Times*, and has appeared in the *Washington Post*, *New York*, *Travel & Leisure*, and dozens of other publications. She teaches writing at New York University and lives in Brooklyn with her husband, Wendell Jamieson, and their two children and golden retriever.

BONNIE SIEGLER is Jules Schulback's granddaughter and founder and creative director of award-winning graphic design studio Eight and a Half. She has worked with *Saturday Night Live*, *Newsweek*, the Brooklyn Public Library, HBO, and the Criterion Collection, among many others. She is also the author of *Dear Client*, a guide for people who work with creatives, from a designer's perspective, and *Signs of Resistance*, a visual history of protest in America, from an activist's perspective. She has taught design at the graduate schools of Yale University and the School of Visual Arts, and has lectured all over the place. She lives in Connecticut with her husband, Jeff Scher, and their two sons, who inspire them (almost) every day.